COLLECTED ESSAYS
OF
EDMUND GOSSE

VOL. IV

FRENCH PROFILES

FRENCH PROFILES

BY

EDMUND WILLIAM GOSSE, C. B.

New Edition

Essay Index Reprint Series

originally published by

WILLIAM HEINEMANN

 BOOKS FOR LIBRARIES PRESS
FREEPORT, NEW YORK

New edition first published 1913
Reprinted 1970

STANDARD BOOK NUMBER:
8369-1574-7

LIBRARY OF CONGRESS CATALOG CARD NUMBER:
70-108638

PRINTED IN THE UNITED STATES OF AMERICA

TO
MY FRIEND
SIR ALFRED BATEMAN, K.C.M.G.
IN MEMORY OF
THE TALKS OF MANY YEARS
I AFFECTIONATELY INSCRIBE
THESE STUDIES

PREFACE

IT is characteristic of native criticism that it contemplates, or should contemplate, the products of native literature from the front; that it looks at them, in other words, from a direct and complete point of view. Foreign criticism must not pretend to do this; unless it is satisfied to be a mere echo or repetition, its point of view must be incomplete and indirect, must be that of one who paints a face in profile. In preparing the following sideviews of some curious figures in modern French literature, I have attempted to keep two aims prominently before me. I have tried to preserve that attitude of sympathy, of general comprehension, for the lack of which some English criticism of foreign authors has been valueless, because proceeding from a point so far out of focus as to make its whole presentation false; and yet I have remembered that it is a foreigner who takes the portrait, and that he takes it for a foreign audience, and not for a native one.

What I have sought in every case to do is to give an impression of the figure before me which shall be in general harmony with the tradition of French criticism, but at the same time to preserve that independence which is the right of a foreign observer, and to illustrate the peculiarities of my subject by references to English poetry and prose.

It should not be difficult to carry out this scheme of portraiture in the case of authors whose work is finished. But the study of contemporary writers, also, is of great interest, and must not be neglected, although its results are incomplete. Several of the authors who are treated here are still alive, and some are younger than myself. It is highly probable that all of these will, in the development of their genius, make some new advance which may render obsolete what the most careful criticism has said about them up to the present time. In these living cases, therefore, it seems more helpful to consider certain books—to take snapshots, as it were, at the authors in the course of their progress—than to attempt a summing-up of what is still fortunately undefined. Of the art with which this can be done, and the permanent value of that art, the French criticism of our generation has given admirable proof.

The last chapter in this book is not in any sense a profile, but the writer trusts that he will be forgiven for introducing it here. Last winter he had the honour of being invited to Paris to deliver an address before the Société des Conférences. The Committee of that Society, consisting of MM. Ferdinand Brunetière, Édouard Rod and Gaston Deschamps, in proposing the subject of the address, asked that it should be delivered in English. In an admirable French translation, made by my accomplished friend, M. Henry D. Davray, it was afterwards published in the *Mercure de France* and then as a separate *brochure*, but the English text is now printed for the first time.

Mr. James Fitzmaurice-Kelly has been so kind as to read the proofs of this volume, and I am indebted to his rare acquaintance with Continental literature for many valuable corrections and suggestions. My thanks are due to the proprietors of the *Fortnightly Review*, the *Contemporary Review*, the *International Quarterly Review*,

the *Saturday Review* and the *Daily Chronicle*, for permission to reprint what originally appeared in their
pages. I regret that in one other case, that of the
useful and unique European review, *Cosmopolis*, there
is no one left who can receive this acknowledgment.

E. G.

ARGELÈS-GAZOST,
   September 1904.

PREFACE TO THE NEW EDITION

CALLED upon after eight years to revise a new impression of this volume, I feel, with regard to parts of it, the inconvenience of studying the characteristics of a living organism. Leighton, I remember, once told me of the heartbreaking anxiety which pursued him while making a very elaborate pencil-study of a lemon-tree. Every morning some shoot had pushed in front of another, some bud had swelled or had burst in blossom, growths in every portion of the tree conspired to defeat the designer. In literature those who have published studies of the living—greater men than I, such as M. Anatole France and M. Jules Lemaître—have bewailed the same phenomenon. I have, therefore, not attempted to follow the later growth or to record the unexpected blossomings of those of my themes who are still happily alive and active. I have confined myself to a careful revision of matters of fact and to a few necessary interpolations. But I have added a chapter, on the same scale, about M. Maurice Barrès, and I have greatly enlarged, or practically re-written, the sketch of Stéphane Mallarmé.

E. G.

May 1913.

CONTENTS

	PAGE
PREFACE	vii
ALFRED DE VIGNY	1
MADEMOISELLE AÏSSÉ	33
A NUN'S LOVE LETTERS	63
BARBEY D'AUREVILLY	87
ALPHONSE DAUDET	103
THE SHORT STORIES OF ZOLA	125
FERDINAND FABRE	149
A FIRST SIGHT OF VERLAINE	177
THE IRONY OF M. ANATOLE FRANCE	185
PIERRE LOTI	199
SOME RECENT BOOKS OF M. PAUL BOURGET	233
M. RENÉ BAZIN	259
M. MAURICE BARRÈS	285
M. HENRI DE RÉGNIER	297

xiv   Contents

PAGE

FOUR POETS :—

    STÉPHANE MALLARMÉ   313

    M. EMILE VERHAEREN   324

    ALBERT SAMAIN   329

    M. PAUL FORT   334

THE INFLUENCE OF FRANCE UPON
    ENGLISH POETRY   339

APPENDIX: MALLARMÉ AND SYMBOLISM 371

INDEX   375

ALFRED DE VIGNY

ALFRED DE VIGNY

THE reputation of Alfred de Vigny has endured extra-ordinary vicissitudes in France. After having taken his place as the precursor of French romantic poetry and as one of the most admired of its proficients, he withdrew from among his noisier and more copious contemporaries into that "ivory tower" of reverie which is the one commonplace of criticism regarding him. He died in as deep a retirement as if his body had lain in the shepherd's hut on wheels upon the open moorland, which he took as the symbol of his isolation.

He had long been neglected, he was almost forgotten, when the publication of his posthumous poems—a handful of unflawed amethysts and sapphires—revived his fame among the enlightened. But the Second Empire was a period deeply unfavourable to such contemplation as the writings of Vigny demand. He sank a second time into semi-oblivion; he became a curiosity of criticism, a hunting-ground for anthology-makers. Within the last ten years, however, a marked revolution of taste has occurred in France. The supre-macy of Victor Hugo has been, if not questioned, since it is above serious attack, at least mitigated. Other poets have recovered from their obscurity; Lamartine, who had been quenched, shines like a lamp relighted; and, above all, the pure and brilliant and profoundly original genius of Alfred de Vigny now takes, for the first time, its proper place as one of the main illuminating

3

forces of the nineteenth century. It was not until about ninety years after this poet's birth that it became clearly recognised that he is one of the most important of all the great poets of France.

The revival of admiration for Vigny has not yet spread to England, where he is perhaps less known than any other French writer of the first class. This is the more to be regretted because he did not, in the brief day of his early glory, contrive to attract many hearers outside his own country. It is not merely regrettable, moreover, it is curiously unjust, because Vigny is of all the great French poets the one who has assimilated most of the English spirit, and has been influenced most by English poetry. André Chénier read Pope and Thomson and the *Faërie Queen*, but he detested the Anglo-Saxon spirit. Alfred de Vigny, on the other hand, delighted in it; he was a convinced Anglophil, and the writers whom he resembles, in his sublime isolation from the tradition of his own country, are Wordsworth and Shelley, Matthew Arnold and Leopardi. He has much of the spirit of Dante and of the attitude of Milton. Wholly independent as he is, one of the most unattached of writers, it is impossible not to feel in him a certain Anglo-Italian gravity and intensity, a certain reserve and resignation in the face of human suffering, which distinguish him from all other French writers of eminence. It is not from any of Alfred de Vigny's great contemporaries that life would have extracted that last cry in the desert :—

> " Seul le silence est grand : tout le reste est faiblesse,"

nor should we look to them for the ambiguous device " Parfaite illusion—Réalité parfaite." The other poets of France have been picturesque, abundant, gregarious, vehement; Alfred de Vigny was not of their class, but we can easily conceive him among those who, in the Cumberland of a hundred years ago, were murmuring by the running brooks a music sweeter than their own.

One word of warning may not be out of place. If Alfred de Vigny was known to English readers of a past generation it was mainly through a brilliant study by Sainte-Beuve in his *Nouveaux Lundis*. This was composed very shortly after the death of Vigny, and, in spite of its excessive critical cleverness, it deserves very little commendation. Sainte-Beuve, who had been more or less intimate with Vigny forty years before, had formed a strange jealousy of him, and in this essay his perfidy runs riot. It is Sainte-Beuve who calls the poet of *Les Destinées* a " beautiful angel who had been drinking vinegar," and the modern reader needs a strong caution against the malice and raillery of the quondam friend who was so patient and who forgot nothing.

I

An image of the youthful Alfred de Vigny is preserved for us in the charming portrait of the Carnavalet Museum. Here he smiles at us out of gentle blue eyes, and under copious yellow curls, candid, dreamy, almost childlike in his magnificent scarlet and gold uniform of the King's Musketeers. This portrait was painted in 1815, when the subject of it was just eighteen, yet had already served in the army for a year. Alfred de Vigny was born at Loches, on March 27, 1797. Aristocrats and of families wholly military, his father and mother had been thrown into prison during the Terror, had escaped with their lives, and had concealed themselves after Thermidor, in the romantic little town of the Touraine. The childhood of the poet was not particularly interesting; what is known about it is recorded in M. Séché's recent volume [1] and elsewhere. But there effervesced in his young soul a burning ambition for arms, and before he was seventeen, he contrived to leave school and enter a squadron of the Gendarmes Rouges. He was full of military pride in his early life, and until his illusions overcame him he hardly knew whether to be more vain of the laurel or of the sword. He says :—

> " J'ai mis sur le cimier doré du gentilhomme
> Une plume de fer qui n'est pas sans beauté ;
> J'ai fait illustre un nom qu'on m'a transmis sans gloire,"

for he knew that the deeds of that " petite noblesse " from which he sprang were excellent, but not magnificent.

No one seems to have discovered under what auspices he began to write verses. There appear in his works two idyls, *La Dryade* and *Symétha*, which are marked as " written in 1815." Sainte-Beuve, with curious coarseness, after Vigny's death, accused him in so many terms of having antedated these pieces by five years in order to escape the reproach of having imitated André Chénier, whose poems were first collected posthumously in 1819. Such a charge is contrary to everything we know of the upright and chivalrous character of Vigny. That the influence of Chénier is strong on these verses is unquestionable. But Sainte-Beuve should not have forgotten that the eclogues of Chénier were quoted by Chateaubriand in a note to the *Génie du Christianisme* in 1802, and that this was quite enough to start the

[1] Léon Séché, *Alfred de Vigny et son Temps*, Paris, Félix Juven, 1902.

youthful talent of Vigny. From this time forth, no attack can be made on the originality of the poet, so far as all French influences are concerned. The next piece of his which we possess, *La Dame Romaine*, is dated 1817; this and *Le Bal*, of 1818, show the attraction which Byron had for him. In these verses the romantic school of French poetry made its earliest appeal to the public, and in 1819 Alfred de Vigny's friendship with the youthful Victor Hugo began.

It was in 1822 that a little volume of the highest historical importance was issued, without the name of its author, and under the modest title of *Poèmes*. It was divided into three parts, *Antiques*, *Judaïques*, and *Modernes*, and the second of these sections contained one poem which can still be read with undiluted pleasure. This is the exquisite lyrical narrative entitled *La Fille de Jephté*, which had been composed in 1820. To realise what were the merits of Alfred de Vigny as a precursor, we have but to compare this faultless Biblical elegy with anything of the kind written up to that date by a French poet, even though his name was Hugo.

Meanwhile the life of Vigny was a picturesque and melancholy one. A certain impression of its features may be gathered, incidentally, from the pages of the *Grandeur et Servitude Militaires*, although that was written long afterwards. He was a soldier from his seventeenth to his thirtieth year, and many of his best poems were written by lamplight, in the corner of a tent, as the young lieutenant lay on his elbow, waiting for the tuck of drum. He· was long in garrison with the Royal Foot Guards at Vincennes, and thence he could slip in to Paris, meet the other budding poets at the rooms of Nodier, and recite verses with Émile

Deschamps and Victor Hugo. But in 1823 he was definitely torn from Paris. The Spanish War took his regiment to the Pyrenean frontier and it was while in camp, close to Roncevaux and Fuentarrabia, that he seems to have heard, one knows not how, of the newly discovered wonders of the *Chanson de Roland*, which was still unknown save to a few English scholars; the result was that he wrote that enchanting poem, *Le Cor*. If the student is challenged, as he sometimes is, to name a lyric in the French language which has the irresistible magic and melody of the best pieces of Coleridge or Keats, that fairy music which is the peculiar birthright of England, he cannot do better than to quote, almost at random, from *Le Cor* :—

> " Sur le plus haut des monts s'arrêtent les chevaux ;
> L'écume le blanchit ; sous leurs pieds, Roncevaux
> Des feux mourants du jour à peine se colore.
> A l'horizon lointain fuit l'étendard du More.
>
> ' Turpin, n'as-tu rien vu dans le fond du torrent ? '
> ' J'y vois deux chevaliers ; l'un mort, l'autre expirant.
> Tous deux sont écrasés sous une roche noire ;
> Le plus fort, dans sa main, élève un Cor d'ivoire,
> Son âme en s'exhalant nous appela deux fois.'
>
> Dieu ! que le son du Cor est triste au fond des bois."

Begun at Roncevaux in 1823, *Le Cor* was finished at Pau in 1825. At the former date, Alfred de Vigny was slightly in love with the fascinating Delphine Gay, and some verses, recently given to the world, lead to the belief that he failed to propose to her because she "*laughed too loudly.*" Already the melancholy and distinguished sobriety of manner which was to be the mark of Alfred de Vigny had begun to settle upon him. Already he shrank from noise, from levity, from hollow and reverberating enthusiasm. His regiment was sent to Strasburg and he became a captain. Returning to the Pyrenees, he wrote *Le Déluge* and *Dolorida ;* in the Vosges he composed the first draft of *Éloa,* which he called *Satan.* In the second edition of his *Poèmes,* there were included a number of pieces vastly superior to those previously published, and Alfred de Vigny boldly claimed for himself that distinction as a precursor, which was long denied to him, and which is now again universally conceded. He wrote that " the only merit of these poems,"—it was not their only or their greatest merit, but it was a distinction,—" c'est d'avoir devancé en France toutes celles de ce genre." . That was absolutely true.

When we reflect that the earliest poems of Victor Hugo which display his characteristic talent, such as *Le Sylphe* and *La Grand'mère,* belong to 1823, the originality of *Moïse,* which was written in 1822, is extraordinary. In spite of all that has been published since, this poem may still be read with complete pleasure ; there are few narratives in the French language more distinguished, more uplifted. Moses stands at sunset on the brow of Nebo ; the land of Canaan lies spread at his feet. He gazes at it with longing and despair, and then he turns to climb the mountain. Amid the hymns of Israel he ascends into the clouds, and in the luminous obscurity he speaks with God. In a majestic soliloquy he expatiates on the illusions of his solitary greatness, and on the disappointment of his finding his own life more isolated and more arid the vaster his destinies become. The angels, themselves, envy his position :—

> " Vos anges sont jaloux et m'admirent entre eux,
> Et cependant, Seigneur, je ne suis pas heureux ;
> Vous m'avez fait vieillir puissant et solitaire,
> Laissez-moi m'endormir du sommeil de la terre."

Here we have at length the master accent of Alfred de
Vigny, that which was to be the central note of his
poetry, a conception of the sublimity of man, who,
having tasted of the water of life, sinks back " dizzy,
lost, yet unbewailing." Nothing could be more poignant
than the melodious reverie of Moses :—

> " J'ai vu l'amour s'éteindre et l'amitié tarir ;
> Les vierges se voilaient et craignaient de mourir.
> M'enveloppant alors de la colonne noire,
> J'ai marché devant tous, triste et seul dans ma gloire,
> Et j'ai dit dans mon cœur : ' Que vouloir à présent ? '
> Pour dormir sur un sein mon front est trop pesant,
> Ma main laisse l'effroi sur la main qu'elle touche,
> L'orage est dans ma voix, l'éclair est sur ma bouche ;
> Aussi, loin de m'aimer, voilà qu'ils tremblent tous,
> Et, quand j'ouvre les bras, on tombe à mes genoux.
> O Seigneur ! j'ai vécu puissant et solitaire,
> Laissez-moi m'endormir du sommeil de la terre ! "

On the morning when these enchanting verses were
composed, poetry was full-grown again in France,
reborn after the long burial of the eighteenth century.

The processes of the poet's mind are still better
observed in *Le Déluge*, a less perfect poem. All was
serene and splendid in the primeval world,

> " Et la beauté du Monde attestait son enfance,"

but there was one blot on the terrestrial paradise, for
" l'Homme était méchant." In consequence of a secret
warning, Noah builds the ark, and enters it with his
family. One of his descendants, however, the young
Sara, refuses to take shelter in it, because she has an
appointment to meet Emmanuel, her angel lover, on
Mount Arar. The deluge arrives ; Sara calls in vain
on her supernatural protector, and, climbing far up the
peak, is the last of mortals to be submerged. The
violence of the flood is rather grotesquely described ;

the succeeding calm is, on the other hand, of the purest
Vigny :—

> " La vague était paisible, et molle et cadencée,
> En berceaux de cristal mollement balancée ;
> Les vents, sans résistance, étaient silencieux ;
> La foudre, sans échos, expirait dans les cieux ;
> Les cieux devenaient purs, et, réfléchis dans l'onde,
> Teignaient d'un azur clair l'immensité profonde."

Written in the Pyrenees in 1823, *Le Déluge* exemplifies
the close attention which Alfred de Vigny paid to
English literature, and particularly to Byron. In
Moïse the sole influences discoverable are those of the
Bible and Milton ; *Le Déluge* shows that the French poet
had just been reading *Heaven and Earth*. This drama
was not published until January 1823, a week after
Moore's *Loves of the Angels*, which also was already
exercising a fascination over the mind of Vigny. The
promptitude with which he transferred these elements
into his own language is very remarkable, and has never,
I think, been noted.

Still more observable are these English influences in
Éloa, which was written in the spring of 1824. This
is the romance of pity, tenderness, and sacrifice, of
vain self-sacrifice and of pity without hands to help.
It was received by the young writers of its own country
with a frenzy of admiration. In *La Muse Française*
Victor Hugo reviewed it in terms of redundant eulogy.
A little later, and when so much more of a brilliant
character had been published, Gautier styled *Éloa* " the
most beautiful and perhaps the most perfect poem in
the French language." As a specimen of idealistic
religious romanticism it will always be a classic and will
always be read with pleasure ; but time has somewhat
tarnished its sentimental beauty. It is another variant

of *The Loves of the Angels*, but treated in a far purer
and more ethereal spirit than that of Moore or Byron.

It would be difficult to point to a more delicate
example of the school of sensibility than *Éloa*. To
submit one's self without reserve to its pellucid charm
is like gazing into the depths of an amethyst. The
subject is sentimental in the highest degree; Éloa is an
angel, who, in her blissful state, hears of the agony of
Satan, and is drawn by curiosity and pity to descend
into his sphere. Her compassion and her imprudence
are rewarded by her falling passionately in love with the
stricken archangel, and resigning herself to his baneful
force. Brought face to face with his crimes, she resists
him, but the wily fiend melts into hypocritical tears,
and Éloa sinks into his arms. Wrapped in a flowing
cloud they pass together down to Hell, and a chorus
of faithful seraphim, winging their way back to Paradise,
overhear this latest and fatal dialogue :—

> " ' Où me conduisez-vous, bel ange ? '   ' Viens toujours.'
> —' Que votre voix est triste, et quel sombre discours !
> N'est-ce pas Éloa qui soulève ta chaîne ?
> J'ai cru t'avoir sauvé.'   ' Non ! c'est moi qui t'entraîne.'
> —' Si nous sommes unis, peu m'importe en quel lieu !
> Nomme-moi donc encore ou ta sœur ou ton dieu ! '
> —' J'enlève mon esclave et je tiens ma victime.'
> —' Tu paraissais si bon !   Oh ! qu'ai-je fait ? '   ' Un crime.'
> —' Seras-tu plus heureux ? du moins, es-tu content ? '
> —' Plus triste que jamais.'   —' Qui donc est-tu ? '   ' Satan.'"

Taste changes, and *Éloa* has too much the appearance,
to our eyes, of a wax-work. But nothing can prevent
our appreciation of the magnificent verses in which it
is written. The design and scheme of colour may be
those of Ary Scheffer, the execution is worthy of
Raphael.

Before we cease to examine these early writings,
however, we must spare a moment—though only a

moment—to the consideration of a work which gave
Vigny the popular celebrity which served to introduce
his verses to a wider public. Early in 1826 he was
presented to Sir Walter Scott in Paris, and, fired with
Anglomaniac ambition, he immediately sat down to
write a French Waverley novel. The result was *Cinq-
Mars*, long the most successful of all his writings,
although not the best. It is a story of the time of
Louis XIII. and of Cardinal Richelieu; it deals with
all the court intrigues which led up to the horrible
assassination of De Thou and of Henri d'Effiat, Marquis
de Cinq-Mars. Anne of Austria is a foremost figure
on the scene of it. *Cinq-Mars*, a very careful study
in the manner of Walter Scott, was afterwards enriched
by notes and historical apparatus, and by an essay
"On Truth in Art," written in 1827. It has passed
through countless editions, but it is overfull of details,
the plot drags, and the reader must be simple to find it
an exciting romance. It is interesting to notice in it
the Anglophil tendencies of its author betrayed in
quotations from Shakespeare, Milton, and Byron, and
the restricted circle of his friends by frequent introduction of the names of Delphine Gay, Soumet, Nodier,
Lammenais. *Cinq-Mars* will always be remembered
as the earliest French romantic novel of the historical
order.

The marriage of Alfred de Vigny, the facts and even
the date of which have been persistently misreported
by his biographers—even by M. Paléologue—took place,
as M. Séché has proved, at Pau, on February 3, 1825. He
married Miss Lydia Bunbury, the daughter of Sir Henry
Edward Bunbury, a soldier and politician not without
eminence in his day. She was twenty-six years of age,
of a " majestic beauty " which soon disappeared under

the attacks of ill-health, and everything about her gratified the excessive Anglomania of the poet. She could not talk French with ease, and curiously enough when she had for many years been the Comtesse Alfred de Vigny, it was observed that she still spoke broken French with a strong English accent. It appears that this was positively agreeable to the poet, who had a little while before written that his only *penates* were his Bible and " a few English engravings," and whose conversation ran incessantly on Byron, Southey, Moore, and Scott. It is certain that some French critics have found it hard to forgive the intensity of Vigny's early love of all things English.

French writers have laboured to prove that the marriage of Alfred de Vigny was an unhappy one. It was certainly both anomalous and unfortunate, but there is not need to exaggerate its misfortunes. Lydia Bunbury appears to have been limited in intelligence and sympathy, and bad health gradually made her fretful. Yet there exists no evidence that she ever lost her liking for her husband or ceased to be soothed by his presence. He, for his part, had never loved when he proposed to Lydia Bunbury, and their relations continued to be as phlegmatic on the one side as on the other. For four or five years they lived together in sober friendship, Lydia sinking deeper and deeper into the condition of a chronic invalid. She was then nursed and tended by her husband with the tenderest assiduity and patience, and in later years he was a constant visitor at her sofa. She had exchanged a husband for a nurse, and doubtless renunciation would have been the greater part for Vigny also to play. But over his calm existence love now, for the first and only time, swept like a whirlwind of fire. In the tumult of this passion it is to his credit that he never forgot to be patient with and solicitous about the helpless invalid at home. If morality is offended, let this at least be recollected, that Lydia de Vigny knew all, and expressed no murmur which has been recorded.

The first period of Alfred de Vigny's life closed in 1827, when he left the army, on the pretext of health. He travelled in England with his wife, and it was at Dieppe, on a return journey in 1828, that he wrote the most splendid of his few lyrical poems, *La Frégate* '*La Sérieuse.*' This ode is too long for its interest, but contains stanzas that have never been surpassed for brilliance, as for example :—

> " Comme un dauphin elle saute,
> Elle plonge comme lui
> Dans la mer profonde et haute
> Où le feu Saint Elme a fui.
> Le feu serpente avec grâce ;
> Du gouvernail qu'il embrasse
> Il marque longtemps la trace,
> Et l'on dirait un éclair
> Qui, n'ayant pu nous atteindre,
> Dans les vagues va s'éteindre,
> Mais ne cesse de les teindre
> Du prisme enflammé de l'air."

II

It is remarkable to notice how many English influences the nature of Alfred de Vigny obeyed. In May 1828 the performances of Edmund Kean in Paris stirred his imagination to its depths. He immediately plunged himself into a fresh study of Shakespeare, and still further exercised his fancy by repeated experiences of the magic of Mrs. Siddons during a long visit he paid to London. The result was soon apparent in his attempts to render Shakespeare vocal to the French, who had welcomed Kean's " Othello " with " un vulgaire le plus profane que jamais l'ignorance parisienne ait déchaîné dans une salle de spectacle " (May 17, 1828). Vigny translated *The Merchant of Venice, Romeo and Juliet*, and, above all, *Othello*, which was acted in October, 1829, amid the plaudits of the whole romantic camp of Paris. That night Vigny, already extremely admired within a limited circle, became universally famous, and a dangerous rival to Victor Hugo, with whose *Hernani* and *Marion de Lorme*, moreover, comparison soon grew inevitable.

But Alfred de Vigny cared little for the jealousies of the Cénacle. He was now absorbed by a very different passion. It appears to have been on May 30, 1829,[1] that, after a performance of Casimir Delavigne's romantic tragedy of *Marino Faliero*, Vigny was presented to the actress, Marie Dorval. This remarkable woman of genius had been born in 1798, had shown from the age of four years a prodigious talent for the stage, had made her *début* in Paris in 1818, and had been a universal favourite since 1822. She was, therefore, neither very young nor very new when she passed across the path of Alfred de Vigny with such fiery results. She was highly practised in the arts of love, and he a timid and fastidious novice. It may even be said, without too great a paradox, that the romance of *Éloa* was now enacted in real life, with the parts reversed, for the poet was the candid angel, drawn to his fall by pity, curiosity, and tenderness, while Madame Dorval was the formidable and fatal demon who dragged him down. " Demon," however, is far too harsh a word to employ, even in jest, for this tremendous and expansive woman, all emotion and undisciplined ardour. M. Séché has put the position very well before us : " When, at the age of thirty-two,

[1] See M. Léon Séché's monograph, pp. 53–56.

she saw kneeling at her feet this gentleman of ancient lineage, his charming face framed in his blond and curly hair and delicately lighted up by the tender azure of his eyes, she experienced a sentiment she had never felt before, as though a cup of cold well-water had been lifted to her burning lips."

Reserved, irreproachable, by temperament obscure and chilly, it was long before Alfred de Vigny succumbed to the tumult of the senses. For a long time the animated and extravagant actress was dazzled by the mystical adoration, the respectful and solemn worship of her new admirer. She was accustomed to the rough way of the world, but she had never been loved like this before. She became hypnotised at last by the gaze of Alfred de Vigny fixed upon her in what Sainte-Beuve has called " a perpetual seraphic hallucination." A transformation appeared to come over herself. She fell in love with Vigny as completely as the poet had with her, and she became, in virtue of the transcendent ductility of her temperament as an actress, a temporary copy of himself. She was all reverie, all abstract devotion, and the strange pair floated through the stormy life of Paris, a marvel to all beholders, in a discreet and delicate rapture, as a poet with his muse, as a nun with her brother. This ecstatic relation continued until 1831, and during these years Alfred de Vigny scarcely wrote anything in prose or verse, entirely supported by the exquisite sentiment of his attachment. He fulfilled the dream of Pascal, " Tant plus le chemin est long dans l'amour, tant plus un esprit délicat sent de plaisir."

The circumstances under which this seraphic and mystical relation came to an end have but recently been made public. The wonder is that Madame Dorval, so romantic, violent, and susceptible, should have been

c

willing so long to preserve such an idyllic or even angelic
reserve.   George Sand, who saw her at this time, selects
other adjectives for her, " Oh ! naïve et passionnée, et
jeune et suave, et tremblante et terrible."   But she
determined at last to play the comedy of renunciation
no longer, and Vigny's subtlety and platonism were
burned up like grass in the flame of her seduction.   He
was Éloa, as I have said; she was the tenebrous and
sinister archangel, and he sank in the ecstatic crisis of
her will.   For the next few years, Mme. Dorval possessed
the life of the poet, swayed his instincts, inspired his
intellect.   His genius enjoyed a new birth in her; she
brought about a palingenesis of his talent, and during
this period he produced some of the most powerful and
the most solid of his works.

Under the influence of these novel and violent emotions, Vigny began at the close of 1831 to write *Stello ;*
he composed it in great heat, and it was finished in
January 1832, and immediately sent to press.   *Stello*
is a book which has been curiously neglected by modern
students of the poet; it is highly characteristic of the
author at this stage of his career, and deserves a closer
examination than it usually receives.   It is a triad of
episodes set in a sort of Shandean framework of fantastic
prose; the influence of Sterne is clearly visible in the
form of it.   It occupies a single night, and presents but
two characters.   Stello, a very happy and successful
poet, wealthy and applauded, nevertheless suffers from
the " spleen."   In a fit of the blue devils, he is stretched
on his sofa, the victim of a headache, which is described
in miraculous and Brobdingnagian terms.   A mystic
personage, the Black Doctor, a physician of souls, attends
the sufferer, and engages him in conversation.   This
conversation is the book called *Stello.*

The Black Doctor will distract the patient by three typical anecdotes of poets, who, in Wordsworth's famous phrase,

> " began in gladness,
> But thereof came, in the end, despondency and madness."

He tells a story of a mad flea, which develops into the relation of the sad end of the poet Gilbert. To this follow the history of Chatterton, and an exceedingly full and close chronicle of the last days of André Chénier. The friends converse on the melancholy topic of the rooted antipathy which exists between the Man of Action and the Man of Art. Poets are the eternal helots of society; modern life results in the perpetual ostracism of genius. Stello, in whom Alfred de Vigny obviously speaks, is roused to indignation at the charge of inutility constantly brought against the fine arts, and charges. Plato with having given the original impetus to this heresy by his exclusion of the poets from his republic. But the Black Doctor is inclined to accept Plato's view, and to hold that the great mistake is made by the men of reverie themselves in attempting to act as social forces. The friends agree that the propaganda of the future must be to separate the Life Poetic from the Life Politic as with a chasm.

Then in eloquent and romantic pages the law of conduct is laid down. The poet must not mix with the world, but in solitude and liberty must withdraw that he may accomplish his mission. He must firmly repudiate the too facile ambitions and enterprises of active life. He must keep firmly before him the image of those martyrs of the mind, Gilbert, Chatterton, and Chénier. He must say to his fellow men, what the swallows say as they gather under our eaves, " Protect

us, but touch us not." Such is the teaching of *Stello*,
a book extraordinary in its own day, and vibrating still;
a book in which for the first time was preached, without
the least reserve, the doctrines of the aristocracy of
imagination and of the illusiveness of any theory of
equality between the artist and the common proletariat
of mankind. Alfred de Vigny wrote *Stello* in a passion
of sincerity, and it is in its pages that we first see him
retiring into his famous " ivory tower." It is the credo
of a poet for whom the charges of arrogance and narrow-
ness do not exist; who doubted as little about the supre-
macy of genius as an anointed emperor does about Right
Divine.

The stage now attracted Vigny. In the summer of
1831 he wrote, and in 1834 brought out on the stage of
the Second Théâtre Français, *La Maréchale d'Ancre*, a
melodrama in prose, of the beginning of the seventeenth
century, a poison and dagger piece, thick with the
intrigues of Concini and Borgia. In May 1833 he produced *Quitte pour la Peur*, a trifle in one act. These
unimportant works lead us up to what is perhaps the
most famous of all Vigny's writings, the epoch-making
tragedy of *Chatterton*. This drama, which is in very
simple prose, was the work of seventeen nights in June
1834, when the poet was at the summit of his infatuation
for Madame Dorval. The subject of *Chatterton* had been
already sketched in *Stello*, and the play is really nothing
more than one of the episodes in that romance, expanded
and dramatised. Vigny published *Chatterton* with a
preface which should be carefully read if we are to
appreciate the point of view from which the poet desired
his play to be observed.

The subject of *Chatterton* is the perpetual and inevitable martyrdom of the Poet, against whom all the

rest of the successful world nourishes an involuntary resentment, because he will take no part in the game of action. Vigny tells the story of the young English writer, with certain necessary modifications. He represents him as a lodger at the inn of John and Kitty Bell, where at the end he tears up his manuscripts and commits suicide. The English reader must try to forgive and forget the lapses against local colour. Chatterton has been a spendthrift at Oxford, and has friends who hunt the wild boar on Primrose Hill; Vigny keeps to history only when it suits him to do so. These eccentricities did not interfere with the frenetic joy with which the play was received by the young writers and artists of Paris, and they ought not to disturb us now. Chatterton drinks opium in the last scene, because a newspaper has said that he is not the author of the " Rowley Poems," and because he has been offered the situation of first flunkey to the Lord Mayor of London. But these things are a symbol.

Much of the plot of *Chatterton* may strike the modern reader as mere extravagance. The logic of the piece is, nevertheless, complete and highly effective. It was the more strikingly effective when it was produced because no drama of pure thought was known to the audience which witnessed it. Classics and romantics alike filled their stage with violent action; this was a play of poignant interest, but that interest was entirely intellectual. The mystical passion of Chatterton and Kitty Bell is subtle, silent, expressed in thoughts; here were brought before the footlights " infinite passion and the pain of finite hearts that yearn " without a sigh. It is a marvellous tribute to genius that such a play could succeed, yet it was precisely in the huge psychological soliloquy in the third act—where the

danger seemed greatest—that success was most eminent.
When the audience listened to Chatterton murmuring
in his garret, with the thick fog at the window, all the
cold and hunger supported by pride alone, and when
they listened to the tremendous words in which
the pagan soul of Alfred de Vigny speaks through
the stoic boy, their emotion was so poignant as to be
insupportable.

The Poet as the imaginative pariah—that is the theme
of *Chatterton ;* the man of idealism crushed by a material-
istic society. It is a case of romantic neurosis, faced
without shrinking. Chatterton, the dramatist admits,
is suffering from a malady of the mind. But why, on
that account, should he be crushed out of existence?
Why should there be no pity for the infirmities of inspiration ? Has the poet really no place in the state ?
Is not the fact that he " reads in the stars the pathway
that the finger of God is pointing out " reason enough
for granting him the trifle that he craves, just leisure
and a little bread ? Why does the man of action
grudge the inspired dreamer his reverie and the necessary
food ? Everybody in the world is right, it appears,
except the poets. I do not know that it has ever been
suggested that, in his picture of Chatterton, Vigny was
thinking of the poet, Hégésippe Moreau, who, in 1833,
was in hospital, and who eminently " n'était pas de
ceux qui se laissent protéger aisément."

Chatterton is Alfred de Vigny's one dramatic success.
Its form is extremely original; it expresses with great
fulness one side of the temperament of the author, and
it suits the taste of the young artist not only in that but
in every age. It is written with simplicity, although
adorned here and there, as by a jewel, with an occasional
startling image, as where the Quaker (a chorus needed

because the passion of Chatterton and Kitty is voiceless) says that " the peace that reigns around you has been as dangerous for the spirit of this dreamer as sleep would be beneath the white tuberose." Whatever is forgotten, *Chatterton* must be remembered, and in each generation fresh young pulses will beat to its generous and hopeless fervour. Vigny was writing little verse at this time, but the curious piece called " Paris : Elevation " belongs to the year 1834, and is interesting as a link between the otherwise unrelated poetry of his youth and the chain of philosophical apologues in which his career as a poet was finally to culminate. But his main interest at this time was in prose.

Tenacity of vision was one of the most remarkable of Vigny's characteristics. When an experience had once made its impression upon him, this became deeper and more vivid as the years went on. He concealed it, he brooded on it, and suddenly the seed shot up and broke in the perfect blossom of imaginative writing. Hence we need not be surprised that the military adventures of his earliest years, when the yellow curls fell round the candid blue eyes of the boy as he rode in his magnificent scarlet uniform, although long put aside, were not forgotten. In the summer of 1835, with that curious activity in creation which always followed his motionless months of reverie, Alfred de Vigny suddenly set about and rapidly carried through the composition of the finest of his prose works, the admirable classic known as *Grandeur et Servitude Militaires*. The subject of this book is the illusion of military glory as exemplified in three episodes of the great war. The form of the volume is very notable; its stories rest in an auto-biographical setting, and it was long supposed that this also was fiction. But a letter has recently been discovered, written to a friend while the *Grandeur et Servitude* was being composed, in which the author says categorically, "wherever I have written 'I,' what I relate is the truth. I was at Vincennes when the poor adjutant died. I saw on the road to Belgium a cart driven by an old commander of a battalion. It was I who galloped along singing *Joconde*." This testimony adds great value to the delightful setting of the three stories, *Laurette*, *La Veillée de Vincennes*, and *La Canne de Jonc*. It is the confession of a sensitive spirit, striking the note of the disappointment of the age.

Laurette is an experience of 1815, in which a tale of 1797 is told; the poet makes a poignant appeal to the feelings by relating a savage crime of the Directory. A blunt sea captain is ordered to take a very young man and his child-wife to the tropics, and on a certain day to open a sealed letter. He becomes exceedingly attached to the charming pair of lovers, but when at last the letter is opened, he finds that he is instructed to shoot the husband for a supposed political offence. This he does, being under the "servitude" of duty, and the little wife goes mad. Nothing can exceed the exquisite simplicity of the scenes on shipboard, and the whole narrative is conducted with a masterly and almost sculptural reserve. The moral of *Laurette* is the illusion of pushing the sentiment of duty to its last and most inhuman consequences.

Somewhat later experiences in Vigny's life inspire *La Veillée de Vincennes*, a story of 1819. This episode opens with a delicious picture of a summer evening in the fortress before the review, the soldiers lounging about in groups, the white hen of the regiment strutting across the courtyard in her scarlet aigrette and her silver collar. It is full of those marvellous sudden images in which Vigny delights, phrases that take possession of the fancy; such as, " Je sentais quelque chose dans ma pensée, comme une tache dans une émeraude."

As a story *La Veillée de Vincennes* is not so interesting as its companions, but as an illustration of the poet's reflection upon life, it has an extreme value. The theme is the illusion of military excitement; the soldier only escapes *ennui* by the magnificent disquietude of danger, and in periods of peace he lacks this tonic. The curious and quite disconnected narrative of the accidental blowing up of the powder magazine, towards the close of this tale, is doubtless drawn directly from the experience of Vigny, who narrates it in a manner which is almost a prediction of that of Tolstoi.

In *La Canne de Jonc* we have the illusion of active glory. In the military life, when it is not stagnant, there is too much violence of action, not space enough for reflection. The moral of this story of disappointment in the person of Napoleon is that we should devote ourselves to principles and not to men. There are two magnificent scenes in *La Canne de Jonc*, the one in which the Pope confronts Napoleon with the cry of " Commediante ! " the other in which the author pays a noble tribute to Collingwood, and paints that great enemy of France as a hero of devotion to public duty. The whole of this book is worthy of close attention. It is one of the most distinguished in modern literature. Nothing could have been more novel than this exposure to the French of the pitiful fallacies of their military glory, of the hollowness of vows of poverty and obedience blindly made to power, whose only design was to surround itself by a bodyguard of gladiators. Of the reserve and sobriety of emotion in *Grandeur et Servitude Militaires*, and of the limpid, delicate elegance of its style, there cannot be any question. It will be a joy to readers of refinement as long as the French language endures.

At the close of 1835 Alfred de Vigny made the distressing discovery—he was the only member of the circle who had remained oblivious of the fact—that Madame Dorval was flagrantly unfaithful to him. He became aware that she was in intrigue with no less a personage than the boisterous Alexandre Dumas. Recent investigations have thrown an ugly light on this humiliating and painful incident. Wounded mortally in his pride and in his passion, he felt, as he says, " the earth give way under his feet." He was from this time forth dead to the world, and, in the fine phrase of M. Paléologue, he withdrew into his own intellect as into " an impenetrable Thebaid where he could be alone in the presence of his own thoughts." Alfred de Vigny survived this blow for more than a quarter of a century, but as a hermit and a stranger among the people.

III

When Alfred de Vigny perceived the treason of Madame Dorval in December 1835, his active life ceased. Something snapped in him—the chords of illusion, of artistic ambition, of the hope of happiness. He never attempted to forgive the deceiver, and he never forgave woman in her person. His pessimism grew upon him; he lost all interest in the public and in his friends; after a brief political effort he sank into a soundless isolation. He possessed a country house, called Le Maine-Giraud, in the west of France, and thither he withdrew, absorbed in the care of his invalid wife, and in the cultivation of his thoughts. His voice was scarcely heard any more in French literature, and gradually he grew to be forgotten. The louder and more active talents of his contemporaries filled up the void; Alfred de Vigny glided into silence, and was not missed. During the last twenty-eight years of his existence, on certain rare occasions, Vigny's intensity of dream, of impassioned reverie, found poetical relief. When he died, ten poems of various length were discovered among his papers, and these were published in 1864, as a very slender volume called *Les Destinées*, by his executor, Louis Ratisbonne.

Several of these posthumous pieces are dated, and the earliest of them seems to be *La Colère de Samson*, written in April 1839, when the Vignys were staying with the Earl of Kilmorey at Shavington Park in Shropshire. It is a curious proof of the intensity with which Alfred de Vigny concentrated himself on his vision that this terrible poem, one of the most powerful in the French language, should have been written in England during a country visit. It would seem that for more than three years the wounded poet had been brooding on his wrongs. Suddenly, without warning, the storm breaks in this tremendous picture of the deceit of woman and the helpless strength of man, in verses the melody and majesty of which are only equalled by their poignant agony :—

" Toujours voir serpenter la vipère dorée
Qui se traîne en sa fange et s'y croit ignorée;
Toujours ce compagnon dont le cœur n'est pas sûr,
La Femme, enfant malade et douze fois impur !
Toujours mettre sa force à garder sa colère
Dans son cœur offensé, comme en un sanctuaire,
D'où le feu s'echappant irait tout dévorer;
Interdire à ses yeux de voir ou de pleurer,
C'est trop ! Dieu, s'il le veut, peut balayer ma cendre,
J'ai donné mon secret, Dalila va le vendre."

He buried the memory of Madame Dorval under *La*

Colère de Samson, as a volcano buries a guilty city beneath a shower of burning ashes, and he turned to the contemplation of the world as he saw it under the soft light of the gentle despair which now more and more completely invaded his spirit.

The genius of Alfred de Vigny as the philosophical exponent of this melancholy composure is displayed in the noble and sculptural elegy, named *Les Destinées*, composed in *terza rima* in 1849; but in a still more natural and personal way in a poem which is among the most fascinating that he has left behind him, *La Maison du Berger*. Here he adopted a stanzaic form closely analogous to *rime royal*, and this adds to the curiously English impression, as of some son of Wordsworth or brother of Matthew Arnold, which this poem produces; it may make a third in our memories with " Laodamia " and " The Scholar-Gipsy." Vigny describes in it the mode in which the soul goes burdened, by the weight of life, like a wounded eagle in captivity, dragging at its chain. The poet must escape from this obsession of the world; he finds a refuge in the shepherd's cabin on wheels, far from all mankind, on a vast, undulating surface of moorland. Here he meditates on man's futility and fever, on the decline of the dignity of conduct, on the public disdain of immortal things. It is remarkable that at this lofty station, no modern institution is too prosaic for his touch; his treatment of the objects and methods of the day is magnificently simple, and he speaks of railways as an ancient Athenian might if restored to breath and vision. A certain mystical Éva is evoked, and a delicate analysis of woman follows. From the solitude of the shepherd's wheeled house the exile looks out on life and sees the face of nature. But here he parts with Wordsworth and the pantheists; for in nature, also, he finds illusion and the reed that runs into the hand :—

> " Vivez, froide Nature, et revivez sans cesse
> Sur nos pieds, sur nos fronts, puisque c'est votre loi ;
> Vivez, et dédaignez, si vous êtes déesse,
> L'homme, humble passager, qui dut vous être un roi ;
> Plus que tout votre règne et que ses splendeurs vaines,
> J'aime la majesté des souffrances humaines ;
> Vous ne recevrez pas un cri d'amour de moi."

Finally, it is in pity, in the tender patience of human sympathy, in the love which is " taciturne et toujours menacé," that the melancholy poet finds the sole solace of a broken and uncertain existence.

It is in the same connection that we must read *La Sauvage* and *La Mort du Loup*, poems which belong to the year 1843. The close of the second of these presents us with the pessimistic philosophy of Vigny in its most concise and penetrating form. The poet has described in his admirable way the scene of a wolf hunt in the woods of a château where he has been staying, and the death of the wolf, while defending his mate and her cubs. He closes his picture with these reflections :—

> " Comment on doit quitter la vie et tous ses maux,—
> C'est vous que le savez, sublimes animaux !
> A voir ce que l'on fut sur terre et ce qu'on laisse,
> Seul le silence est grand : tout le reste est faiblesse ;
> Ah ! je t'ai bien compris, sauvage voyageur,
> Et ton dernier regard m'est allé jusqu'au cœur !
> Il disait : ' Si tu peux, fais que ton âme arrive
> A force de rester studieuse et pensive,
> Jusqu'à ce haut degré de stoïque fierté
> Où, naissant dans les bois, j'ai tout d'abord monté.
> Gémir, pleurer, prier, est également lâche.
> Fais énergiquement ta longue et lourde tâche
> Dans la voie où le sort a voulu t'appeler—
> Puis, après, comme moi, souffre et meurs sans parler.' " [1]

It was in nourishing such lofty thoughts as these that

[1] We have here, doubtless, a reminiscence of Byron and *Childe Harold*,—" And the wolf dies in silence."

Alfred de Vigny lived the life of a country gentleman at Maine-Giraud, reading, dreaming, cultivating his vines, sitting for hours by the bedside of his helpless Lydia.

"Silence is Poetry itself for me," Alfred de Vigny says in one of his private letters, and as time went on he had scarcely energy enough to write down his thoughts. When he braced himself to the effort of doing so, as when in 1858 he contrived to compose *La Bouteille à la Mer*, his accent was found to be as clear and his music as vivid and resonant as ever. The reason was that although he was so solitary and silent, the labour of the brain was unceasing; under the ashes the fire burned hot and red. He has a very curious phrase about the action of his mind; he says, " Mon cerveau, toujours mobile, travaille et tourbillonne sous mon front immobile avec une vitesse effrayante; des mondes passent devant mes yeux entre un mot qu'on me dit et le mot que je réponds." Dumas, who was peculiarly predisposed to miscomprehend Vigny, could not reconcile himself, in younger days, to his " immateriality," to what another observer called his " perpetual seraphic hallucination "; after 1835, this disconcerting remoteness and abstraction grew upon the poet so markedly as to cut him off from easy contact with other men. But his isolation, even his pessimism, failed to harden him; on the contrary, by a divine indulgence, they increased his sensibility, the enthusiasm of his pity, his passion for the welfare of others.

Death found him at last, and in one of its most cruel forms. Soon after he had passed his sixtieth year, he began to be subjected to vague pains, which became intenser, and which presently proved to be the symptoms of cancer. He bore this final trial with heroic fortitude, and as the physical suffering grew more extreme, the intellectual serenity prevailed above the anguish. In the very last year of his life, the poetical faculty awakened in him again, and he wrote *Les Oracles*, the incomparably solemn and bold apologue of *Le Mont des Oliviers*, and the mystical ode entitled *L'Esprit Pur*. This last poem closed with the ominous words, " et pour moi c'est assez." On September 17, 1863, his soul was released at length from the tortured and exhausted body, and the weary Stello was at peace.

It is not to be pretended that the poetry of Alfred de Vigny is to every one's taste. He was too indifferent to the public, too austere and arrogant in his address, to attract the masses, and to them he will remain perpetually unknown. But he is a writer, in his best prose as well as in the greater part of his scanty verse, who has only to become familiar to a reader susceptible to beauty, to grow more and more beloved. The other poets of his age were fluent and tumultuous; Alfred de Vigny was taciturn, stoical, one who had lost faith in glory, in life, perhaps even in himself. While the flute and the trumpet sounded, his hunter's horn, blown far away in the melancholy woodland, could scarcely raise an echo in the heart of a warrior or banqueter. But those who visit Vigny in the forest will be in no hurry to return. He shall entertain them there with such high thoughts and such proud music that they will follow him wherever his dream may take him. They may admit that he is sometimes hard, often obscure, always in a certain facile sense unsympathetic, but they will find their taste for more redundant melodies than his a good deal marred for the future. And some among them, if they are sincere, will admit that, so far as they are concerned, he is the most majestic poet whom France produced in the rich course of the nineteenth century.

MADEMOISELLE   AÏSSÉ

MADEMOISELLE AÏSSÉ

LITERATURE presents us with no more pathetic figure
of a waif or stray than that of the poor little Circassian
slave whom her friends called Mademoiselle Aïssé.
But interesting and touching as is the romance of her
history, it is surpassed by the rare distinction of her
character and the delicacy of her mind. Placed in the
centre of the most depraved society of modern Europe,
protected from ruin by none of those common bulwarks
which proved too frail to sustain the high-born virtues
of the Tencins and the Parabères, exposed by her wit
and beauty to all the treachery of fashionable Paris
unabashed, this little Oriental orphan preserved an
exquisite refinement of nature, a conscience as sensitive
as a nerve. If she had been *dévote*, if she had retired
to a nunnery, the lesson of her life would have been
less wholesome than it is; we may go further and admit
that it would be less poignant than it is but for the
single frailty of her conduct. She sinned once, and
expiated her sin with tears; but in an age when love
was reduced to a caprice and intrigue governed by
cynical maxims, Aïssé's fault, her solitary abandonment
to a sincere passion, almost takes the proportions of a
virtue. Ruskin has somewhere recommended Swiss
travellers who find themselves physically exhausted
by the pomp of Alpine landscape, to sink on their knees
and concentrate their attention on the petals of a rock-
rose. In comparison with the vast expanse of French

literature the pretensions of Aïssé are little more than those of a flower, but she has no small share of a flower's perfume and beauty.

In her lifetime Mademoiselle Aïssé associated with some of the great writers of her time. Yet if any one had told her that she would live in literature with such friends as Montesquieu and Destouches her modesty would have been overwhelmed with confusion. She made no pretensions to being a blue-stocking; she would have told us that she did not know how to write a page. An exact coeval of hers was the sarcastic and brilliant young man who called himself Voltaire; he was strangely gentle to Aïssé, but she would have been amazed to learn that he would long survive her, and would annotate her works in his old age. Her works! Her only works, she would have told us, were the coloured embroideries with which, in some tradition of a Turkish taste, she adorned her own rooms in the Hôtel Ferriol. Notwithstanding all this, no history of French literature would have any pretensions to completeness if it omitted Aïssé's name. Among all the memoir-writers, letter-writers, and pamphleteers of the early eighteenth century she stands in some respects pre-eminent. As a correspondent pure and simple there is a significance in the fact that her life exactly fills the space between the death of Sévigné, which occurred when Aïssé was about two years old, and the birth of L'Espinasse, which happened a few months before Aïssé's death. During this period of nearly forty years no woman in France wrote letters which could be placed beside theirs except our Circassian. They form a singularly interesting trio; and if Aïssé can no more pretend to possess the breadth of vision and rich imagination of Madame de Sévigné than to command the incomparable accent of passion

which cries through the correspondence of Mademoiselle
de L'Espinasse, she has qualities which are not unworthy
to be named with these—an exquisite sincerity, an
observation of men and things which could hardly be
more picturesque, a note of pensive and thrilling tenderness, and a candour which melts the very soul to pity.

In the winter of 1697 or spring of 1698, a dissipated
and eccentric old bachelor, Charles de Ferriol, Baron
d'Argental, who was French Envoy at the court of the
Grand Vizier, bought a little Circassian child of about
four years old in one of the bazaars of Constantinople.
He had often bought slaves in the Turkish market before,
and not to the honour of his memory. But this time
he was actuated by a genuine kindly impulse. He was
fifty-one years of age; he did not intend to marry, and
he seems to have thought that he would supply himself
with a beautiful daughter for the care of his old age.
Sainte-Beuve, with his unfailing intuition, insisted on
this interpretation, and since his essay was written, in
1846, various documents have turned up, proving beyond
a doubt that the intentions of the Envoy were parental.
The little girl said that her name was Haidée. She
preserved in later life an impression of a large house,
and many servants running hither and thither. Her
friends agreed to consider her as the daughter of a
Circassian prince, and the very large price (1500 livres)
which M. de Ferriol paid for her, as well as the singular
distinction of her beauty, to some extent support the
legend. In August 1698, M. de Ferriol, who had held
temporary missions in Turkey for seven years, was
recalled to France, to be sent out again as French
ambassador to the Porte in 1699. He brought his little
Circassian orphan with him, and placed her in the charge
of his sister-in-law, Madame de Ferriol, in Paris. She

was immediately christened as Charlotte Haidée, but
she preserved neither of these names in ordinary life;
Charlotte was dropped at once, and Haidée on the lips
of her new French relations became the softer Aïssé.

Aïssé's adopted aunt, as we may call her, Madame de
Ferriol, was a very fair average specimen of the fashionable lady of the Regency.   She belonged to the notorious
family of Tencin, whose mark on the early part of the
eighteenth century is so ineffaceable.   Of Madame de
Ferriol it may be said by her defenders that she was not
so openly scandalous as her sister the Canoness, who
appears in a very curious light in the letters of Aïssé.
Born in 1674, Madame de Ferriol was still quite a young
woman, and her sons, the Marquis de Pont-de-Veyle
and Comte d'Argental, were little children, fit to become
the playmates of Aïssé.   Indeed these two boys were
regarded almost as the Circassian's brothers, and the
family documents speak of all three as " nos enfants."
She was put to school—it is believed, from a phrase of
her own, " Je viens de me ressouvenir "—with the
Nouvelles Catholiques, a community of nuns, whose
house was a few doors away from the Hôtel Ferriol,
and there for a few years we may suppose her to have
passed the happy life of a child.   From this life she
herself, in one of the most charming of her letters, draws
aside the curtain for a moment.   In 1731 some gossip
accused her of a passion for the Duc de Gesvres, and her
jealous mentor in Geneva wrote to know if there was
any truth in the report.   Aïssé, then about thirty-seven
years of age, wrote back as follows :—

" I admit, Madame, notwithstanding your anger and
the respect which I owe you, that I have had a violent
fancy for M. le Duc de Gesvres, and that I even carried
this great sin to confession.   It is true that my confessor

did not think it necessary to impose any penance on me.
I was eight years old when this passion began, and at
twelve I laughed at the whole affair, not that I did not
still like M. de Gesvres, but that I saw how ludicrous
it had been of me to be so anxious to be talking and
playing in the garden with him and his brothers. He
was two or three years older than I, and we thought
ourselves a great deal more grown up than the rest.
We liked to be conversing while the others were playing
at hide-and-seek. We set up for reasonable people;
we met regularly every day : we never talked about
love, for the fact was that neither of us knew what
that meant. The window of the little drawing-room
opened upon a balcony, where he often came; we made
signs to each other; he took us out to see the fireworks,
and often to Saint Ouen. As we were always together,
the people in charge of us began to joke about us and
it came to the ears of my aga (the Ambassador), who,
as you can imagine, made a fine romance out of all this.
I found it out; it distressed me; I thought that, as a
discreet person, I ought to watch my own behaviour,
and the result was that I persuaded myself that I must
really be in love with M. de Gesvres. I was *dévote*, and
went to confession; I first mentioned all my little sins,
and then I had to mention this big sin; I could scarcely
make up my mind to do so, but as a girl that had been
well brought up, I determined to hide nothing. I
confessed that I was in love with a young man. My
director seemed astonished; he asked me how old he
was. I told him he was eleven. He laughed, and told
me that there was no penance for that sin; that I had
only to keep on being a good girl, and that he had nothing
more to say to me for the time being."

It is like a page of Hans Andersen; there is the same

innocence, the same suspicion that all the world may not be so innocent.

The incidents of the early womanhood of Aïssé are known to us only through an anonymous sketch of her life, printed in 1787, when her *Letters* first appeared. This short life, which has been attributed to Mademoiselle Rieu, the granddaughter of the lady to whom the letters were addressed, informs us that Aïssé was carefully educated, so far as the head went, but more than neglected in the lessons of the heart. " From the moment when Mademoiselle Aïssé began to lisp," says this rather pedantic memoir, " she heard none but dangerous maxims. Surrounded by voluptuous and intriguing women, she was constantly being reminded that the only occupation of a woman without a fortune ought to be to secure one." But she found protectors. The two sons of Madame de Ferriol, though themselves no better than their neighbours, guarded her as though she had really been their sister; and in her own soul there were no germs of the fashionable depravity. When she was seventeen, her " aga " came back from his long exile in Constantinople, broken in health, even, it is said, more than a little disturbed in intellect. To the annoyance of his relatives he nourished the design of being made a cardinal; he was lodged, for safety's sake, close to the family of his brother. From Ferriol's return in 1711 to his death in 1722, we have considerable difficulty in realising what Aïssé's existence was.

There is some reason to suppose that it was Lord Bolingbroke who first perceived the exceptional charm of Aïssé's mind. When the illustrious English exile came to France in 1715, he was almost immediately drawn into the society of the Hôtel Ferriol. One of Aïssé's kindest friends was that wise and charming

woman, the Marquise de Villette, whom Bolingbroke
somewhat tardily married about 1720, and it was doubtless through her introduction that he became intimate
with Madame de Ferriol. As early as 1719 Bolingbroke
writes of Aïssé as of an intimate friend, and speaks of
her as threatened by a " disadvantageous metamor-
phosis," by which he probably refers to an attack of
the small-pox. It appears to have been during a visit
to the château of Lord and Lady Bolingbroke that Aïssé
first met Voltaire; and later on we shall see that these
persons played a singular but very important part in
the drama of her life. There seems no doubt that,
however little Madame de Villette and Lord Bolingbroke
could claim the white flower of a spotless life, they were
judicious and useful friends at this perilous moment of
her career. Aïssé's beauty, which was extraordinary,
and her dubious social station, made the young Circassian
peculiarly liable to attack from the men of fashion who
passed from alcove to alcove in search of the indulgence
of some ephemeral caprice. The poets turned their
rhymes in her honour, and one of their effusions, that
of the Swiss Vernet, was so far esteemed that it was
engraved fifty years afterwards underneath her portrait.
It may thus be paraphrased :—

> " Aïssé's beauty is all Greek;
>   Yet was she wise in youth to borrow
> From France the charming tongue we speak,
>   And wit, and airs that banish sorrow :
>
> A theme like this deserves a verse
>   As warm and clear as mine is cold,
> For has there been a heart like hers
>   Since our Astrean age of gold ? "

Aïssé received all this homage unmoved. The Duke
of Orleans one day met her in the salon of Madame de

Parabère, was enchanted with her beauty, and declared his passion to Madame de Ferriol. To the lasting shame of this woman, she agreed to support his claim, and the Regent imagined that the little Greek would fall an easy prey. To his amazement, and to the indignation of Madame de Ferriol, he was indignantly repulsed; and when further pressure was brought to bear upon her, Aïssé threatened to retire at once to a convent if the proposition was so much as repeated. She was one of the principal attractions of Madame de Ferriol's salon, and, says the memoir, " as Aïssé was useful to her, fearing to lose her, she consented, though most unwillingly, to say no more to her " about the Duke. This was but one, though certainly the most alarming, of the traps set for her feet in the brilliant and depraved society of her guardians. The habitual life of the Tencins and Parabères of 1720 was something to us quite incredible. Such a " moral dialogue " as *Le Hasard au Coin du Feu* would be rejected as the dream of a licentious satirist, if the memoirs and correspondence of the Cidalises and the Clitandres of the age did not fully convince us that the novelists merely repeated what they saw around them. We must bear in mind what an extraordinary condition of roseate semi-nudity this politest of generations lived in, to understand the excellence as well as the frailty of Aïssé. We must also bear in mind, when our Puritan indignation is ready to carry us away in profuse condemnation of this whole society, that extremely shrewd remark of Duclos : " Le peuple français est le seul peuple qui puisse perdre ses mœurs sans se corrompre."

In 1720 the old ex-ambassador fell ill. Aïssé immediately took up her abode with him, and nursed him assiduously until he died. That he was not an easy invalid to cherish we gather from a phrase in one of her own letters, as well as from hints in those of Bolingbroke. In October 1722 he died, leaving to Aïssé a considerable fortune in the form of an annuity, as well as a sum of money in a bill on the estate. The sister-in-law, Madame de Ferriol, to whose guardianship Aïssé had been consigned, thought her own sons injured by the ambassador's generosity, and had the extreme bad taste to upbraid Aïssé. The note had not yet been cashed, and at the first word from Madame de Ferriol, Aïssé fetched it and threw it into the fire. This little anecdote speaks worlds for the sensitive and independent character of the Circassian; one almost blushes to complete it by adding that Madame de Ferriol took advantage of her ward's hasty act of injured pride. Aïssé, however, had other things to think of; " the birthday of her life was come, her love was come to her." As early as 1721, we find Lord Bolingbroke saying, in a letter to Madame de Ferriol, " I fully expect you to come; I even flatter myself that we shall see Madame du Deffand; but as for Mademoiselle Aïssé, I do not expect her. The Turk will be her excuse, and a certain Christian of my acquaintance her reason." This seems to mean that Aïssé would give as her excuse for not coming to stay with the Bolingbrokes that she was needed at the Ambassador's pillow; but that her real reason would be that she wished to stay in Paris to be near " a certain Christian." That which had been vainly attempted by so many august and eminent personages, namely, the capture of Aïssé's heart, was now being pursued with alarming success by a very modest candidate for her affections.

The Chevalier Blaise Marie d'Aydie, the hope of an impoverished Périgord family who claimed descent, with a blot on their escutcheon, from the noble house

of Foix, was, in 1721, about thirty years of age.   He had
lived a passably dissipated life, after the fashion of the
Clitandres of the age, and if Mademoiselle Rieu is to be
believed, Madame la Duchesse de Berry herself had
passed through the fires on his behalf.   He was poor;
he was brave and handsome and rather stupid; he was
expected one of these days to break his vows as a Knight
of Malta and redeem the family fortunes by a good
marriage.   We have a portrait of him by Madame du
Deffand, written in her delicate, persistent way, touch
upon touch, with a result that reminds one of Mr. Henry
James's pictures of character.   Voltaire, more rapidly
and more enthusiastically, called him the " chevalier
sans peur et sans reproche," and drew him as the hero
of his tragedy of *Adélaïde du Guesclin*.   He had the
superficial vices of his time; but his tenderness, loyalty,
and goodness of heart were infinite, and if we judge him
by the morals of his own age and not of ours, he was a
very fine fellow.   His principal fault seems to have been
that he was rather dull.   As Madame du Deffand puts
it, " They say of Fontenelle that instead of a heart he
has a second brain; one might believe that the head of
the Chevalier contained another heart."   All evidence
goes to prove that from the moment when he first met
Aïssé no other woman existed for him, and if their
union was blameworthy, let it be at least admitted that
it lasted, with impassioned fidelity on both sides, for
twelve years and until Aïssé's death.

It would appear that until the Ambassador passed
away, and the irksome life at the Hôtel Ferriol began
again, Aïssé contrived to keep her ardent admirer within
bounds.   To us it seems amazingly perverse that the
lovers did not marry; but Aïssé herself was the first to
insist that a Chevalier d'Aydie could not and should not

offend his relations by a *mésalliance* with a Circassian slave. At last she yielded; but, as Mademoiselle Rieu tells us, " he loved her so delicately that he was jealous of her reputation; he adored her, and would have sacrificed everything for her; while she, on her part, loving the Chevalier, found his fame, his fortune, his honour, dearer to her than her own." In 1724 she found it absolutely necessary to disappear from her circle of acquaintance. She did not dare to confide her secret to the unscrupulous Madame de Ferriol, and in her despair she examined the circle of her friends for the most sympathetic face. She decided to trust Lady Bolingbroke, and she could not have made a wiser choice. That tender-hearted and deeply-experienced lady was equal to the delicate emergency. She announced her intention of spending a few months in England, and she begged Madame de Ferriol to allow Aïssé to accompany her. They started as if for Calais, but only to double upon their steps. Aïssé, in company with her maid, Sophie, and a confidential English man-servant, was installed in a remote suburb of Paris, under the care of the Chevalier d'Aydie, while Lady Bolingbroke hastened on to England, and amused herself with inventing anecdotes and messages from Aïssé. In the fulness of time Lady Bolingbroke returned and took care to " collect " Aïssé before she presented herself at the Hôtel Ferriol. Meanwhile a daughter had been born, who was christened Célénie Leblond, and who was placed in a convent at Sens, under the name of Miss Black, as a niece of Lord Bolingbroke. The abbess of this convent was a Mademoiselle de Villette, the daughter of Lady Bolingbroke. No novelist would dare to describe so improbable a stratagem; let us make the story complete by adding that it succeeded to perfection, and that Madame de Ferriol herself never seems to have suspected the truth. This daughter, whom we shall presently meet again, grew up to be a charming woman, and adorned society in the next generation as the Vicomtesse de Nanthia. If the story of Aïssé ended here it would not appeal to a Richardson, or even to an Abbé Prévost d'Exiles, as a moral tale.

Between 1723 and 1726 Aïssé's life passed quietly enough. The Chevalier d'Aydie was constantly at the Hôtel Ferriol, but the two lovers were not any longer in their first youth. A little prudence went a long way in a society adorned by Madame de Parabère and Madame de Tencin. No breath of scandal seems to have troubled Aïssé, and when her cares came, they all began from within. We do not possess the letters of Aïssé to her lover. I hope I am not a Philistine if I admit that I sincerely hope they will never be discovered. We possess the love letters of Mademoiselle de L'Espinasse; this should be enough of that kind of literature for one century at least—it would be a terrible thing to come down one morning to see announced a collection of the letters of Aïssé to her Chevalier, edited by M. Edmond de Goncourt! In the summer of 1726 there arrived from Geneva a lady about twenty years older than Aïssé, the wife of a M. Calandrini; she was a step-aunt, if such a relationship be recognised, of Lord Bolingbroke, and so was intimately connected with the Ferriol circle. Research, which really is far too busy in our days, has found out that Madame de Calandrini herself had not been all that could be desired; but in 1726 she was *dévote*, yet not to such an extent as to throw any barrier between herself and the confidences of a younger woman. Aïssé received her warmly, gave her heart to her without reserve, and when the lady went back to Geneva Aïssé discovered that she was the first and best friend that she had ever possessed. Madame Calandrini carried home with her the inmost and most dangerous secrets of Aïssé's history, and it is evident that she immediately planned her young friend's conversion.

The *Letters* of Aïssé are exclusively composed of her correspondence with this Madame Calandrini from the autumn of 1726 to her own fatal illness in January 1733. They remained in Geneva until, in 1758, they were lent to Voltaire, who enriched them with very interesting and important notes. Nearly thirty years more passed, and at length, in 1787, they saw the light. Next year they were reprinted, with a very delightful portrait of Aïssé. In this she appears as a decided beauty, with very fair hair, an elegant and spirited head lightly poised on delicate shoulders, and nothing Oriental in her appearance except the large, oval, dark eyes, languishing with incredible length of eyelash. The text was confused and difficult in these early editions, and in successive reprints has occupied various biographers—M. de Barante, M. Ravenel, M. Piedagnal. I suppose, however, that I do no injustice to those writers if I claim for M. Eugène Asse the credit of having done more than any other man, by patient annotation and collection of explicatory documents, to render the reading of Aïssé's letters interesting and agreeable.

The letters of Aïssé to Madame Calandrini are the history of an awakening conscience. It is this fact, and the slow development of the inevitable moral plot, which give them their singular psychological value. As the letters approach their close, our attention is entirely riveted by the spectacle of this tender and passionate spirit tortured by remorse and yearning for expiation. But at the outset there is no moral passion expressed,

and we think less of Aïssé herself than of the society to
which she belonged by her age and education.   As it
seems impossible, from other sources of information, to
believe that Madame Calandrini was what is commonly
thought to be an amiable woman, we take from Aïssé's
praise of her something of the same impression that we
obtain from Madame de Sévigné's affectionate addresses
to Madame de Grignan.   Indeed, the opening letter of
Aïssé's series, with its indescribable tone of the seventeenth century, reads so much like one of the Sévigné's
letters to her daughter that one wonders whether the
semblance can be wholly accidental.   There is a childish
archness in the way in which Aïssé jests about all her
own adorers—the susceptible abbés, and the councillors
whose neglected passion has comfortably subsided into
friendship.   There are little picturesque touches—the
black spaniel yelping in his lady's lap, and upsetting the
coffee-pot in his eagerness to greet a new-comer.   There
are charming bits of self-portraiture : " I used to flatter
myself that I was a little philosopher, but I never shall
be one in matters of sentiment."   It is all so youthful,
so girlish, that we have to remind ourselves that the
author of such a passage as the following was in her
thirty-third year :—

" I spend my days in shooting little birds; this does
me a great deal of good.   Exercise and distraction are
excellent remedies for the vapours.   The ardour of the
chase makes me walk, although my feet are bruised; the
perspiration that this exercise causes is good for me.   I
am as sun-burned as a crow; you would be frightened
if you saw me, but I scarcely mind it.   How happy
should I be if I were still with you !   I would willingly
give a pint of my blood if we could be together at this
moment."

Here Aïssé anticipates by a year or two Matthew Green's famous " Fling but a stone, the giant dies." She has told Madame Calandrini everything. The Chevalier is away in Périgord, which adds to her vapours ; but his letters breathe the sweetest constancy. She would like to send them to Geneva, but she dares not ; they are too full of her own praises. She has been to see the first performance of a new comedy, *Pyrame et Thisbé*, and giggles over its disastrous fate. This gives us firm ground in dating this first letter, for this comedy, or rather opera, was played on the 17th of October, 1726. Nothing could be more gay or sparkling than Aïssé's tone.

But soon there comes a change. We find that she is not happy in the Hôtel Ferriol. Her friend and foster-brother, Comte d'Argental, who lived on until 1788 to be the last survivor of her circle, is away " with his sweetheart in the Enchanted Island," and she has his room while hers is being refurnished. But it will cost her one hundred pistoles, for Madame de Ferriol makes her pay for everything. The subjects which she writes about in all light-heartedness are extraordinary. She cannot resist, from sheer ebullience of mirth, copying out a letter of amazing impudence written by a certain officer of dragoons to the bishop of his diocese. Can she or can she not continue to know the beautiful brazen Madame de Parabère, whose behaviour is of a lightness, but oh ! of such a lightness ? Yet " her carriage is always at my service, and don't you think it would be ridiculous not to visit her at all ? " If one desires a marvellous tale of the ways and the manners of the great world under Louis XV., there is the astounding story of Madame la Princesse de Bournonville, and how she was publicly engaged to marry the Duc de Ruffec

E

fifteen minutes after her first husband's death; it is told, with perfect calmness, in Aïssé's best manner. The Prince was one of Aïssé's numerous rejected adorers; she rejoices that he has left her no compromising legacy. There is a certain affair, on the 10th of January 1727, " which would make your hair stand on end; but it really is too infamous to be written down." A wonderful world, so elegant and so debased, so enthusiastic and so cynical, so full of beauty and so full of corruption, that we find no name but Louis Quinze to qualify its paradoxes.

In her earlier letters Aïssé reveals herself as a patron of the stage, and a dramatic critic of marked views. Her foster-brothers, Pont-de-Veyle and Argental, were deeply stage-stricken; the " Enchanted Island " of the latter seems to have been situated somewhere in that ocean, the Théâtre de l'Opéra. Aïssé threw herself with heart and soul into the famous rivalry between the two operatic stars of Paris; she was all for the enchanting Lemaure, and when that public favourite wilfully retired to private life Aïssé found that the Pellissier " fait horriblement mal." She tells with infinite zest a rather scurrilous story of how a certain famous Jansenist canon, seventy years of age, fearing to die without having ever seen a dramatic performance, dressed himself up in his deceased grandmother's garments and made his appearance in the pit, creating, by his incredible oddity of garb and feature, such a sensation that the actor Armand stopped playing, and desired him, amid the shrieks of laughter of the audience, to decamp as fast as possible. Voltaire vouches for the absolute truth of this anecdote. But before Aïssé begins to lose the gaiety of her spirits it may be well to let her give in her own language, or as near as I can reach it, a sample of her powers as an artist in anecdote.

" A little while ago there happened a little adventure which has made a good deal of noise. I will tell you about it. Six weeks ago Isez, the surgeon [one of the most eminent practitioners of his time] received a note, begging him, at six o'clock on the afternoon of the next day, to be in the Rue du Pot-de-Fer, close to the Luxembourg. He did not fail to be there; he found waiting for him a man, who conducted him for a few steps, and then made him enter a house, shutting the door on the surgeon, so as, himself, to remain in the street. Isez was surprised that this man did not at once take him where he was wanted. But the *portier* of the house appeared, and told him that he was expected on the first floor, and asked him to step up, which he did. He opened an ante-chamber all hung with white; a lackey, made to be put in a picture, dressed in white, nicely curled, nicely powdered, and with a pouch of white hair and two dusters in his hand, came to meet him, and told him that he must have his shoes wiped. After this ceremony, he was conducted into a room also hung with white. Another lackey, dressed like the first, went through the same ceremony with the shoes; he was then taken into a room where everything was white, bed, carpet, tapestry, *fauteuils*, chairs, tables, and floor. A tall figure in a night-cap and a perfectly white dressing-gown, and a white mask, was seated near the fire. When this kind of phantom perceived Isez, he said to him, ' I have the devil in my body,' and spoke no more; for three-quarters of an hour he did nothing but put on and pull off six pairs of white gloves which he had on a table by his side. Isez was frightened, but he grew more so when, glancing round the room, he saw several fire-arms; he was taken with such a trembling that he was obliged to sit down for fear of falling. At last, to break the silence, he asked the figure in white what was wanted of him, because he had an engagement, and his time belonged to the public. The white figure dryly replied, ' What does it matter to you, if you are paid well ? ' and said nothing more. Another quarter of an hour passed in silence; at last the phantom pulled the bell-rope. The two white lackeys reappeared; the phantom asked for bandages, and told Isez to draw five pounds of blood.''

We must spoil the story by finishing it abruptly. Isez bleeds the phantom not in the arm, on account of the monstrous quantity of blood, but in the foot, a very beautiful woman's foot, apparently, when he gets to the last of six pairs of white silk stockings. He is presently, after various other adventures, turned out of the mysterious house, and nobody, not even the King himself, can tell what it all means.

But very soon the picture of Aïssé's life begins to be clouded over. In the spring of 1727, she is in a peck of troubles. The periodical reduction of the State annuities, which had been carried out once more during the preceding winter by the new Minister of Finance, had brought misery to many gentlefolks of France. In Aïssé's early letters, she and her acquaintances appear much as Irish landlords do now; in her latest letters they remind us of what these landlords would be if the National party realised its dream. The Chevalier does not seem to have been a sufferer personally; he had not much to lose, but we find him sympathising with Aïssé, and drawing up an appealing letter for her to send to the Cardinal de Fleury. Aïssé begins to feel the shadows falling across her future. If ever she marries, she says, she will put into the contract a clause by which she retains the right to go to Geneva whenever she likes,

for she longs to tell her troubles to Madame Calandrini.
And thus is first sounded the mournful key to which we
soon become accustomed :—

" Every day I see that there is nothing but virtue that
is any good for this world and the next. As for myself,
who have not been lucky enough to behave properly,
but who respect and admire virtuous people, the simple
wish to belong to the number attracts to me all sorts of
flattering things; the pity which every one shows me
[for her money losses, doubtless] almost prevents me
from being miserable. I have just 2000 francs of income
at most left. My jewels and my diamonds are sold."

The result of her sudden poverty appears to have
been that the Chevalier d'Aydie, sorely against his
inclination, but actuated by a generous impulse, offered
to marry her. She was not less generous than he, and
almost Quixotically rejected what would have been her
greatest satisfaction. To Madame Calandrini, who was
plainly one of those who urged her to accept this act of
restitution, the orphan-mother answers thus :—

" Think, Madame, of what the world would say if he
married a nobody, and one who depended entirely on
the charity of the Ferriol family. No; I love his fame
too much, and I have myself at the same time too much
pride, to allow him to commit such an act of folly. He
would be sure to repent of having followed the bent of
his absurd passion, and I could not survive the pain of
having made him wretched, and of being myself no
longer loved."

The Chevalier, unable to live in Paris without being
at her side, fled for a five months' exile to the parental
château in Périgord. Aïssé had expressed a mild surprise that he could not contrive to be more calm, but
their discussions had always ended in a joke. Yet it is

plain that all these circumstances made her regard life more seriously than she had ever done before. In her next letter (August 1727) we learn how miserable a home the Hôtel Ferriol had now become for her. " The mistress of this house," she says, " is much more difficult to live with than the poor Ambassador was." As for the Chevalier, he had scarcely reached Périgueux, when he forgot all about the months he wished to spend in the country, and hastened back to Paris to be near Aïssé. The latter writes, in her prim way, " I admit I was very agreeably surprised to see him enter my room yesterday. How happy I should be if I could only love him without having to reproach myself for it ! " It is plain, in spite of the always modest, and now timid way in which she writes, that her moral worth and delicate judgment were estimated at their true value even by the frivolous women who surrounded her. The Duchess of Fitz-James asks her advice as to whether she shall or shall not accept the hand of the Duc d'Aumont. The dissolute Madame de Tencin cannot forgive or forget Aïssé's tacit disapproval of her conduct. The gentler, but not less naughty, Madame de Parabère purrs around her like a cat, exquisitely assiduous not entirely to lose the esteem of one whose position in the world can have offered nothing to such a personage, but by whose intelligence and sympathetic goodness she could not help being fascinated. In recording all this, without in the least being aware of it, Aïssé gives us an impression of her own simple sweetness as of a touchstone by which radically evil natures were distinguished from those whose voluntary abasement was not the sign of a complete corruption of spirit.

We are made to feel in Aïssé's letters, that, without being in any degree a blue-stocking, she was eager to

form her own impression on the various intellectual
questions of the hour. *Gulliver's Travels* had only been
published in England in the autumn of 1726; in the
spring of 1727 Aïssé had read it, in Desfontaine's translation, knew that it was the work of Swift, and praised it
in the very same terms that the world has since agreed
to bestow upon it. Destouches seems to have been a
friend of hers, but when in the same year she went to
see his new comedy *Le Philosophe Marié*, she was not
blinded by friendship. " It is a very charming comedy,"
she wrote, " full of sentiment, full of delicacy; but it
does not possess the genius of Molière." Nor is she less
judicious in what she says about the masterpiece of
another friend, the Abbé Prévost d'Exiles. She writes
in October 1728, " We have a new book here entitled
Mémoires d'un Homme de Qualité retiré du Monde, it is
not worth much, except one hundred and ninety pages
which make one burst out crying." These one hundred
and ninety pages were that immortal supplement to a
dull book which we call *Manon Lescaut*, over which as
many tears are shed nowadays as were dropped a century
and a half ago. It is said by those who have read
Prévost's forgotten romance, *Histoire d'une Grecque
Moderne*, published long afterwards in 1741, that it
contains a full-length portrait of the author's old friend
Aïssé. It might be amusing to compare this with
Voltaire's portrait of her chevalier in *Adélaïde du Guesclin*.

She was evidently a centre of light and activity. The
young woman with whom, at all events during certain
periods, Bolingbroke corresponded by every post, could
be no commonplace person. Voltaire vouches for her
exact and independent knowledge of events. When
Madame Calandrini is anxious to know how a certain
incident at court will turn out, Aïssé says, " You shall

know before the people who make the Gazette do," and
her letters differ from the poet Gray's, which otherwise
they often curiously resemble, that she seems to know
at first hand the class of news that Gray only repeats.
She sometimes shows her first-hand knowledge by her
very inaccuracy.   She gives, for instance, a long account,
which we follow with breathless interest, of the death of
Adrienne Lecouvreur, the event, probably, which moved
Paris more vehemently than any other during the year
1730.   Aïssé directly charges the young Duchesse de
Bouillon with the murder of the actress, and supports
her charge with an amazing array of horrible details.
The affair was mysterious, and Aïssé was evidently
minutely informed; yet Voltaire, in whose arms Adrienne
Lecouvreur died, declares that her account is not the
true one.   On one point her knowledge of her contemporaries is very useful to us.   The priceless correspondence of Madame du Deffand makes the latter, as
an old woman, an exceedingly life-like figure, but we
know little of her early life; Aïssé's sketches of her,
therefore, and to say the truth, cruelly penetrating
analysis of her character at the age of thirty, are most
valuable.   The Madame du Deffand we know seems a
wiser woman than Aïssé's friend; but the fact is that
many of these witty Frenchwomen only became tolerable,
like remarkable vintages, when they were growing a little
crusted.

Among the brightest sections of Aïssé's correspondence
are those in which she speaks of her high-spirited and
somewhat dissolute foster-brothers, Pont-de-Veyle and
D'Argental.   These two men were sowing their wild
oats very hard, in the fashion of the day, and although
they were passing the solemn age of thirty, the sacks
seemed inexhaustible.   But so far as regarded Aïssé,

their conduct was all that was chivalrous, all that was honourably fraternal. Pont-de-Veyle she calls an angel, but it was D'Argental whom she loved the most, and nothing is more touching than an account she gives, with the *naïveté* of a child, of a quarrel she had with him. This quarrel lasted eight days, and Aïssé kept her letter open until she could add, in a postscript, the desired information that, she having drunk his health at dinner and afterwards kissed him, they have made it up without any formal explanation. " Since then," she adds in that tone of hers which makes the eyes of a middle-aged citizen of perfidious Albion quite dim after a hundred and fifty years, " Since then we have been a great deal together."

In 1728 she had need of all the kindness she could get. The Chevalier was so ill in June that she was obliged to face the prospect of his death. " Duty, love, inquietude, and friendship, are for ever troubling my thoughts and my body; I am in a cruel agitation; my body is giving way, for I am overwhelmed with vapours and with grief; and, if any misfortune should happen to that man, I feel I should not be able to endure the horrible sorrow of it. He is more attached to me than ever; he encourages me to perform my duties. Sometimes I cannot help telling him, that if he gets any worse it will be impossible for me to leave him; and then he scolds me." The dreadful condition of genteel poverty in which the Ferriol family were now living did not tend to make Aïssé's home a bed of roses. In the winter of 1728 these famous people of quality were " dying of hunger." There was not, that is to say, as much food upon their table as their appetites required, and Aïssé expected to share the fate of the horse whose master gave him one grain less of oats each day until he died

from starvation. In this there was of course a little
playful exaggeration, but her poverty weighed heavily
on Aïssé. She had scarcely enough money for her daily
wants, and envied the Chevalier, who was saving that
he might form a dowry for the little daughter at Sens,
the "*pauvre petite*" in the convent, after whom Aïssé's
heart yearned, and whom she might but very rarely
visit as a stranger.

She spent the autumn of 1729 at Pont-de-Veyle, the
country seat of the Ferriol family, a château between
Macon and Bourg. She took advantage of this neighbourhood to Switzerland, and paid the long-pro iised
visit to Madame Calandrini in Geneva. The incident
was a momentous one in the history of her soul. She
came back more uneasy, more irresolute than ever, and
in deep depression of spirits. Her first instinct, on
being left to her own thoughts again, was to enter a
convent, but Madame Calandrini did not encourage this
idea, and Aïssé soon relinquished it. She saw, herself,
that duty called her to stay with Madame de Ferriol,
who was now growing an invalid. Before leaving Geneva
Madame Calandrini had made a solemn attempt to
persuade her to conclude her dubious relations with the
Chevalier. She tried to extract a promise from Aïssé
that she would either marry D'Aydie or cease to see
him. But it is easy for comfortable matrons in their
own boudoirs to urge a line of conduct; it is less simple
for the unfortunate to carry out these maxims in the
hard light of day. Aïssé wrote: "All that I can
promise you is that nothing shall be spared to bring
about one or other of these things. But, Madame, it
may cost me my life." Such words are lightly said; but
in Aïssé's case they came from the heart. She made the
sacrifice, and it did cost her her life. She attempted to

melt the severe censor at Geneva by extracts from the
Chevalier's letters, and finally she made an appeal which
goes straight to our sympathy. " How can I cut to the
quick a violent passion, and the tenderest and firmest
friendship ? Add to all this, gratitude : it is frightful !
Death would not be worse ! However, since you wish
me to make an effort, I will do so." Conscience and the
Calandrini were inexorable.

In the dull house at Pont-de-Veyle Aïssé was thrown
upon her own consciousness more than in Paris. She
gives us a picture of her dreary existence. The Archbishop of Lyons, who was Madame de Ferriol's brother,
was the only intelligent companion she had, and he was
locked up all day with Jesuit priests. The young
Ferriols were in Paris; their mother, jealous, pietistic,
and peevish, wore Aïssé out with *ennui*. It was in this
tension of the nervous system, this irritation and depression of spirits, that on her way back to Paris in November
she paid a stolen visit to Sens to see her little daughter.
The letter in which she describes the interview is simply
heartrending. The little delicate child, with an exquisite
instinct, clung to this unknown friend, and when at last
Aïssé had to say farewell, her daughter—whom she
must not call her daughter—wrung the mother's heart
with mingled anguish and delight by throwing her arms
round her neck and crying out, " I have no father or
mother; please, you be my mother, for I love you as
much as if you really were ! " Aïssé could not tear
herself away; she remained a fortnight at the convent,
more unhappy than happy, and so afflicted in spirits
that she positively had to take to her bed. The little
" Miss Black " waited upon her with a child's enthusiasm, refusing to play with her companions, and lavish-
ing her caresses upon her. At last the poor mother

forced herself to depart, fearing lest she should expose her secret by her emotion. She made her way to Paris, where she found the Chevalier waiting for her, and all her good resolutions were shattered by the passionate joy of his welcome. She did not know what to do or where to turn.

In the beginning of 1730 the Chevalier had another dangerous illness, and Aïssé was obliged to postpone the crisis. He got well and she was so happy that she could not but postpone it a little longer. Slowly, as she herself perceived, her bodily strength began to waste away under the agitations of her conscience. We may pass over the slow progress of the spiritual complaint, which took more than three years to destroy her healthy constitution. We must push on to the end. In 1732 her health gave serious alarm to all those who surrounded her. That few of her friends suspected the real state of the case, or the hidden griefs that were destroying her, is proved among other things by a little copy of verses which has been preserved in the works of a great man. Voltaire, who made a joke of his own supposed passion for Aïssé, sent her in 1732 a packet of ratafia, to relieve a painful symptom of her complaint, and he accompanied it by a flippant versicle, which may thus be rendered :—

" Hence ! Through her veins like subtle anguish fleet !
Change to desires the snows that thro' them roll !
So may she feel the heat
That burns within my soul."

But the women about her knew that she was dying. The Parabère to whom we may forgive much, because she loved Aïssé so well, fluttered around her with pathetic tenderness; and we find her forcing upon her friend the most beautiful of her personal possessions, a splendid box of crimson jasper. Even Madame de Tencin, whom she had always kept at arm's length, and who had rewarded her with aversion, startled her now with expressions and proofs of affection. Madame de Ferriol herself, with her sharp temper and her ugly speeches, urged upon her the attentions of a Jansenist confessor. The Chevalier, understanding at last that he was about to lose her, was distracted with anxiety, and hung around the room until the ladies were put to their wits' end to get rid of him. In her next letter, written about Christmas of 1732, Aïssé expresses herself thus :—

" I have to be very careful how I deal with you know whom. He has been talking to me about a certain matter as reasonably and affectionately as possible. All his goodness, his delicate way of thinking, loving me for my own self, the interest of the poor little one, to whom one could not give a position, all these things force me to be very careful how I deal with him. For a long time I have been tortured with remorse; the carrying out of this would sustain me. If the Chevalier does not keep to what he has promised, I will see him no more. You see, Madame, what my resolutions are; I will keep to them. But they will probably shorten my life."

The explanation of this passage seems to be that the Chevalier, having put off marriage so long, was anxious not to break his vows for a merely sentimental union, that could last but a few weeks. She had extracted, it would seem, a sort of promise from him, but he did not keep it, and Aïssé died unmarried.

In her last hours Aïssé became completely *dévote*, but not to such an extent as to be unable to see the humour of sending such light ladies as Madame de Parabère and Madame du Deffand through the length

and breadth of Paris to search for a director to under-
take her conversion. At last these inexperienced
emissaries discovered a Père Boursault, who was perhaps
of their world, for he was the son of the dramatist, the
enemy of Molière; from him Aïssé received the consola-
tions of religion. A few days before she died she wrote
once more to Madame Calandrini, and these are the last
words which we possess from the pen of Aïssé :—

" I say nothing to you about the Chevalier. He is
in despair at seeing me so ill. You never witnessed a
passion so violent, more delicacy, more sentiment, more
greatness and generosity. I am not anxious about the
poor little one; she has a friend and protector who loves
her tenderly. Good-bye, dear Madame; I am too weak
to write any more. It is still infinitely sweet to me to
think of you; but I cannot yield to this happiness
without tears, my dear friend. The life I have led has
been very wretched. Have I ever had a moment's
enjoyment? I could not be happy alone; I was afraid
to think; my remorse has never once left me since the
instant when I began to have my eyes open to my mis-
conduct. Why should I be alarmed at my soul being
separated, since I am persuaded that God is all good, and
that the moment when I begin to enjoy happiness will
be that in which I leave this miserable body ? "

On the 14th of March 1733, Charlotte Elizabeth
Aïssé, spinster, aged about forty years, was buried in
the chapel of the Ferriol family, in the Church of St.
Roch, in Paris.

A NUN'S LOVE LETTERS

A NUN'S LOVE LETTERS

BRIEF and unobtrusive as was the volume of *Lettres Portugaises* published in Paris in 1669, it exercised an influence on the sentimental literature of Europe which was very extraordinary, and to which we have not yet ceased to be subject. Since the revival of learning there had been no collection of documents dealing with the experiences of emotion in which an element of Renaissance feeling had not shown itself in some touch of rhetoric, in some flower of ornament, in some trick of language that concealed what it desired to expose. The *Portuguese Letters*, slight as they were, pleased instantly and universally because they were entirely modern. The seventeenth century, especially in France, had cultivated epistolary literature with care, even with too much care. There had been letter-writers by profession, and the value of their correspondence has been weighed and found wanting. Even in England, where the French were held up as models of letter-writing, there were not wanting critics. Howell wrote in 1625 :—

" Others there are among our next transmarine neighbours eastward, who write in their own language, but their style is so soft and easy that their letters may be said to be like bodies of loose flesh without sinews; they have neither joints of art nor arteries in them. They have a kind of simpering and lank hectic expression, made up of a bombast of words and finical affected compliments only. I cannot well away with such fleasy

F   65

stuff, with such cobweb compositions, where there is no strength of matter—nothing for the reader to carry away with him that may enlarge the notions of his soul."

We may be quite sure that Howell had Balzac in his eye when he wrote this passage, and to Balzac presently succeeded Voiture. To the qualities of Voiture's famous correspondence, to its emptiness, flatness, and rhetorical elegance, signifying nothing and telling us nothing, M. Gaston Boissier has lately dedicated a very amusing page of criticism. Even in the middle of the seventeenth century the French were conscious of their deficiency as letter-writers, and were anxious to remove it. Mademoiselle de Scudéry, who was as awkward as the best of them, saw that girls ought to know how to express their feelings briefly, plainly, and sincerely. In the depths of the wilderness of *Clélie* may still be found rules for letter-writing. But the time was not quite ripe, and it is noticeable that it was just before the publication of the *Portuguese Letters* that Mademoiselle, in the agonies of her grotesque passion, turned over the pages of Corneille for phrases which might express the complex emotions of her heart. If she had waited a few months a manual of the tender passion would have lain at her hand. At all events, the power to analyse the feelings in simple language, to chronicle the minute symptoms of emotion without rhetoric, closely succeeds the great success of these letters; nor is it unworthy of notice that they appear to have exercised an instant influence on no less a personage than Madame de Sévigné, who alludes to them certainly twice, if not oftener, and whose great epoch of letter-writing, following upon the marriage of Madame de Grignan, begins with this very year, 1669. In England the influence of the *Portuguese Letters*, as we shall presently see, was scarcely less sudden than

decisive. That we in England needed such an influence
on our letter-writers is not to be questioned, although the
faults of English correspondence were not those of the
admirers of Voiture and Balzac. The French needed
to throw off a rhetorical insipidity; the English were
still in the toils of the ornamental allusiveness of the
Renaissance. We find such a sentence as the following,
written by Mrs. Penruddock, in 1655, on the night before
her husband's execution, in a letter which has been
preserved just because it seemed direct, tender, and
sincere :—

" Those dear embraces which I yet feel and shall never
lose, being the faithful testimonies of a loving husband,
have charmed my soul to such a reverence of your
remembrance, that, were it possible, I would, with my
own blood, cement your dead limbs to live again, and
(with reverence) think it no sin to rob Heaven a little
longer of a martyr."

Such persons as Mrs. Penruddock never again on such
occasions as this wrote in this particular manner, when
Europe had once read the *Portuguese Letters*. The secret
of saying what was in the heart in a straightforward way
was discovered, and was at once adopted by men and
women a hundred times more accomplished and adroit
than the Canoness of Beja.

A romantic and mysterious story had quite as much
to do with the success of the *Portuguese Letters* as any
directness in their style. In January 1669 a little
duodecimo of 182 pages, entitled simply *Lettres Portugaises*, was issued by Barbin, the leading Paris publisher.
The Letters were five in number; they were neither
signed nor addressed, and there was no indication of
date or place. A prefatory note stated that they were a
translation of certain Portuguese letters written to a

gentleman of quality who had been serving in Portugal, and that the publisher did not know the name of the writer. He abstained from saying that he knew to whom they were addressed. Internal evidence showed that the writer was a nun in a Portuguese convent, and that she had been forsaken, after an impassioned episode, by a French cavalry officer who had loved and had ridden away. Like the hero of a Border ballad, he had passed, at the head of his regiment, through the narrow streets of the town where she lived. He had ridden not a bowshot from her bower-eaves, and she had leaned over her balcony, for a fatal instant, and all was lost and won. The little book was read and continued to be read; edition after edition was called for, and in 1678 the letters were stated to be written by " le Chevalier de C. . . ." Saint Simon and Duclos each informed the world that the male personage was the Marquis of Chamilly, long after-wards Marshal of France, and a mighty warrior before the Roi-Soleil. But no indiscretion of memoir-writers gave the slightest information regarding the lady. All that appeared was that her name was Mariana and that her chamber-window looked across to the only place mentioned in the letters—Mertola, a little town on the right bank of the Guadiana. But in 1810 Boissonade, in a copy of the first edition, found a note in a con-temporary hand, stating in French that the letters were written by Mariana Alcaforada, a nun in a convent at Beja, in the province of Alem-Tejo.

Beja, the theatre of the *Portuguese Letters*, is a small mediæval city, perched on a hill in the midst of the vast fertile plain of central Portugal, and boasting to this day a ring of walls and a lofty citadel, which make it a beacon from all parts of the surrounding province. What the Marquis of Chamilly was doing at Beja may now be explained, especially as, owing to the recent researches of M. Beauvois, we can for the first time follow him with some exactness. The French were in a very equivocal position with regard to Portugal. The Queen of Portugal was a French princess, and the court of Lisbon was full of Frenchmen, but Louis XIV. did not find it convenient to give Don Alfonso his open support. The fact was that Mazarin, anxious to meet the Spaniards half-way, had sacrificed Portugal in the negotiations of the Ile des Faisans. He had no intention, however, of really leaving his old allies to the tender mercies of Madrid, and he secretly encouraged the Portuguese to fight for their independence. The Spaniards had no sooner seen France sign the Treaty of the Pyrenees, late in 1659, than they threw themselves on the frontier of Portugal, and a guerilla war began that lasted for nine years. All France could openly do was to permit her own recently disbanded foreign auxiliaries to take up service with the King of Portugal; and as a general for these somewhat dubiously constituted troops, the Count of Schomberg offered peculiar advantages, as a Huguenot and a citizen of Heidelberg. Schomberg arrived late in 1660, and from this time forward success leaned to the side of Portugal. M. Beauvois has discovered that it was not until 1663 that a young cavalry officer of great promise accompanied the non-official envoy of France, Ablancourt, to the court of Lisbon. This young soldier was Noël Bouton, then known under the title of Count of St. Léger-sur-Dheune, who had already, although only twenty-six years of age, seen a great deal of service in the field. He was the eleventh child of a fine old Burgundy noble, who had trained him to arms. In 1656 he had been taken prisoner at the siege of Valenciennes, and had attracted the notice of the king by a succession of gallant exploits.   He is the hero, though in a most unheroic light, of the *Portuguese Letters*.

His first mission to Portugal seems to have been diplomatic; but on the 30th of April 1664, being at Estremoz, on the Spanish frontier, and in the heart of the fighting, he received from Schomberg the command of a regiment of cavalry, and at once took his place in the forefront of the work in hand.   His name is henceforth connected with the little victories of this obscure and provincial war, the results of which, none the less, were highly important to Portugal.   The theatre of the campaign was the hilly district lying between the Douro and that part of the Guadiana which flows westward before its course changes at Juramenha.   Chamilly is first mentioned with glory for his part in the ten days' siege of Valença-de-Alcantara, in Spain, in June 1664. A month later he helped to defeat the Spaniards under the walls of Castello Rodrigo, a mountain fastness in the valley of the Douro.   By this victory the independence of Northern Portugal was secured.   All through 1665 Chamilly and his dragoons hovered around Badajos, winning laurels in June at the great battle of Villa Viçosa; and in October, in the flight on Badajos, after the victory of Rio Xevora.   The war now sank to a series of marches and countermarches, diversified by a few skirmishes between the Tagus and Badajos.   But in September 1667, after the Count of St. Léger, who is now Marquis of Chamilly, has been more than three years in Portugal, we find him for the first time distinguishing himself in the plains of southern Alam-Tejo by an attack on the Castle of Ferreira, a few miles from Beja.   It is scarcely too much to conjecture that it was either while advancing on, or more probably while returning from Ferreira, that he passed under the balcony of the Franciscan convent of the Conception, and won the heart of the susceptible canoness. So long as the war was being prosecuted with ardour Chamilly could have had no time for such a *liaison*, but all the troubles of the Portuguese were practically over when Ferreira fell. Six months later, on the 13th of February 1668, peace was proclaimed, and Spain accepted the independence of Portugal.[1]

A glance at the map will show the importance of these dates and names in judging the authenticity of the letters of Mariana. Without them the critics of those letters have been left with no basis for conjecturing when or how, between 1661 and 1668, the Portuguese nun and the French officer met and parted. We now see that for the first arduous years of the campaign the young Frenchman was not near Beja, but that he may well have spent the last six months of his campaigning in peace within or beside its walls. One or two otherwise meaningless phrases in the letters are now easily explicable; and the probability that the story, as tradition has sketched it for us, is mainly correct, becomes vastly greater. Before considering what these expressions are, however, it may be best to take the *Letters* themselves into our hands.

---

[1] The important sequence of facts here given with regard to the military record of Chamilly in Portugal has never been used before in any critical examination of the *Portuguese Letters*. That I am able to give it is owing to the kindness of my friend M. Jusserand, who has pointed out to me a very learned memoir on the Chamilly family, full of fresh facts, buried by a Burgundian historian, M. E. Beauvois, in the transactions for 1884 of a local society, the "Société d'Histoire" of Beaune. I think I never saw so valuable a contribution to history concealed with so successful a modesty. I am the more anxious to express my debt to M. Beauvois for his facts, in that I wholly disagree with his conclusions when he comes to deal with the *Portuguese Letters*.

It is with some trepidation that I confess that, in my judgment, the central fact on which the chronicle of the *Portuguese Letters* hangs has hitherto been overlooked by all their editors and critics. As the *Letters* were published without dates, without indications of place or address, they took a sequence which has ever since been religiously adhered to. But reading them through very carefully—as Mark Pattison used to say all books should be read, pencil in hand—I had come to the conclusion that this order was not merely incorrect, but fatal, if persevered in, to any historic credence in the *Letters* as a whole. The fourth has all the appearance of being the earliest in date, and M. Beauvois' discoveries make this almost certain. We must understand that all the five letters are the successive appeals of a forsaken woman, who repeats her expressions of love and lamentation without much indication of scene or reason. But some such indication may, by reading the text with great care, be discovered. The fourth letter, which I believe to be the first, opens thus abruptly :—

" Your lieutenant tells me that a storm forced you to put into port in the kingdom of Algarve. I am afraid that you must have greatly suffered on the sea, and this fear has so occupied me that I have thought no more about all my own troubles. Are you quite sure that your lieutenant takes more interest than I do in all that happens to you ? Why then do you keep him better informed ? And, finally, why have you not written to me ? I am very unfortunate if you found no opportunity of writing to me before you started, and I am still more so if you did find one without using it to write to me. Your injustice and your ingratitude are extreme, yet I should be in despair if they brought you misfortune."

The tone of this is angry and indignant, but it is not the tone of a woman who considers herself abandoned. She has evidently parted with her lover unwillingly, and with suspicion, but she does not resign the right to scold him. Moreover, it is noticeable that he has but just started, and that he had hardly put to sea before he was driven into a port in Algarve. Not a critic of the *Portuguese Letters* has known what to make of this latter point, for Algarve is the strip running along the extreme south coast of Portugal, and no ship leaving Lisbon for France could possibly be driven into ports that look right across into Africa. But as we now see Chamilly slowly descending the frontier from the Douro to Beja, and as we presently find Mariana overwhelmed with emotion at the sight of the road to Mertola, we have but to look again at the map to observe that Mertola would be naturally the first stage in a journey continued south to the mouth of the Guadiana, which is navigable from that town onwards. On reaching the sea Chamilly would take ship, and would most naturally be driven by the first storm into some port of Algarve, from which the news would promptly be brought back to Beja. When we find the Portuguese nun speaking of some early confidences as made " five or six months ago," and when we recollect that the capture of Ferreira took place five months before the peace with Spain, we can hardly doubt that the events upon which the *Letters* are founded took place between September 1667 and February 1668, soon after which latter date Chamilly doubtless made an excuse for setting forth for France. Thus a series of minute expressions in this so-called fourth letter— expressions hitherto meaningless or misleading—are shown to be of vital importance in testifying to the genuineness of the correspondence.

Another fragment from this same letter will help to complete the picture of Chamilly's desertion :—

" You have taken advantage of the excuses which you had for going back to France. A ship was starting. Why did you not let her start ? Your family had written to you. Do you not know what persecutions I have endured from mine ? Your honour compelled you to forsake me. Have I been so solicitous about my honour ? You were forced to go to serve your king. If all that is said of him be true, he has no need of your help, and he would have excused you. I should have been only too happy had we passed our lives together; but since a cruel absence had to divide us, it seems to me that I ought to be satisfied in knowing that I am not faithless to you. Indeed, for all the world contains would I not commit so base an action. What ! have you known the depths of my heart and my affection, and have yet been able to persuade yourself to abandon me for ever, and to expose me to the terror of believing that you will for the future only think of me to sacrifice the memory of me to some new passion ! "

The freedom with which this cloistered lady and her foreign lover met has been objected to as improbable. But the manners of Portugal in the seventeenth century gave to women of the religious orders a social freedom denied to ordinary wives and daughters. In the *Mémoires* of Ablancourt, whom Chamilly attended on his first mission to Lisbon, we read of royal parties of pleasure at the Convent of Santa Speranza, where the nuns and courtiers mingled in theatrical representations before the king and queen. Another contemporary account admits that the French and English were so much beloved in Portugal that some liberty was allowed to them beyond what a Portuguese gentleman might indulge in.

It is easy to see that if convents might without scandal be opened to men in social intercourse, it is not probable that they would be closed to a brilliant foreign ally fresh from Villa Viçosa or Ferreira. But we must again allow Mariana Alcaforada to tell her own tale :—

" Every one has noticed the entire change in my mood, my manners, and my person. My mother has spoken to me about it, with bitterness at first, and then with a certain kindliness. I do not know what I said to her in reply; I fancy I must have confessed everything to her. The strictest of the nuns here are sorry to see what a condition I am in; they even treat me on account of it with some consideration and some tenderness. Everybody is touched at my love, and you alone remain perfectly indifferent, writing me only cold letters, full of repetitions; half the paper is not filled, and you are rude enough to let me see that you are dying with impatience to be done writing. Doña Brites has been persecuting me these last days to get me to leave my room; and fancying that it would amuse me, she took me for a turn on the balcony from which one has a view of Mertola; I went with her, and at once a cruel memory came back to me, a memory which kept me weeping all the remainder of the day. She brought me back, and I threw myself on my bed, where I could but reflect a thousand times over how little chance there was of my ever being cured. Whatever is done to solace me augments my suffering, and in the remedies themselves I find intimate reasons why I should be wretched. I have often seen you pass that spot with an air that charmed me, and I was on that balcony on that fatal day when I first began to feel the symptoms of my ill-starred passion. I fancied that you wished to please me, although you did not know me. I persuaded myself

that you had noticed me among all the ladies that were
with me. I imagined that when you drew rein, you
were well pleased that I should have a better sight of
you, and that I should admire your skill and how graceful
you looked on horseback. I was surprised to notice
that I was frightened when you took your horse through
a difficult place; the fact is that I was taking a secret
interest in all your actions."

We see that he wrote to her at first, although not from
that port of Algarve, in which he had thought of nothing
but business. It does not appear that after this he ever
wrote again, nor as her memory loses its sharpness does
she ever, after this first letter, regain the same clearness
of reminiscence. We may quote once more from this,
the most interesting of the famous five. It is thus that
Mariana closes her pathetic appeal :—

" I want to have the portraits of your brother and of
your sister-in-law. Whatever is anything to you is very
dear to me, and I am wholly devoted to what concerns
you. I have no will of my own left. There are moments
in which it seems to me that I should be humble enough
to serve her whom you love. . . . An officer has been
waiting for this letter for a long time; I had made up
my mind to write it in such a way that you may not be
disgusted when you receive it, but I see I have made it
too extravagant. I must close it. Alas ! it is out of my
power to do so. I seem to be talking to you when I
write to you, and you become a little more present to
me then. . . . The officer who is to take this letter
reminds me for the fourth time that he wishes to start.
What a hurry he is in ! He, no doubt, is forsaking some
unhappy lady in this country. Farewell ! it is harder
for me to finish my letter than it was for you to abandon
me, perhaps for ever."

The remaining letters give fewer indications of date and sequence than the fourth, nor are they so picturesque. But the reader will not seek the *Portuguese Letters*, as he seeks the *Mémoires* of Madame de Motteville, or even the correspondence of Madame de Sévigné, mainly for sparkling incident and the pretty details of contemporary life. The value of these epistles rests in their sincerity as a revelation of the heart. Poor Mariana had no inclination to describe the daily life of her fellow-nuns or the intrigues of society in Beja. She has been deceived, the man she loves is absent, and as she weeps without cessation, she cannot help confessing to herself that she does not expect to see him back again.

" I resigned my life to you," she says in the so-called first letter, " as soon as I saw you, and I feel some pleasure now in sacrificing to you what you will not accept. A thousand times a day I send my sighs out after you; they search for you everywhere, and for all reward of so much disquietude what do they bring me back but too sincere a warning from my evil fortune, which is too cruel to suffer me to deceive myself, and which says to me every moment, Cease, cease, unfortunate Mariana ! vainly thou dost consume thyself, vainly dost seek a lover whom thou shalt never see again, who has crost the ocean to escape from thee, who is now in France in the midst of pleasures, who gives no single moment to the thought of thy sufferings, and who can well dispense with all these thy needless transports."

She will not, however, yet admit that she is wholly deserted. She has received a letter from him, and though its tone was so far from responding to her own that it threw her beside herself for three hours, it has re-awakened her hopes.

" Can you ever be contented by a passion less ardent

than mine ?   You will, perhaps, find elsewhere more
beauty (although you used to tell me that I was beautiful
enough) but you will never find so much love again, and
all the rest is nothing.   Do not fill out your letters with
needless matter, and you may save yourself the trouble
of reminding me to remember you.   I cannot forget you,
and I cannot forget, too, that you made me hope that
you would come back to me for awhile.   Ah ! why will
you not spend all your life here ?   Were it possible for
me to quit this wretched cloister, I would not stay in
Portugal to see whether you performed your promises.
I would not count the cost, but would fly to seek you,
to follow you, to love you.   I dare not persuade myself
that this will be ; I will not nourish such a hope (though
there might be pleasure in delusion), for since I am
doomed to be unhappy, I will have no feelings incon-
sistent with my lot."

The violent and wretched tone of the *Letters*
culminates in the third, which is unsurpassed as a revelation of the ingenious self-torture of a sensitive mind
brooding upon its own despair.   The women of Paris
were astonished to read such pages as the following,
where complex emotions which they had often experienced or imagined, but had never been able to
formulate, suddenly found perfectly direct and limpid
expression :—

" I cannot persuade myself to wish that you may no
longer be thinking about me ; and, indeed, to speak
sincerely, I am furiously jealous of whatever may give
you happiness, and of all that may touch your heart
and your tastes in France.   I do not know why I write
to you.   I see well enough that you will only pity me,
and I do not wish for your pity.   I am very angry with
myself when I reflect upon all that I have sacrificed for

you. I have exposed myself to the rage of my relatives, to the severity of the laws of this country against nuns, and to your ingratitude, which appears to me the greatest of all misfortunes. Yet, all the while, I am conscious that my remorse is not sincere, and that for the love of you I would with all my heart run into far greater dangers than any of these."

The extraordinary and at that time the unique merit of the Portuguese Nun, as a letter-writer, lies in the fact that, in the full tempest and turmoil of her passion, she never yields to the temptation of giving herself up to rhetoric, or rather that whenever she does make a momentary concession to this habit of her age, she doubles on herself immediately, and is the first to deprecate such false flowers of speech. She knows that her letters are too long, although she cannot keep them within bounds. It is part of the torture of her spirit that she recognises better than any monitor from without could teach her, that her lamentations, reproaches, and entreaties are as little calculated as a material flood of tears would be to revive the fire upon a hearth of sunken embers. As she clamours at the door of memory, and makes the air resound with her importunity, she is sane enough to be aware all the while that these are no seductions by which a weary heart may be refreshed and re-awakened; yet is she absolutely powerless to moderate her own emotion. The result is poignant to the last degree; and from the absence of all, or almost all, surrounding local colour of incident or tradition, the spectacle of this distress moves and excites the reader in somewhat the same fashion as the loud crying of an unseen figure out-of-doors in the darkness of the night may move the helpless sympathy of one who listens from a window.

Nothing more is known of this shadowy Mariana Alcaforada, but the author of her misfortunes figures long and gloriously in French history. His fatuity, if not his heartlessness, in allowing her letters to be immediately printed, is a blot upon his humanity in our eyes, but seems to have abated his magnificence not a whit among his contemporaries. It would be idle to inquire by what means the letters came into the hands of a publisher. In 1690, upon the death of the translator, it was admitted that they had been turned out of Portuguese into excellent French by Pierre Girardin de Guilleragues, a " Gascon gourmand," as Saint-Simon calls him, immortalised moreover by Boileau, in a graceful couplet, as being—

> " Born master of all arts a court can teach,
> And skilled alike in silence and in speech."

It was Guilleragues who said of Pelisson that " he abused the permission that men have to be ugly." He was patronised by Madame de Maintenon and died French ambassador to the Porte in 1689. To Guilleragues is attributed the composition of the *Portuguese Letters* by those who seek to deny that Mariana Alcaforada ever existed. But in their own day no one doubted that the actors in this little drama were real persons. Chamilly is described by Saint-Simon as a tall, heavy man, extremely good-natured and gallant in fight, although to listen to and to look at, giving little suggestion that he could ever have inspired so romantic a passion as that revealed by the *Portuguese Letters*. To this there is an obvious reply, that Saint-Simon only knew Chamilly in his mature years, and that there is no reason why a heavy dragoon should not have been very attractive to a Portuguese maiden at twenty-six and yet

seem most unattractive at forty-six to the wittiest of
memoir-writers. To the Portuguese nun he undoubtedly
behaved disgracefully ill, and not at all like a Christian
gentleman; but we must remember that his own age
judged such bad deeds as peccadillos in the free campaign
of love and war. Chamilly's subsequent career was
unquestionably glorious. He fought the Turks in
Candia, he commanded the troops of the Electors of
Cologne and of Munster, he won deathless laurels at the
famous siege of Grave; and, finally, after twenty-five
campaigns, he ended as Marshal of France, and married
a wife who was, as we may smile maliciously to read in
our Saint-Simon, " singularly ugly."

The success of the *Portuguese Letters* was attested not
merely by the multitude of successive editions of the
text, but by the imitations and continuations which
were foisted upon a credulous public. Only seven
months after the original publication there appeared a
second part containing seven letters, with the same date,
1669, on the title-page. These did not, however,
pretend to be written by Mariana, but by a Portuguese
lady of quality. The style was very different, as the
publisher admitted, and the letters bear every stamp
of artifice and fiction. They were, however, greedily
accepted as genuine, and the " Dame Portugaise " took
her place beside the " Religieuse." The temptation to
prolong the romance was irresistible, and there was
immediately published a pamphlet of " Replies," five in
number, supposed to be sent by the French officer to
the Portuguese nun in answer to each of her letters.
This came from a Parisian press; but the idea of publishing the officer's letters had occurred simultaneously to
a provincial bookseller, and still in the same year, 1669,
there appeared at Grenoble a volume of *New Replies*,

G

six in number, the first being not properly a reply, but an introductory letter. This last publication openly professes to be fiction. The editor states in the preface that being " neither a girl, nor a nun, nor even perhaps in love," he cannot pretend to express the sentiments of the heart with the genuine vigour of the original letters; but that, as Aulus Sabinus ventured to reply to certain of the heroic epistles of Ovid, though with so little success as merely to heighten the lustre of those originals, so he hopes by these inventions, and a mere *jeu d'esprit*, to increase the admiration of readers for Mariana's genuine correspondence. All this is very honest and very legitimate, but so eager were the ladies of the seventeenth century to be deluded that this preface of the guileless editor was taken to be a mere mystification, and the Grenoble *New Replies* were swallowed like the rest. Some idea of the popularity of the *Portuguese Letters* may be gained, not merely from the vogue of these successive imitations, but from the fact that M. Eugène Asse, the latest and best of Mariana's editors, has described no fewer than sixteen editions of the *Letters* themselves, issued before the close of the seventeenth century, a list which would seem to be very far indeed from being complete.

Rousseau was the first to start the idea that the *Portuguese Letters* were written by a man. He went upon no external evidence, but on subtle and in truth very fanciful arguments regarding the point of view taken by the writer. No one else has seriously questioned their authenticity, until quite recently, when M. Beauvois, a Burgundian antiquary, has endeavoured to destroy our faith in the existence of the Portuguese nun. This gentleman is an impassioned admirer of the exploits of the Marquis of Chamilly, and it is not difficult

to perceive that his wish to discredit the *Letters* is
due to his desire to whitewash the character of his hero,
blackened for the present, at all events to modern eyes,
by the cruel abandonment of this poor religious lady
in the Beja convent. This critic goes to the opposite
extreme, and allows himself to speak of Mariana's letters
as " the obsessions of a Mænad." Many of M. Beauvois's
acute objections are met by the rearrangement of the
letters which I have suggested above, and particularly
by the fact that the fourth of them should certainly
stand the first. After a careful examination of his
criticism, and particularly in the light of the important
historical dates, with regard to Chamilly's record in the
Portuguese war, which M. Beauvois has himself brought
forward, I for one am more persuaded than ever that
the outline of the story as we know it is true, and that
the letters, or something Portuguese which was very
like them, were actually sent after the rascally *bellâtre*
when he made his way back to France in 1668.

Bare as the letters are, there are nevertheless little
touches of detail here and there, little inexplicable allusions, such as a real correspondence would possess, and
such as no forger would introduce. It would be tedious
in this place to dwell minutely on this sort of evidence,
but a single example may be given. In one passage the
nun writes, " Ah! how I envy the happiness of Emmanuel
and of Francisque. Why am not I always with you, as
they are!" Nothing more is said of these beings. We
are left to conjecture whether they were fellow-officers,
or servants, or dogs, or even perhaps parrots. A forger
would scarcely leave two meaningless names in the body
of his text without some indication of his idea. The
sincerity, moreover, of the style and sentiments is
extraordinary, and is observed to great advantage by

comparing the various continuations and replies with the five original letters. To suppose the first little volume of 1669 to be a deliberate fiction would be to land us in the more serious difficulty of discovering in its inventor a great imaginative creator of emotional romance. The hero-worship of M. Beauvois has not convinced me that Mariana never gazed across the olives and oranges to Mertola, nor watched the cavalcade of her false dragoon file down into the gorge of the Guadiana.

The French critics have not taken any interest in the influence of the *Portuguese Letters* in England. Yet translations and imitations of these letters became very numerous in this country before the close of the seventeenth century. The earliest version which I have been able to trace is that of Sir Roger L'Estrange, published as a very tiny little book of *Five Love-Letters from a Nun to a Cavalier*, in 1678 (December 28, 1677). In a short preface to the reader, the translator says, " These five letters are here at your service. You will find in them the lively image of an extravagant and an unfortunate passion, and that a woman may be flesh and blood in a cloister as well as in a palace." This translation of L'Estrange's went on being reprinted for fifty years, and was attended on its successful course from one toilet to another by a variety of imitations, the liveliest of which is attributed to the pen of the vivacious Major Richardson Pack. From the first the *Portuguese Letters* were not presented to the women of England as literature, but as models of sincere letter-writing, and hence they escaped mention in our solemn handbooks of bibliography and literary history. But their influence was extraordinary, and by the time that the *Spectator* had come into existence, and Richard Steele was sitting over his wine, " the slave of beauty," writing out of his heart to

Mary Scurlock, the men and women of England had learned the lesson which the nun of Beja was betrayed to teach them, and they could say in plain, straightforward sentences exactly what it was in their souls to express to one another, without any sort of trope or rhetorical ornament.

JULES BARBEY D'AUREVILLY

JULES BARBEY D'AUREVILLY

THOSE who can endure an excursion into the backwaters of literature may contemplate, neither too seriously nor too lengthily, the career and writings of Barbey d'Aurevilly. Very obscure in his youth, he lived so long, and preserved his force so consistently, that in his old age he became, if not quite a celebrity, most certainly a notoriety. At the close of his life—he reached his eighty-first year—he was still to be seen walking the streets or haunting the churches of Paris, his long, sparse hair flying in the wind, his fierce eyes flashing about him, his hat poised on the side of his head, his famous lace frills turned back over the cuff of his coat, his attitude always erect, defiant, and formidable. Down to the winter of 1888 he preserved the dandy dress of 1840, and never appeared but as M. de Pontmartin has described him, in black satin trousers, which fitted his old legs like a glove, in a flapping, brigand wideawake, in a velvet waistcoat, which revealed diamond studs and a lace cravat, and in a wonderful shirt that covered the most artful pair of stays. In every action, in every glance, he seemed to be defying the natural decay of years, and to be forcing old age to forget him by dint of spirited and ceaseless self-assertion. He was himself the prototype of all the Brassards and Misnilgrands of his stories, the dandy of dandies, the mummied and immortal beau.

His intellectual condition was not unlike his physical one. He was a survival—of the most persistent. The last, by far the last, of the Romantiques of 1835, Barbey d'Aurevilly lived on into an age wholly given over to other aims and ambitions, without changing his own ideals by an iota.   He was to the great man who began the revival, to figures like Alfred de Vigny, as Shirley was to the early Elizabethans.   He continued the old tradition, without resigning a single habit or prejudice, until his mind was not a whit less old-fashioned than his garments.   Victor Hugo, who hated him, is said to have dedicated an unpublished verse to his portrait :—

" Barbey d'Aurevilly, formidable imbécile,"

But *imbécile* was not at all the right word.   He was absurd; he was outrageous; he had, perhaps, by dint of resisting the decrepitude of his natural powers, become a little crazy.   But imbecility is the very last word to use of this mutinous, dogged, implacable old pirate of letters.

Jules Barbey d'Aurevilly was born near Valognes (the " V——" which figures in several of his stories) on the 2nd of November 1808.   He liked to represent himself as a scion of the bluest nobility of Normandy, and he communicated to the makers of dictionaries the fact that the name of his direct ancestor is engraved on the tomb of William the Conqueror.   But some have said that the names of his father and mother were never known, and others (poor d'Aurevilly !) have set him down as the son of a butcher in the village of Saint-Sauveur-le-Vicomte.   While yet a school-boy in 1825, he published an elegy *Aux héros desThermopyles*, and dedicated it to Casimir Delavigne.   He was at college with Maurice de Guérin, and quite early he became personally acquainted with Chateaubriand.   His youth seems to be wrapped up in mystery; according to one of the best-informed of his biographers, he vanished in 1831, and was not heard of again until 1851. To these twenty years of alleged disappearance, one or two remarkable books of his are, however, ascribed. So characteristic a novel as *L'Amour Impossible* saw the light in 1841, and it appears that what is perhaps the most characteristic of all his writings, *Du Dandyisme et de Georges Brummell*, was written as early as 1842. In 1845 a very small edition of it was printed by an admirer of the name of Trebutien, to whose affection d'Aurevilly seems to have owed his very existence. It is strange that so little is distinctly known about a man who, late in life, attracted much curiosity and attention. He was a consummate romancer, and he liked to hint that he was engaged during early life in intrigues of a corsair description. The truth seems to be that he lived, in great obscurity, in the neighbourhood of Caen, probably by the aid of journalism.

Of all the productions of his youth, the only one which can now be met with is the prose poem of *Amaïdée*, written, I suppose, about 1835; this was published by M. Paul Bourget as a curiosity immediately after Barbey d'Aurevilly's death. Judged as a story, *Amaïdée* is puerile; it describes how to a certain poet, called Somegod, who dwelt on a lonely cliff, there came a young man altogether wise and stately named Altaï, and a frail daughter of passion, who gives her name to the book. These three personages converse in magnificent language, and, the visitors presently departing, the volume closes. But an interest attaches to the fact that in Somegod (*Quelque Dieu!*) the author was painting a portrait of Maurice de Guérin, while the majestic Altaï is himself. The conception of this book is Ossianic; but the style is often singularly beautiful, with a marmoreal splendour founded on a study of Chateaubriand, and, perhaps, of Goethe, and not without relation to that of Guérin himself.

The earliest surviving production of d'Aurevilly, if we except *Amaïdée*, is *L'Amour Impossible*, a novel published with the object of correcting the effects of the poisonous *Lélia* of George Sand. Already, in the crude book, we see something of the Barbey d'Aurevilly of the future, the Dandy-Paladin, the Catholic Sensualist or Diavolist, the author of the few poor thoughts and the sonorous, paroxysmal, abundant style. I forget whether it is here or in a slightly later novel that, in hastily turning the pages, I detect the sentiment, " Our fore-fathers were wise to cut the throats of the Huguenots, and very stupid not to burn Luther." The late Master of Balliol is said to have asked a reactionary under-graduate, " What, Sir! would you burn, would you burn ? " If he had put the question to Barbey d'Aure-villy, the scented hand would have been laid on the cambric bosom, and the answer would have been, " Certainly I should." In the midst of the infidel society and literature of the Second Empire, d'Aurevilly persisted in the most noisy profession of his entire loyalty to Rome, but his methods of proclaiming his attachment were so violent and outrageous that the Church showed no gratitude to her volunteer defender. This was a source of much bitterness and recrimination, but it is difficult to see how the author of *Le Prêtre Marié* (1864) and *Une Histoire sans Nom* (1882) could expect pious Catholics to smile on his very peculiar treatment of ecclesiastical life.

Barbey d'Aurevilly undertook to continue the work of Chateaubriand, and he gave his full attention to a development of the monarchical neo-catholicism which that great inaugurator had sketched out. He was im-pressed by the beauty of the Roman ceremonial, and he determined to express with poetic emotion the mystical majesty of the symbol. It must be admitted that, although his work never suggests any knowledge of or sympathy with the spiritual part of religion, he has a genuine appreciation of its externals. It would be difficult to point to a more delicate and full impression of the solemnity which attends the crepuscular light of a church at vespers than is given in the opening pages of *A un Dîner d'Athées*. In *L'Ensorcelée* (1854), too, we find the author piously following a chanting procession round a church, and ejaculating, " Rien n'est beau comme cet instant solennel des cérémonies catholiques." Almost every one of his novels deals by preference with ecclesiastical subjects, or introduces some powerful figure of a priest. But it is very difficult to believe that his interest in it all is other than histrionic or phenomenal. He likes the business of a priest, he likes the furniture of a church, but there, in spite of his vehement protestations, his piety seems to a candid reader to have begun and ended.

For a humble and reverent child of the Catholic Church, it must be confessed that Barbey d'Aurevilly takes strange liberties. The mother would seem to have had little control over the caprices of her extremely unruly son. There is scarcely one of these ultra-catholic novels of his which it is conceivable that a pious family would like to see lying upon its parlour table. The Devil takes a prominent part in many of them, for d'Aurevilly's whim is to see Satanism everywhere, and to consider it matter of mirth; he is like a naughty boy, giggling when a rude man breaks his mother's crockery. He loves to play with dangerous and forbidden notions. In *Le Prêtre Marié* (which, to his lofty indignation, was forbidden to be sold in Catholic shops) the hero is a renegade and incestuous priest, who loves his own

daughter, and makes a hypocritical confession of error
in order that, by that act of perjury, he may save her
life, as she is dying of the agony of knowing him to be
an atheist. This man, the Abbé Sombreval, is bewitched,
is possessed of the Devil, and so is Ryno de Marigny in
Une Vieille Maîtresse, and Lasthénie de Ferjol in *Une
Histoire sans Nom*. This is one of Barbey d'Aurevilly's
favourite tricks, to paint an extraordinary, an abnormal
condition of spirit, and to avoid the psychological
difficulty by simply attributing it to sorcery. But he
is all the time rather amused by the wickedness than
shocked at it. In *Le Bonheur dans le Crime*—the moral
of which is that people of a certain grandeur of temperament can be absolutely wicked with impunity—he
frankly confesses his partiality for " la plaisanterie
légèrement sacrilège," and all the philosophy of d'Aurevilly is revealed in that rash phrase. It is not a matter of
a wounded conscience expressing itself with a brutal
fervour, but the gusto of conscious wickedness. His
mind is intimately akin with that of the Neapolitan lady,
whose story he was perhaps the first to tell, who wished
that it only were a sin to drink iced sherbet. Barbey
d'Aurevilly is a devil who may or may not believe, but
who always makes a point of trembling.

The most interesting feature of Barbey d'Aurevilly's
temperament, as revealed in his imaginative work, is,
however, his pre-occupation with his own physical life.
In his youth, Byron and Alfieri were the objects of his
deepest idolatry; he envied their disdainful splendour
of passion; and he fashioned his dream in poverty and
obscurity so as to make himself believe that he was of
their race. He was a Disraeli—with whom, indeed, he
has certain relations of style—but with none of Disraeli's
social advantages, and with a more inconsequent and

violent habit of imagination. Unable, from want of wealth and position, to carry his dreams into effect, they became exasperated and intensified, and at an age when the real dandy is settling down into a man of the world, Barbey d'Aurevilly was spreading the wings of his fancy into the infinite azure of imaginary experience. He had convinced himself that he was a Lovelace, a Lauzun, a Brummell, and the philosophy of dandyism filled his thoughts far more than if he had really been able to spend a stormy youth among marchionesses who carried, set in diamonds in a bracelet, the ends of the moustaches of viscounts. In the novels of his maturity and his old age, therefore, Barbey d'Aurevilly loved to introduce magnificent aged dandies, whose fatuity he dwelt upon with ecstasy, and in whom there is no question that he saw reflections of his imaginary self. No better type of this can be found than that Vicomte de Brassard, an elaborate, almost enamoured, portrait of whom fills the earlier pages of what is else a rather dull story, *Le Rideau Cramoisi.* The very clever, very immoral tale called *Le Plus Bel Amour de Don Juan*—which relates how a superannuated but still incredibly vigorous old beau gives a supper to the beautiful women of quality whom he has known, and recounts to them the most piquant adventure of his life—is redolent of this intense delight in the prolongation of enjoyment by sheer refusal to admit the ravages of age. Although my space forbids quotation, I cannot resist repeating a passage which illustrates this horrible fear of the loss of youth and the struggle against it, more especially as it is a good example of d'Aurevilly's surcharged and intrepid style :—

"Il n'y avait pas là de ces jeunesses vert tendre, de ces petites demoiselles qu'exécrait Byron, qui sentent la tartelette et qui, par la tournure, ne sont encore que des épluchettes, mais tous étés splendides et savoureux, plantureux automnes, épanouissements et plénitudes, seins éblouissants battant leur plein majestueux au bord découvert des corsages, et, sous les camées de l'épaule nue, des bras de tout galbe, mais surtout des bras puissants, de ces biceps de Sabines qui ont lutté avec les Romains, et qui seraient capables de s'entrelacer, pour l'arrêter, dans les rayons de la roue du char de la vie."

This obsession of vanishing youth, this intense determination to preserve the semblance and colour of vitality. in spite of the passage of years, is, however, seen to greatest advantage in a very curious book of Barbey d'Aurevilly's, in some aspects, indeed, the most curious which he has left behind him, *Du Dandyisme et de Georges Brummell*. This is really a work of his early maturity, for, as I have said, it was printed so long ago as 1845. It was not published, however, until 1861, when it may be said to have introduced its author to the world of France. Later on he wrote a curious study of the fascination exercised over La Grande Mademoiselle by Lauzun, *Un Dandy d'avant les Dandys*, and these two are now published in one volume, which forms that section of the immense work of d'Aurevilly which best rewards the curious reader.

Many writers in England, from Thomas Carlyle in *Sartor Resartus* to our ingenious young forger of paradoxes, Mr. Max Beerbohm, have dealt upon that semifeminine passion in fatuity, that sublime attention to costume and deportment, which marks the dandy. The type has been, as d'Aurevilly does not fail to observe, mainly an English one. We point to Beau Nash, to Byron, to Lord Yarmouth, to Sheridan, and, above all, "à ce Dandy royal, S. M. Georges IV. ;" but the star of each of these must pale before that of Brummell.

These others, as was said in a different matter, had
" other preoccupations," but Brummell was entirely
absorbed, as by a solemn mission, by the conduct of
his person and his clothes. So far, in the portraiture
of such a figure, there is nothing very singular in what
the French novelist has skilfully and nimbly done, but
it is his own attitude which is so original. All other
writers on the dandies have had their tongues in their
cheeks. If they have commended, it is because to be
preposterous is to be amusing. When we read that
" dandyism is the least selfish of all the arts," we smile,
for we know that the author's design is to be entertaining.
But Barbey d'Aurevilly is doggedly in earnest. He
loves the great dandies of the past as other men contemplate with ardour dead poets and dead musicians. He
is seriously enamoured of their mode of life. He sees
nothing ridiculous, nothing even limited, in their self-
concentration. It reminds him of the tiger and of the
condor; it recalls to his imagination the vast, solitary
forces of Nature; and when he contemplates Beau
Brummell, his eyes fill with tears of nostalgia. So would
he have desired to live; thus, and not otherwise, would
he fain have strutted and trampled through that
eighteenth century to which he is for ever gazing back
with a fond regret. " To dress one's self," he says,
" should be the main business of life," and with great
ingenuity he dwells upon the latent but positive influence
which dress has had on men of a nature apparently
furthest removed from its trivialities; upon Pascal,
for instance, upon Buffon, upon Wagner.

It was natural that a writer who delighted in this
patrician ideal of conquering man should have a limited
conception of life. Women to Barbey d'Aurevilly were
of two varieties—either nuns or amorous tigresses; they

H

were sometimes both in one. He had no idea of soft
gradations in society: there were the tempestuous
marchioness and her intriguing maid on one side; on
the other, emptiness, the sordid hovels of the *bourgeoisie*.
This absence of observation or recognition of life d'Aurevilly shared with the other Romantiques, but in his
sinister and contemptuous aristocracy he passed beyond
them all. Had he lived to become acquainted with the
writings of Nietzsche, he would have hailed a brother-
spirit, one who loathed democracy and the humanitarian
temper as much as he did himself. But there is no
philosophy in Barbey d'Aurevilly, nothing but a prejudice fostered and a sentiment indulged.

In referring to *Nicholas Nickleby*, a novel which he
vainly endeavoured to get through, d'Aurevilly remarks:
" I wish to write an essay on Dickens, and at present
I have only read one hundred pages of his writings. But
I consider that if *one hundred pages* do not give the talent
of a man, they give his spirit, and the spirit of Dickens
is odious to me." " The vulgar Dickens," he calmly
remarks in *Journalistes et Polémistes*, and we laugh
at the idea of sweeping away such a record of genius
on the strength of a chapter or two misread in *Nicholas
Nickleby*. But Barbey d'Aurevilly was not Dickens,
and it really is not necessary to study closely the vast
body of his writings. The same characteristics recur in
them all, and the impression may easily be weakened
by vain repetition. In particular, a great part of the
later life of d'Aurevilly was occupied in writing
critical notices and studies for newspapers and reviews. He made this, I suppose, his principal source
of income; and from the moment when, in 1851, he
became literary critic to *Le Pays* to that of his death,
nearly forty years later, he was incessantly dogmatising

about literature and art. He never became a critical force, he was too violent and, indeed, too empty for that; but a pen so brilliant as his is always welcome with editors whose design is not to be true, but to be noticeable, and to escape " the obvious." The most cruel of Barbey d'Aurevilly's enemies could not charge his criticism with being obvious. It is intensely contentious and contradictory. It treats all writers and artists on the accepted nursery principle of " Go and see what baby's doing, and tell him not to." This is entertaining for a moment; and if the shower of abuse is spread broadly enough, some of it must come down on shoulders that deserve it. But the " slashing " review of yester-year is dismal reading, and it cannot be said that the library of reprinted criticism to which d'Aurevilly gave the general title of *Les Œuvres et les Hommes* (1861–65) is very enticing.

He had a great contempt for Goethe and for Sainte-Beuve, in whom he saw false priests constantly leading the public away from the true principle of literary expression, " le couronnement, la gloire et la force de toute critique, que je cherche en vain." A very ingenious writer, M. Ernest Tissot, has paid Barbey d'Aurevilly the compliment of taking him seriously in this matter, and has written an elaborate study on what his *criterium* was. But this is, perhaps, to inquire too kindly. I doubt whether he sought with any very sincere expectation of finding; like the Persian sage, " he swore, but was he sober when he swore ? " Was he not rather intoxicated with his self-encouraged romantic exasperation, and determined to be fierce, independent, and uncompromising at all hazards ? Such are, at all events, the doubts awakened by his indignant diatribes, which once amused Paris so much, and now influence no living creature. Some of his dicta, in their showy way, are

forcible. " La critique a pour blason la croix, la balance
et la glaive;" that is a capital phrase on the lips of a
reviewer, who makes himself the appointed Catholic
censor of worldly letters, and is willing to assume at
once the cross, the scales, and the sword. More of the
hoof peeps out in this : " La critique, c'est une intrépidité
de l'esprit et du caractère." To a nature like that of
d'Aurevilly, the distinction between intrepidity and
arrogance is never clearly defined.

It is, after all, in his novels that Barbey d'Aurevilly
displays his talent in its most interesting form. His
powers developed late; and perhaps the best constructed of all his tales is *Une Histoire sans Nom*, which
dates from 1882, when he was quite an old man. In
this, as in all the rest, a surprising narrative is well,
although extremely leisurely, told, but without a trace
of psychology. It was impossible for d'Aurevilly to
close his stories effectively; in almost every case,
the futility and extravagance of the last few pages
destroys the effect of the rest. Like the Fat Boy, he
wanted to make your flesh creep, to leave you cataleptic
with horror at the end, but he had none of Poe's skill
in producing an effect of terror. In *Le Rideau Cramoisi*
(which is considered, I cannot tell why, one of his successes) the heroine dies at an embarrassing moment,
without any disease or cause of death being suggested—
she simply dies. But he is generally much more violent
than this; at the close of *A un Dîner d'Athées*, which up
to a certain point is an extremely fine piece of writing,
the angry parents pelt one another with the mummied
heart of their only child; in *Le Dessous des Cartes*, the
key of all the intrigue is discovered at last in the skeleton
of an infant buried in a box of mignonette. If it is
not by a monstrous fact, it is by an audacious feat of

anti-morality, that Barbey d'Aurevilly seeks to harrow and terrify our imaginations. In *Le Bonheur dans le Crime*, Hauteclaire Stassin, the woman-fencer, and the Count of Savigny, pursue their wild intrigue and murder the Countess slowly, and then marry each other, and live, with youth far prolonged (d'Aurevilly's special idea of divine blessing), without a pang of remorse, without a crumpled rose-leaf in their felicity, like two magnificent plants spreading in the violent moisture of a tropical forest.

On the whole, it is as a writer, pure and simple, that Barbey d'Aurevilly claims most attention. His style, which Paul de Saint-Victor (quite in his own spirit) described as a mixture of tiger's blood and honey, is full of extravagant beauty. He has a strange intensity, a sensual and fantastic force, in his torrent of intertwined sentences and preposterous exclamations. The volume called *Les Diaboliques*, which contains a group of his most characteristic stories, published in 1874, may be recommended to those who wish, in a single example, compendiously to test the quality of Barbey d'Aurevilly. He has a curious love of punning, not for purposes of humour, but to intensify his style : " Quel oubli et quelle oubliette " (*Le Dessous des Cartes*), " boudoir fleur de pêcher ou de péché " (*Le Plus bel Amour*), " renoncer à l'amour malpropre, mais jamais à l'amour propre " (*A un Dîner d'Athées*). He has audacious phrases which linger in the memory : " Le Profil, c'est l'écueil de la beauté " (*Le Bonheur dans le Crime*); " Les verres à champagne de France, un lotus qui faisait [les Anglais] oublier les sombres et religieuses habitudes de la patrie ; " " Elle avait l'air de monter vers Dieu, las mains toutes pleines de bonnes œuvres " (*Memoranda*).

That Barbey d'Aurevilly will take any prominent

place in the history of literature is improbable. He was a curiosity, a droll, obstinate survival. We like to think of him in his incredible dress, strolling through the streets of Paris, with his clouded cane like a sceptre in one hand, and in the other that small mirror by which every few minutes he adjusted the poise of his cravat, or the studious tempest of his hair. He was a wonderful old fop or beau of the forties handed down to the eighties in perfect preservation. As a writer he was fervid, sumptuous, magnificently puerile; I have been told that he was a superb talker, that his conversation was like his books, a flood of paradoxical, flamboyant rhetoric. He made a gallant stand against old age, he defied it long with success, and when it conquered him at last, he retired to his hole like a rat, and died with stoic fortitude, alone, without a friend to close his eyelids. It was in a wretched lodging high up in a house in the Rue Rousselet, all his finery cast aside, and three melancholy cats the sole mourners by his body, that they found, on an April morning of 1889, the ruins of what had once been Barbey d'Aurevilly.

ALPHONSE DAUDET

ALPHONSE DAUDET

AFTER spending the summer, as usual, in his country place at Champrosay, Alphonse Daudet came back no more to winter in those historic rooms in the Rue de Belchasse where all the world had laid at his feet the tribute of its homage and curiosity. His growing infirmities had made the mounting of five flights of stairs finally intolerable to him. He took an apartment on the first floor, No. 41, Rue de l'Université, which was far better suited to his condition, and here, in excellent spirits, charmed with the change, and eager for the spring to blossom in the surrounding gardens, he was proposing to receive his friends at Christmas. But another guest long since due, but not at that moment expected, knocked first at the door of the still unfinished house. On the evening of December 16, 1897, while he was chatting gaily at the dinner-table in company with his wife and children, Alphonse Daudet uttered a cry and fell back in his chair. His sons flew for a doctor, but in vain; the end had come —the terrible spectre so long waited, so mysteriously dreaded for its attendant horrors of pain and intolerable decay, had appeared alone, and in the guise of a beneficent angel. The last page of *Ma Douleur*, when it comes into our hands, will be the record, by another voice than Daudet's, of a death as peaceful and as benign in all its circumstances as death can be.

I

It is not possible to discuss the character of Alphonse Daudet without some consideration of his personal conditions. In every page of his brilliant, variegated, emotional books, ever trembling into tears or flashing into laughter, the writer is present to the mind of the instructed reader. Few men have been born with a keener appetite for life or an aptitude for more intense enjoyment. Daudet was of the tribe of those who, as Keats says, " burst joy's grape against their palate fine." It is highly possible that, with this temperament and a southern habit of life, advancing years might have tended to exaggerate in him the tumult of the senses; he might have become a little gross, a little noisy. But fortune willed it otherwise, and this exquisite hedonist, so amorous of life and youth, was refined and etherealised by a mysterious and wasting anguish. It was about the close of 1881 that, while engaged in writing *Sapho*, Daudet became conscious of sudden thrills of agonising pain in his limbs, which attacked him unexpectedly, and lacerated every part of his frame in turn. From this time forth, he was never free from the terror of the pang, and he once used a phrase regarding it, which awakens a vision of Prometheus stretched on Caucasus. " La souffrance, chez moi," he said, " c'est un oiseau qui se pose partout, tantôt ici, tantôt là."

It will be remembered that when Daudet published *L'Évangéliste* in 1883, he dedicated it to Charcot. It was that great master of diagnosis who detected in what the family physician had supposed to be neuralgia the first symptoms of that malady of the spinal cord to which the novelist now slowly succumbed. The ravages of this terrible disease, while they gradually affected more and more completely his powers of locomotion, spared all the functions of the head. Since the completion of *Sapho*, it is true, there has been apparent a flagging in Daudet's constructive power; but this need

not be attributed to disease. In agility of conversation, in refinement of style, in alertness and lucidity of
mind, Daudet showed to the last hour no observable
decline. His courage, on the other hand, his heroic
resignation and patience were qualities that raised him
to a sort of moral sublimity. They would have done
credit to the most placid of northerners, but as the ornament of a Provençal in early middle life, the blood in
whose veins was quicksilver, they were exquisite and
astonishing. There are not many finer pictures in the
cabinet of modern literary history than that of Alphonse
Daudet waiting to be racked with anguish from moment
to moment, a shawl wrapped round his poor knees,
lifting the ivory lines of his face with rapture to the
beauty of a flower, or pouring from his delicate lips a
flood of wit and tenderness and enthusiasm. It carries
the thought back to Scarron, who " souffrit mille fois
la mort avant que de perdre la vie ; " and the modern
instance, while no less brave, is of a rarer beauty.

These physical considerations are so important,
they form so essential a part of our conception of Daudet
and of Daudet's conception of literature, that they
cannot be passed over, even in a brief outline of his place
in the world of writers. He was not one of those who
shrink from being contemplated. His work was not
objective as regarded his own person, it was intensely—
one had almost said it was exclusively—subjective.
Large portions of his fiction are nothing more or less
than selected autobiography, and he had no scruple in
letting this be perceived. He took in later life to writing
prefaces to his old novels, explaining the conditions
in which they were composed. He published *Trente Ans
de Paris* in 1882 ; what it was not quite convenient that
he should narrate himself was confessed by M. Ernest

Daudet, in *Mon Frère et Moi*. The early writings of Alphonse Daudet, up to *Fromont Jeune et Risler Aîné* at least, resolve themselves, it is plain, into autobiography. His only long romance of the early period, *Le Petit Chose*, begins with the sentence " Je suis né le 13 Mai 18—, dans une ville du Languedoc." So speaks the hero, and presently, we calculate from facts recorded, that 18— stands for 1840. Well, Alphonse Daudet was born at Nîmes on May 31, 1840. This changing of 31 into 13 is very characteristic; an analogous alteration is often the only one which the author makes in turning reality into a novel.

The drawback of such a practice is that in reading the charming works of Alphonse Daudet's first thirty-five years, we are divided in allegiance between the artist and the man. This is the danger of the autobiographical method when carried to so great an extreme, and confessed so openly. The poor little hero of *Petit Chose* flying from his tormentors, comes up to Paris in a pair of india-rubber goloshes, having no shoes, and the author makes very happy and pathetic use of this little incident. I remember, however, being much annoyed (I hardly know why) by discovering, as I read *Mon Frère et Moi*, that Alphonse really did come up to Paris thus, in goloshes, but without shoes. By some perversity of temper, I felt vexed that a real person should have plagiarised from the invented history of *Petit Chose*, and to this day I think it would have been better if this piece of personal history had not been unveiled by M. Ernest Daudet. But as a family the Daudets are unsurpassed in the active way in which they take their musical-box to pieces, the result being that we scarcely know, at last, whether the music was the primary object, or was merely secondary to the mechanical ingenuity. This is a doubt which never enhances our pleasure in the fine arts.

The self-consciousness which coloured all the manifestations of the mind of Alphonse Daudet had much to do with his pathos, his really very remarkable command over our tears. There is no recent French writer with whom we weep so easily, and the reason, without doubt, is to be found in his own aptitude for weeping. If his nature were harder, if he were not so sorry for himself, we should not be so sorry for his creations. The intense and sincere sensibility of Daudet disarms the nerves; there is no resisting his pathos. When he chooses to melt his audience he can scarcely be heard for their sobbing. I am bound to say that I think he sometimes carries this sensibility to an illegitimate extreme; it makes, for instance, a great part of *Jack* too painful for endurance. In this otherwise admirable book the author becomes like the too emotional attorney, Baines Carew, in the *Bab Ballads;* he seems to " lie flat upon the floor, convulsed with sympathetic sob," until the reader, bent on pleasure, " toddles off next door," and gives the case to M. de Maupassant or M. Bourget.

Yet this pathetic sensibility, if occasionally pushed to excess, has been one of the most vivid of the qualities which have endeared Alphonse Daudet to thousands of readers. He has a sense of the hysterical sadness of life, the melancholy which arises in the breast without cause at some commonplace conjunction of incidents, the terror of vague future ill, the groundless depressions and faint forebodings which strike men and women like the vision of a spectre at noon-day. Of these neurotic fallacies Daudet is a master; he knows how to make us shudder with the pictures of them, as, consummately, in *Avec Trois Mille Cent Francs.* Pure melodious pathos, produced by the careful balance of elements common to all human frailty, and harmonised by a beautiful balance of style, we discover frequently in the *Contes du Lundi*, in the Alsatian stories, and everywhere in *Jack*. To the last, a novel in Alphonse Daudet's hands was apt to be, what he calls one of his great books, " un livre de pitié, de colère et d'ironie," and the irony and anger were commonly founded upon pity. In particular, *Le Petit Chose* is all pity : the arrival of the telegram that the boy is afraid to deliver, the extreme lachrymosity of Jacques, the agony of the *pion* in sound of the keys of M. Viot (a species of educational Mr. Carker), the fate of Mme. Eyssette taking refuge among her stingy provincial relations—almost every incident in this very pretty book is founded upon the exercise of slightly exaggerated sensibility. The author's voice trembles as he tells the tale; when he laughs, as every now and then he does so gaily, we give a sigh of relief, for we were beginning to fear that he would break down altogether.

II

From this dangerous facility in telling a tale of tears about himself Alphonse Daudet was delivered by developing a really marvellous talent for expatiating on the external and decorative side of life. Out of the wreckage of his experimental writings he has saved for us the *Lettres de mon Moulin* and the *Contes Choisis* which contain, with *Le Petit Chose*, all that needs trouble the general reader, although the amateur of literature examines with interest (and finds entirely Daudesque) those early volumes of verse, *Les Amoureuses*, of 1858, and *La Double Conversion* of 1861. But *Lettres de mon Moulin* (1869) is the one youthful book of A. Daudet which the most hurried student of modern French literature cannot afford to overlook. In its own way, and at its best, there is simply nothing that surpasses it. A short story of mediæval court life better than *La Mule du Pape* has not been told. It is not possible to point to an idyll of pastoral adventure of the meditative class more classic in its graceful purity than *Les Étoiles.* As a masterpiece of picturesque and ironic study of the life of elderly persons in a village, *Les Vieux* stands where *Cranford* stands, since sheer perfection knows neither first nor last. There are Corsican and Algerian sketches in this incomparable volume; but those which rise to the memory first, and are most thoroughly characteristic, are surely those which deal with country life and legend in the dreamy heart of Provence. " Dance and Provençal song and sunburnt mirth "—that is what we recall when we think of the *Lettres de mon Moulin.*

From his ruined mill at Fortvielle, " situated in the valley of the Rhone, in the very heart of Provence, on a hillside clothed with pine-trees and green oaks, the said mill, deserted for more than twenty years and incapable of grinding, as appeareth from the wild vines, mosses, rosemaries, and other parasitic growths which climb to the ends of its sails," from this mill, honourably leased at Pampérigouste, in presence of two witnesses. Francet Mamai, fife-player, and Louiset, called Le Quique, cross-bearer to the White Penitents, Alphonse Daudet writes to his friends, or records a story, as the whim takes him. He recounts legends that illustrate the habits and prejudices of the folks around. He visits the poet Mistral, he accompanies local sportsmen on their walks, he spends his nights with the customs officers. Sometimes, to gain intenser *naïveté*, to get closer still to the heart of things, he borrows the voice of a goat, of a partridge, of a butterfly. And the main object of it all is to render the external impression of this Provençal life more delicately, more radiantly, more intimately than has ever been done before.

It is very difficult to analyse the skill with which Daudet contrives to produce this sense of real things seen intensely through the bright-coloured atmosphere of his talent. His economy of words in the best examples of this branch of his work is notable. The curious reader of his little story, " The Beacon of the Bloody Isles," may ask himself how it would be possible to enhance the mysterious dazzlement caused by the emerging of the writer from the dark winding stairs up into the blaze of light exhibited above :—

" En entrant j'étais ébloui. Ces cuivres, ces étains, ces réflecteurs de métal blanc, ces murs de cristal bombé qui tournaient avec des grands cercles bleuâtres, tout ce miroitement, tout ce cliquetis de lumières, me donnait un moment de vertige."

What could be more masterly than that ? It is said in the fewest possible words, yet so that an impression, in a high degree bewildering and complex, is accurately presented to us. Scarcely less marvellous is the interior, in *Les Vieux*, where, under the miraculous influence of the Life of St. Irenæus, read aloud by a little pensioner in a blue blouse, not the old gentleman and lady only, but the canaries in their cage, the flies on the pane, and all the other elements of still life are plunged in deepest sleep at noon. And of the fantasia about Valencia oranges in the winter streets of Paris, and of the scene in " The Two Inns," which every one has praised, and of the description of the phantom visitors who come uninvited to supper with M. Majesté, and of the series of idyllic vignettes " en Camargue," what shall be said ?—the enumeration of Alphonse

Daudet's successes in this direction becomes a mere catalogue. It is particularly to be observed that with his incessant verbal invention, we are conscious of no strain after effect. Daudet is never pretentious, and it requires some concentration of mind, some going backward over the steps of his sentences, to perceive what a magic of continual buoyancy it is that has carried us along with so swift a precision.

When Alphonse Daudet began to write in Paris, a new set of critical ideas and creative aspirations were setting the young men in motion. In poetry, the example of Baudelaire in noting impressions, and in widening the artistic repertory, was having an electrical influence, while Daudet and Zola, in conjunction with those elder brethren of theirs, Flaubert and the Goncourts, were endeavouring to make of the practice of novel-writing something more solid, brilliant, and exact than had been attempted before. This is no place to touch on what will eventually occupy the historian of literature, Alphonse Daudet's place in the ranks of the naturalists. But it is important to note that he possessed one quality denied to his distinguished friends, denied even to Flaubert, namely, his graceful rapidity. As M. Jules Claretie said of him the other day, he was " un réaliste ailé," and he was preserved from the dulness and pedestrian jog-trot of prosy naturalism by this winged lightness of his, this agility in sensation, and illuminating promptitude in expression. His hand was always light, among the tribe of those who never knew when to stop. Daudet could not fall into the error of Zola in his " symphonies of odours," nor destroy the vitality of a study like *Chérie*, as Edmond de Goncourt did, by the pedantic superfetation of documentary evidence. He was a creature of the sun and wind, like the cicala that the

I

Greek poets sung of, intoxicated with a dew-drop, and flinging itself impetuously into the air, while it struck melody from its wings with its own flying feet.

III

Thus palpitating with observation, thus, as he himself said, " hypnotisé par la réalité," filled to the brim of his quivering nature by the twin sources of pictorial and of moral sensitiveness, seeing and feeling with almost abnormal intensity, his sails puffed out with the pride of life and the glory of visual sensation, Daudet prepared himself by a myriad experiments for the true business of his career. After a somewhat lengthy and arduous apprenticeship as an observer of nature and of himself, armed with those little green books of notes, those *cahiers* of which we have heard so much, he set out to be a great historian of French manners in the second half of the nineteenth century. In 1874 he made a notable sensation with *Fromont Jeune et Risler Aîné*, and, almost simultaneously, with *Jack*. But these were immediately excelled by *Le Nabab* (1877), a trenchant satire of the Second Empire and the Third Republic. Then followed, in a very different key, that extremely delicate study of the dynastic idea in bankruptcy, which he called *Les Rois en Exil* (1879). Daudet had built up an edifice of fiction about his old patron, the Duc de Morny, in *Le Nabab ;* he returned to politics in *Numa Roumestan* (1881), and crystallised his invention round the legend of Gambetta. This book, in my judgment, marked the apogee of Alphonse Daudet's genius; never again, so it seems to me, did he write a novel quite so large, quite so masterly in all its parts, as *Numa Roumestan*. But *L'Évangéliste* (1883), a satiric picture of fanatical Protestantism, had brilliant parts, and a

great simplicity of action; while in *Sapho* (1884), which
M. Jules Lemaitre has called " simplement la *Manon
Lescaut* de ce siècle," Daudet produced an elaborate
study of that obsession of the feminine which is so dear
to our Gallic neighbours. The consensus of French
criticism, I think, puts *Sapho*, where I venture to put
Numa Roumestan, at the head of Daudet's novels.
After this came *L'Immortel* (1888), *Rose et Ninette* (1892),
even later stories, never quite without charm, but
steadily declining in imagination and vitality, so that the
books on which Daudet bases his claim to be regarded
as a great novelist are seven, and they range from *Jack*
to *Sapho*, culminating as I most obstinately hold, in
Numa Roumestan.

In looking over these seven extraordinary books,
which we read in succession at their first appearance
with an enthusiasm that may have carried the critical
faculty away, we are conscious of the brilliant and solid
effect which they still produce. They stand midway
between the rigidly naturalistic and the consciously
psychological sets of novels which France has seen
flourish during the last twenty-five years, and on the
whole, perhaps, they are standing the test of time better
than either. The moment we were fairly launched,
so long ago, upon the narrative of *Fromont Jeune et Risler
Aîné*, as soon as we became acquainted with " the
blooming and sonorous Delobelle," as Mr. Henry James
so happily calls him, when, again, a very little later, we
were introduced to all the flatulent humbugs of the
Maison Moronval in *Jack*, we acknowledged that here
was come at last a great French novelist, with whom the
Anglo-Saxon reader could commune with unspeakable
delight. This *méridional*, who cared so little for England,
who could never read an English sentence, seemed from a

certain limited point of view to run in the very channel of British fiction. He has been called (alas ! poor man, it was a thorn in his flesh !) the French Dickens, but he has aspects in which he seems Mrs. Gaskell and Anthony Trollope as well, even Robert Louis Stevenson and Rudyard Kipling. A whole repertory of such parallelisms might be drawn out, if we examined Daudet not wisely but too well.

The truth seems to be that, with all his violent southern colour and temperament, his pathos, his humour, his preference for the extravagant and superficial parts of character and conduct had a greater resemblance to the English than to the French tradition of invented narrative. This is true of works written before Alphonse Daudet could possibly have touched an English story. We talk of his affinity to Dickens, but that relation is much more strongly marked in *Le Petit Chose* than in any of Daudet's mature works. In the very beginning of that story, the formidable rage of M. Eyssette, and the episode of Annou who marries in desperation because she has lost her " place," are more like pure Dickens than anything in *Fromont Jeune*. It is quite certain, from what he has protested over and over again (and did he not fight poor M. Albert Delpit that he might seal his protest in blood ?), that Daudet's knowledge of all English literature, the works of Dickens included, was extremely exiguous. You could probably have drawn it through the eye of a needle without crushing it. It remains true, none the less, that in his idea of how to entertain by a novel, how to write a thrilling story of pity, anger, and irony, he came much nearer than any other Frenchman to the English standpoint. When we add to this the really extraordinary chastity and delicacy of his language, the tact with which, even in a book like

Sapho, he avoids all occasion of offence, and has therefore been a well of pure and safe delight to thousands of young Englishwomen, it is not to be wondered at that the non-critical class of British readers look upon Alphonse Daudet as the most sympathetic of Continental novelists. He is certainly the one who offers them the smallest chance of springes and pitfalls along their innocent pathway.

In his great novels, the art of Daudet is seen in his arrangement and adaptation of things that he has experienced, not in his invention. He was never happy when he detached himself from the thing absolutely observed and noted. For most readers, I suppose, the later chapters of *Le Petit Chose* are ruined by the absurd episode of Irma Borel, the Creole, a figure laboriously invented *à la* Paul de Kock, with no faint knowledge of any actual prototype. It is interesting to compare this failure with the solid success of the portrait of Sapho fifteen years later, when Daudet had made himself acquainted with this type of woman, and had noted her characteristics with his mature clairvoyance. Even in his more purely fantastic creations, surely, the difference between what Daudet has seen and has not seen is instantly felt. What a distinction there is between Tartarin in Tarascon, in Algeria, on the Righi—where Daudet had accompanied him—and Tartarin in the South Seas, where his creator had to trust to books and fancy! I am inclined to push this so far as even to question the value of *Wood's Town*, a story which many admirers of Daudet have signalled for special eulogy. This is a tale of a peninsula somewhere in the Gulf of Mexico, where a tropic city is built, at first with success, but only to be presently overwhelmed by the onset of the virgin forest, which defies all the exertions of the inhabi-

tants; lianas are flung from roof to roof, the municipal
buildings are roped to one another by chains of prickly-
pear, yuccas pierce the floors with their spines, and fig-
trees rend the walls apart; at last the population has
to take flight in ships, the masts of which are already
like forest-trees, so laden are they with parasitic vegetation. The whole forms a fine piece of melodramatic
extravagance, but one feels what an infinitely truer, and,
therefore, infinitely more vivid picture of such a scene
Mr. Cable could have written in the days when he was
still interested in *The Grandissimes* and *Mme. Delphine.*

IV

In all the creations of Daudet, as we have said, the
fountain of tears lies very close to the surface. There
is, however, one eminent exception, and it is possible
that this, in its sunny gaiety, its unruffled high spirits,
may eventually outlast the remainder. All his life
through, Daudet was fascinated by the mirthful side
of southern exaggeration. He set himself to invent
a figure which should unite all the qualities of the
méridional, a being in whom the hallucination of adven-
turous experiences should be carried to its drollest
excess. The result was pure frolic : the *Prodigious
Feats of Tartarin de Tarascon* (1872). Tartarin the
boaster, the mighty hunter before the Lord, " le roi des
chasseurs de casquettes," has bragged so long and so
loudly that even Tarascon demands confirmation. And
so he sets forth, and at Algiers he shoots a lion—an
old, tame, blind lion that has been taught to hold a
platter in its mouth and beg at the doors of mosques.
He returns to Tarascon, still boasting, and bringing
with him a mangy camel, " which has seen me shoot
all my lions." He reposes again on the confidence of

Tarascon.   Then in 1885, Tartarin sets forth anew, this
ime to climb the Alps, being President of the Tarascon
Alpine Club, and once more forced to prove his prowess.
Glorious are his incredible ascents and accidental adventures.   After a thousand farcical drolleries, gulled and
gulling, back he comes to Tarascon, with its blinding
dust and its blinding sunlight, to the country where it
is too bright and too hot to attempt to tell the truth.
Still later, Daudet made an effort to carry a colony from
Tarascon to the shores of the Pacific Ocean; but this
time he was less vivacious and more cynical.   For sheer
fun and merriment, the two earlier books about Tartarin
remain, however, unexcelled.   There is nothing else
like them in recent French literature, and those who
object to Daudet's other stories here confess themselves
disarmed.   Tarascon itself, the little dry town on the
Rhone, meanwhile accentuates the joke and adds to it
by an increasing exasperation against the great man of
letters who has made its tragi-comical exaltations so
ridiculous and famous.   I have but recently made the
personal observation that it is impossible to purchase
the works of Daudet in the book-shops of the still-
indignant Tarascon.

V

Two years before his death M. Alphonse Daudet paid
his first and only visit to London, accompanied by his
entire family—by his whole *smala*, as he said, like an
Arab sheikh.   Those who are privileged to meet him
then for the first time were astonished at the inconsistencies of his physical condition.   To see Daudet strug-
gling with infinite distress up a low flight of stairs was to
witness what seemed the last caducity of a worn-out
frame.   But his lower limbs only were paralysed; and

once seated at table, and a little rested after the tortures of locomotion, a sort of youth reblossomed in him. Under the wild locks of hair, still thick though striped with grey, the eyes preserved their vivacity—large and liquid eyes, intermittently concentrated in the effort to see distinctly, now floating in a dream, now focussed (as it were) in an act of curiosity. The entire physical and phenomenal aspect of Alphonse Daudet in these late years presented these contradictions. He would sit silent and almost motionless; suddenly his head, arms, and chest would be vibrated with electrical movements, the long white fingers would twitch in his beard, and then from the lips a tide of speech would pour—a flood of coloured words. On the occasion when I met him at dinner, I recollect that at dessert, after a long silence, he was suddenly moved to describe, quite briefly, the melon-harvest at Nîmes when he was a boy. It was an instance, no doubt, of the habitual magic of his style, sensuous and pictorial at its best; in a moment we saw before us the masses of golden-yellow and crimson and sea-green fruit in the little white market-place, with the incomparable light of a Provençal morning bathing it all in crystal. Every word seemed the freshest and the most inevitable that a man could possibly use in painting such a scene, and there was not a superfluous epithet.

This little apologue about the melons took us back to the Daudet with whom we first made acquaintance, the magician of the *Lettres de mon Moulin*. That aged figure, trembling with the inroads of paralysis, became in a flash our charming friend, Petit Chose, sobbing under the boughs of the pomegranate for a blood-red flower to remind him of his childish joys. Those loose wisps of hair had been dark clusters of firm curls around the brows of the poet of *Les Amoureuses*. It was pleasant for one fated to see this beloved writer only in the period of his decay to feel thus that the emblems of youth were still about him. The spirit had not surrendered to the sad physical decline, and so, for all its distressing obviousness, the latter did not produce an overpowering sensation of melancholy. It emphasised the impression one had formed in reading his books; with Daudet all the ideas were concrete and positive. He had no thought, properly speaking, but only a ceaseless flow of violent and pictorial observations, as intense as they were volatile. These had to be noted down in haste as they arrived, or else a fresh sensation would come and banish them for ever. He was an impressionist painter, the colours on whose palette were words of an indescribable abundance, variety, and exactitude.

For some years, it is hardly to be questioned that Alphonse Daudet was the leading novelist of the world. From 1877, when he published *Le Nabab*, to 1881, when he reached the apex of his glory in *Numa Roumestan*, he had no rival. That was a position which it was impossible that he should retain.

It is too early to attempt to fix the position which Alphonse Daudet will hold in French literature. In spite of the extraordinary professional manifestation produced immediately after his death in Paris, it was easy to see that he no longer stood in the affections of unprejudiced readers quite where he did. In 1888 it would have required considerable courage to suggest that Daudet was not in the very first rank of novelwriters; in 1898, even the special pleading of friendship scarcely urged so much as this. It is inevitable, if we subject Daudet to the only test which suits his very splendid and honourable career, that we should hesitate in placing him with the great creative minds. His

beautiful talent is dwarfed when we compare it with
Balzac, with Tourgenieff, with Flaubert, even with
Maupassant. He is vivacious, brilliant, pathetic,
exuberant, but he is not subtle; his gifts are on the surface. He observes rather than imagines; he belongs
to the fascinating, but too often ephemeral class of
writers who manufacture types, and develop what the
Elizabethans used to call " humours." And this he does,
not by an exercise of fancy, not by a penetrating flash
of intuition, but as a " realist," as one who depends on
little green books of notes, and docketed bundles of
pièces justificatives.

But we need not be ungracious and dwell on these
shortcomings in a genius so charming, so intimately
designed to please. Whether his figures were invented
or noted, they live brilliantly in our memories. Who
will lose the impression, so amazingly vivid, left by the
" Cabecilla " in the *Contes Choisis*, or by *Les Femmes
d'Artistes*, " ce livre si beau, si cruel," as Guy de Maupassant called it ? Who will forget the cunning, timid
Jansoulet as he came out of Tunis to seek his fortune
in Paris ? Who the turbulent Numa Roumestan, or
that barber's block, the handsome Valmajour, with his
languishing airs and his tambourine ? Who Queen
Frédérique when she discovers that the diamonds of
Illyria are paste ? and who Mme. Ebsen in her final
interview with Eline ? The love of life, of light, of the
surface of all beautiful things, the ornament of all
human creations, illuminates the books of Alphonse
Daudet. The only thing he hated was the horrible little
octopus-woman, the Fanny Legrand or Sidonie Chèbe,
who has no other object or function than to wreck the
lives of weak young men. To her, perhaps, he is cruel ;
she was hardly worth his steel. But everything else

he loves to contemplate; even when he laughs at Tarascon he loves it; and in an age when the cynical and the sinister take so wide a possession of literature, our thanks are eternally due to a man who built up for us a world of hope and light and benignity.

1898.

THE SHORT STORIES OF ZOLA

THE SHORT STORIES OF ZOLA

It is by his huge novels, and principally by those of the Rougon-Macquart series, that Zola is known to the public and to the critics. Nevertheless, he found time during the forty years of his busy literary career to publish about as many small stories, now comprised in four separate volumes. It is natural that his novels should present so very much wider and more attractive a subject for analysis that, so far as I can discover, even in France no critic has hitherto taken the shorter productions separately, and discussed Zola as a maker of *contes*. Yet there is very distinct interest in seeing how such a thunderer or bellower on the trumpet can breathe through silver; and, as a matter of fact, the short stories reveal a Zola considerably dissimilar to the author of *Nana* and of *La Terre*—a much more optimistic, romantic, and gentle writer. If, moreover, he had nowhere assailed the decencies more severely than he does in these thirty or forty short stories, he would never have been named among the enemies of Mrs. Grundy, and the gates of the Palais Mazarin would long ago have been opened to receive him. It is, indeed, to a lion with his mane *en papillotes* that I here desire to attract the attention of English readers ; to a man-eating monster, indeed, but to one who is on his best behaviour and blinking in the warm sunshine of Provence.

I

The first public appearance of Zola in any form was made as a writer of a short story. A southern journal,

127

La Provence, published at Aix, brought out in 1859 a little *conte* entitled *La Fée Amoureuse*. When this was written, in 1858, the future novelist was a student of eighteen, attending the rhetoric classes at the Lycée St. Louis; when it was printed, life in Paris, far from his delicious South, was beginning to open before him, harsh, vague, with a threat of poverty and failure. *La Fée Amoureuse* may still be read by the curious in the *Contes à Ninon*. It is a fantastic little piece, in the taste of the eighteenth-century trifles of Crébillon or Boufflers, written with considerable care in an over-luscious vein— a fairy tale about an enchanted bud of sweet marjoram, which expands and reveals the amorous fay, guardian of the loves of Prince Loïs and the fair Odette. This is a moonlight-coloured piece of unrecognisable Zola, indeed, belonging to the period of his lost essay on " The Blind Milton dictating to his Elder Daughter, while the Younger accompanies him upon the Harp," a piece which many have sighed in vain to see.

He was twenty when, in 1860, during the course of blackening reams of paper with poems *à la Musset*, he turned, in the aërial garret, or lantern above the garret of 35 Rue St. Victor, to the composition of a second story—*Le Carnet de Danse*. This is addressed to Ninon, the ideal lady of all Zola's early writings—the fleet and jocund virgin of the South, in whom he romantically personifies the Provence after which his whole soul was thirsting in the desert of Paris. This is an exquisite piece of writing—a little too studied, perhaps, too full of opulent and voluptuous adjectives; written, as we may plainly see, under the influence of Théophile Gautier. The story, such as it is, is a conversation between Georgette and the programme-card of her last night's ball. What interest *Le Carnet de Danse* possesses it owes to the style, especially that of the opening pages, in which the joyous Provençal life is elegantly described. The young man, still stumbling in the wrong path, had at least become a writer.

For the next two years Zola was starving, and vainly striving to be a poet. Another " belvédère," as Paul Aléxis calls it, another glazed garret above the garret, received him in the Rue Neuve St. Étienne du Mont. Here the squalor of Paris was around him; the young idealist from the forests and lagoons of Provence found himself lost in a loud and horrid world of quarrels, oaths, and dirt, of popping beer-bottles and yelling women. A year, at the age of two-and-twenty, spent in this atmosphere of sordid and noisy vice, left its mark for ever on the spirit of the young observer. He lived on bread and coffee, with two sous' worth of apples upon gala days. He had, on one occasion, even to make an Arab of himself, sitting with the bed-wraps draped about him, because he had pawned his clothes. All the time, serene and ardent, he was writing modern imitations of Dante's *Divina Commedia*, epics on the genesis of the world, didactic hymns to Religion, and love-songs by the gross. Towards the close of 1861 this happy misery, this wise folly, came to an end; he obtained a clerkship in the famous publishing house of M. Hachette.

But after these two years of poverty and hardship he began to write a few things which were not in verse. Early in 1862 he again addressed to the visionary Ninon a short story called *Le Sang*. He confesses himself weary, as Ninon also must be, of the coquettings of the rose and the infidelities of the butterfly. He will tell her a terrible tale of real life. But, in fact, he is absolutely in the clouds of the worst romanticism. Four soldiers, round a camp-fire, suffer agonies of ghostly

K

adventure, in the manner of Hofmann or of Petrus
Borel. We seem to have returned to the age of 1830,
with its vampires and its ghouls. *Simplice*, which comes
next in point of date, is far more characteristic, and
here, indeed, we find one talent of the future novelist
already developed. Simplice is the son of a worldly
king, who despises him for his innocence; the prince
slips away into the primeval forest and lives with dragon-
flies and water-lilies. In the personal life given to the
forest itself, as well as to its inhabitants, we have something very like the future idealisations in *L'Abbé Mouret*,
although the touch is yet timid and the flashes of
romantic insight fugitive. *Simplice* is an exceedingly
pretty fairy story, curiously like what Mrs. Alfred Gatty
used to write for sentimental English girls and boys :
it was probably inspired to some extent by George Sand.

On a somewhat larger scale is *Les Voleurs et l'Âne*,
which belongs to the same period of composition. It
is delightful to find Zola describing his garret as " full
of flowers and of light, and so high up that sometimes
one hears the angels talking on the roof." His
story describes a summer day's adventure on the
Seine, an improvised picnic of strangers on a grassy
island of elms, a siesta disturbed by the somewhat
stagey trick of a fantastic coquette. According to his
faithful biographer, Paul Aléxis, the author, towards the
close of 1862, chose another lodging, again a romantic
chamber, overlooking this time the whole extent of the
cemetery of Montparnasse. In this elegiacal retreat
he composed two short stories, *Sœurs des Pauvres* and
Celle qui m'aime. Of these, the former was written
as a commission for the young Zola's employer, M.
Hachette, who wanted a tale appropriate for a children's
newspaper which his firm was publishing. After reading

what his clerk submitted to him, the publisher is said
to have remarked, " Vous êtes un révolté," and to have
returned him the manuscript as " too revolutionary."
Sœurs des Pauvres is a tiresome fable, and it is difficult
to understand why Zola has continued to preserve it
among his writings. It belongs to the class of semi-
realistic stories which Tolstoi has since then composed with such admirable skill. But Zola is not
happy among saintly visitants to little holy girls, nor
among pieces of gold that turn into bats and rats in
the hands of selfish peasants. Why this anodyne little
religious fable should ever have heen considered revolutionary, it is impossible to conceive.

Of a very different order is *Celle qui m'aime*, a story
of real power. Outside a tent, in the suburbs of Paris,
a man in a magician's dress stands beating a drum and
inviting the passers-by to enter and gaze on the realisation of their dreams, the face of her who loves you. The
author is persuaded to go in, and he finds himself in
the midst of an assemblage of men and boys, women and
girls, who pass up in turn to look through a glass trap
in a box. In the description of the various types, as
they file by, of the aspect of the interior of the tent,
there is the touch of a new hand. The vividness of the
study is not maintained; it passes off into romanesque
extravagance, but for a few moments the attentive
listener, who goes back to these early stories, is conscious
that he has heard the genuine accent of the master
of Naturalism.

Months passed, and the young Provençal seemed to
be making but little progress in the world. His poems
definitely failed to find a publisher, and for a while he
seems to have flagged even in the production of prose.
Towards the beginning of 1864, however, he put together

the seven stories which I have already mentioned, added to them a short novel entitled *Aventures du Grand Sidoine*, prefixed a fanciful and very prettily turned address *À Ninon*, and carried off the collection to a new publisher, M. Hetzel. It was accepted, and issued in October of the same year. Zola's first book appeared under the title of *Contes à Ninon*. This volume was very well received by the reviewers, but ten years passed before the growing fame of its author carried it beyond its first edition of one thousand copies.

There is no critical impropriety in considering these early stories, since Zola never allowed them, as he allowed several of his subsequent novels, to pass out of print. Nor, from the point of view of style, is there anything to be ashamed of in them. They are written with an uncertain and an imitative, but always with a careful hand, and some passages of natural description, if a little too precious, are excellently modulated. What is really very curious in the first *Contes à Ninon* is the optimistic tone, the sentimentality, the luscious idealism. The young man takes a cobweb for his canvas, and paints upon it a rainbow-dew with a peacock's feather. Except, for a brief moment, in *Celle qui m'aime*, there is not a phrase that suggests the naturalism of the Rougon-Macquart novels, and it is an amusing circumstance that, while Zola was not only practising, but very sternly and vivaciously preaching, the gospel of Realism, this innocent volume of fairy stories should all the time have figured among his works. The humble student who should turn from the master's criticism to find an example in his writings, and who should fall by chance on the *Contes à Ninon*, would be liable to no small distress of bewilderment.

II

Ten years later, in 1874, Zola published a second volume of short stories, entitled *Nouveaux Contes à Ninon*. His position, his literary character, had in the meantime undergone a profound modification. In 1874 he was no longer unknown to the public or to himself. He had already published four of the Rougon-Macquart novels, embodying the natural and social history of a French family during the Second Empire. He was scandalous and famous, and already bore a great turbulent name in literature and criticism. The *Nouveaux Contes à Ninon*, composed at intervals during that period of stormy evolution, have the extraordinary interest which attends the incidental work thrown off by a great author during the early and noisy manhood of his talent. After 1864 Zola had written one unsuccessful novel after another, until at last, in *Thérèse Raquin*, with its magnificent study of crime chastised by its own hideous after-gust, he produced a really remarkable performance. The scene in which the paralytic mother tries to denounce the domestic murderers was in itself enough to prove that France possessed one novelist the more.

This was late in 1867, when M. Zola was in his twenty-eighth year. A phrase of Louis Ulbach's, in reviewing *Thérèse Raquin*, which he called " litérature putride," is regarded as having started the question of Naturalism, and M. Zola, who had not, up to that time, had any notion of founding a school, or even of moving in any definite direction, was led to adopt the theories which we identify with his name during the angry dispute with Ulbach. In 1865 he had begun to be drawn towards Edmond and Jules de Goncourt, and to feel, as he puts it, that in the *salons* of the Parnassians he was growing more and more out of his element " among so many impenitent *romantiques*." Meanwhile he was for ever feeding the furnaces of journalism, scorched and desiccated by the blaze of public life, by the daily struggle for bread. He was roughly affronting the taste of those who differed from him, with rude hands he was thrusting out of his path the timid, the dull, the old-fashioned. The spectacle of these years of Zola's life is not altogether a pleasant one, but it leaves on us the impression of a colossal purpose pursued with force and courage. In 1871 the first of the Rougon-Macquart novels appeared, and the author was fairly launched on his career. He was writing books of large size, in which he was endeavouring to tell the truth about modern life with absolute veracity, no matter how squalid, or ugly, or venomous that truth might be.

But during the whole of this tempestuous decade Zola, in his hot battlefield of Paris, heard the voice of Ninon calling to him from the leafy hollows, from behind the hawthorn hedges, of his own dewy Provence—the cool Provence of earliest flowery spring. When he caught these accents whistling to his memory from the past, and could no longer resist answering them, he was accustomed to write a little *conte*, light and innocent, and brief enough to be the note of a caged bird from indoors answering its mate in the trees of the garden. This is the real secret of the utterly incongruous tone of the *Nouveaux Contes* when we compare them with the *Curée* and *Madeleine Férat* of the same period. It would be utterly to misunderstand the nature of Zola to complain, as Pierre Loti did the other day, that the coarseness and cynicism of the naturalistic novel, the tone of a ball at Belleville, could not sincerely co-exist with a love of beauty, or with a nostalgia for youth and country pleasures. In the short stories of the period of which we are speaking, that poet who dies in most middle-aged men lived on for Zola, artificially, in a crystal box carefully addressed " à Ninon là-bas," a box into which, at intervals, the master of the Realists slipped a document of the most refined ideality.

Of these tiny stories—there are twelve of them within one hundred pages—not all are quite worthy of his genius. He grimaces a little too much in *Les Epaules de la Marquise*, and M. Bourget has since analysed the little self-indulgent *dévote* of quality more successfully than Zola did in *Le Jeûne*. But most of them are very charming. Here is *Le Grand Michu*, a study of gallant, stupid boyhood; here *Les Paradis des Chats*, one of the author's rare escapes into humour. In *Le Forgeron*, with its story of the jaded and cynical town-man, who finds health and happiness by retiring to a lodging within the very thunders of a village blacksmith, we have a profound criticism of life. *Le Petit Village* is interesting to us here, because, with its pathetic picture of Woerth in Alsace, it is the earliest of Zola's studies of war. In other of these stories the spirit of Watteau seems to inspire the sooty Vulcan of Naturalism. He prattles of moss-grown fountains, of alleys of wild strawberries, of rendezvous under the wings of the larks, of moonlight strolls in the bosquets of a château. In every one, without exception, is absent that tone of brutality which we associate with the notion of Zola's genius. All is gentle irony and pastoral sweetness, or else downright pathetic sentiment.

The volume of *Nouveaux Contes à Ninon* closes with a story which is much longer and considerably more important than the rest. *Les Quatre Journées de Jean*

Gourdon deserves to rank among the very best things
to which Zola has signed his name. It is a study of
four typical days in the life of a Provençal peasant of
the better sort, told by the man himself. In the first
of these it is spring : Jean Gourdon is eighteen years
of age, and he steals away from the house of his uncle
Lazare, a country priest, that he may meet his coy
sweetheart Babet by the waters of the broad Durance.
His uncle follows and captures him, but the threatened
sermon turns into a benediction, the priestly male-
diction into an impassioned song to the blossoming
springtide. Babet and Jean receive the old man's
blessing on their betrothal.

Next follows a day in summer, five years later; Jean,
as a soldier in the Italian war, goes through the horrors
of a battle and is wounded, but not dangerously, in the
shoulder. Just as he marches into action he receives a
letter from Uncle Lazare and Babet, full of tender fears
and tremors; he reads it when he recovers consciousness after the battle. Presently he creeps off to help
his excellent colonel, and they support one another
till both are carried off to hospital. This episode,
which has something in common with the *Sevastopol* of
Tolstoi, is exceedingly ingenious in its observation of the
sentiments of a common man under fire.

The third part of the story occurs fifteen years later.
Jean and Babet have now long been married, and Uncle
Lazare, in extreme old age, has given up his cure, and
lives with them in their farm by the river. All things
have prospered with them save one. They are rich,
healthy, devoted to one another, respected by all their
neighbours; but there is a single happiness lacking—
they have no child. And now, in the high autumn
splendour—when the corn and the grapes are ripe, and

the lovely Durance winds like a riband of white satin
through the gold and purple of the landscape—this gift
also is to be theirs. A little son is born to them in the
midst of the vintage weather, and the old uncle, to whom
life has now no further good thing to offer, drops pain-
lessly from life, shaken down like a blown leaf by his
excess of joy, on the evening of the birthday of the child.

The optimistic tone has hitherto been so consistently
preserved, that we must almost resent the tragedy of
the fourth day. This is eighteen years later, and Jean
is now an elderly man. His son Jacques is in early
manhood. In the midst of their felicity, on a winter's
night, the Durance rises in spate, and all are swept away.
It is impossible, in a brief sketch, to give an impression
of the charm and romantic sweetness of this little masterpiece, a veritable hymn to the Ninon of Provence; but
it raises many curious reflections to consider that this
exquisitely pathetic pastoral, with all its gracious and
tender personages, should have been written by the
master of Naturalism, the author of *Germinal* and of
Pot-Bouille.

III

In 1878, Zola, who had long been wishing for a place
whither to escape from the roar of Paris, bought a little
property on the right bank of the Seine, between Poissy
and Meulan, where he built himself the house which he
inhabited to the last, and which he made so famous.
Médan, the village in which this property is placed, is
a very quiet hamlet of less than two hundred inhabitants,
absolutely unillustrious, save that, according to tradition,
Charles the Bold was baptized in the font of its parish
church. The river lies before it, with its rich meadows,
its poplars, its willow groves; a delicious and somnolent

air of peace hangs over it, though so close to Paris. Thither the master's particular friends and disciples soon began to gather : that enthusiastic Boswell, Paul Aléxis; Guy de Maupassant, a stalwart oarsman, in his skiff, from Rouen; others, whose names were soon to come prominently forward in connection with that naturalistic school of which Zola was the leader.

It was in 1880 that the little hamlet on the Poissy Road awoke to find itself made famous by the publication of a volume which marks an epoch in French literature, and still more in the history of the short story. *Les Soirées de Médan* was a manifesto by the naturalists, the most definite and the most defiant which had up to that time been made. It consisted of six short stories, several of which were of remarkable excellence, and all of which awakened an amount of discussion almost unprecedented. Zola came first with *L'Attaque du Moulin*, which is rather a short novel than a genuine *conte*. The next story was *Boule de Suif*, a veritable masterpiece in a new vein, by an entirely new novelist, a certain M. Guy de Maupassant, thirty years of age, who had been presented to Zola, with warm recommendations, by Gustave Flaubert. The other contributors were M. Henri Céard, who also had as yet published nothing, a man who seems to have greatly impressed all his associates, but who has done little or nothing to justify their hopes; M. Joris Karel Huysmans, older than the rest, and already somewhat distinguished for picturesque, malodorous novels; M. Léon Hennique, a youth from Guadeloupe, who had attracted attention by a very odd and powerful novel, *La Dévouée*, the story of an inventor who murders his daughter that he may employ her fortune on perfecting his machine; and finally, the faithful Paul Aléxis, a native, like Zola

himself, of Aix in Provence, and full of the perfervid
extravagance of the South. The thread on which the
whole book is hung is the supposition that these stories
are brought to Médan to be read of an evening to Zola,
and that he leads off by telling a tale of his own.

Nothing need be said here, however, of the works of
those disciples who placed themselves under the flag
of Médan, and little of that story in which, with his
accustomed *bonhomie* of a good giant, Zola accepted their
comradeship and consented to march with them. *The
Attack on the Mill* is very well known to English readers,
who, even when they have not met with it in the original,
have been empowered to estimate its force and truth as
a narrative. Whenever Zola writes of war, he writes
seriously and well. Like the Julien of his late reminiscences, he has never loved war for its own sake. He has
little of the mad and pompous chivalry of the typical
Frenchman in his nature. He sees war as the disturber,
the annihilator; he recognises in it mainly a destructive,
stupid, unintelligible force, set in motion by those in
power for the discomfort of ordinary beings, of workers
like himself. But in the course of three European wars
—those of his childhood, of his youth, of his maturity—
he has come to see beneath the surface, and in *La Débâcle*
he almost agrees with our young Jacobin poets of one
hundred years ago, that Slaughter is God's daughter.

In this connection, and as a commentary on *The
Attack on the Mill*, I would commend to the earnest
attention of readers the three short papers entitled *Trois
Guerres*. Nothing on the subject has been written more
picturesque, nor, in its simple way, more poignant, than
this triple chain of reminiscences. Whether Louis and
Julien existed under those forms, or whether the episodes
which they illustrate are fictitious, matters little or

nothing. The brothers are natural enough, delightful enough, to belong to the world of fiction, and if their story is, in the historical sense, true, it is one of those rare instances in which fact is better than fancy. The crisis under which the timid Julien, having learned the death of his spirited martial brother, is not broken down, but merely frozen into a cold soldierly passion, and spends the remainder of the campaign—he, the poet, the nestler by the fireside, the timid club-man— in watching behind hedges for Prussians to shoot or stab, is one of the most extraordinary and most interesting that a novelist has ever tried to describe. And the light that it throws on war as a disturber of the moral nature, as a dynamitic force exploding in the midst of an elaborately co-related society, is unsurpassed, even by the studies which Count Lyof Tolstoi has made in a similar direction. It is unsurpassed, because it is essentially without prejudice. It admits the discomfort, the horrible vexation and shame of war, and it tears aside the conventional purple and tinsel of it; but at the same time it admits, not without a sigh, that even this clumsy artifice may be the only one available for the cleansing of the people.

IV

In 1883, Zola published a third volume of short stories, under the title of the opening one, *Le Capitaine Burle*. This collection contains the delicate series of brief semi-autobiographical essays called *Aux Champs*, little studies of past impression, touched with a charm which is almost kindred to that of Robert Louis Stevenson's memories. With this exception, the volume consists of four short stories, and of a set of little death-bed anecdotes, called *Comment on Meurt*. This latter is hardly in the writer's best style, and suffers by suggesting the immeasurably finer and deeper studies of the same kind which the genius of Tolstoi has elaborated. Of these little sketches of death, one alone, that of Madame Rousseau, the stationer's wife, is quite of the best class. This is an excellent episode from the sort of Parisian life which Zola understands best, the lower middle class, the small and active shopkeeper, who just contrives to be respectable and no more. The others seem to be invented rather than observed.

The four stories which make up the bulk of this book are almost typical examples of Zola's mature style. They are worked out with extreme care, they display in every turn the skill of the practised narrator, they are solid and yet buoyant in style, and the construction of each may be said to be faultless. It is faultless to a fault; in other words, the error of the author is to be mechanically and inevitably correct. It is difficult to define wherein the over-elaboration shows itself, but in every case the close of the story leaves us sceptical and cold. The *dénouêment* is too brilliant and conclusive, the threads are drawn together with too much evidence of preoccupation. The impression is not so much of a true tale told as of an extraordinary situation frigidly written up to and accounted for. In each case a certain social condition is described at the beginning, and a totally opposite condition is discovered at the end of the story. We are tempted to believe that the author determined to do this, to turn the whole box of bricks absolutely topsy-turvy. This disregard of the soft and supple contours of nature, this rugged air of molten metal, takes away from the pleasure we should otherwise legitimately receive from the exhibition of so much fancy, so much knowledge, so many proofs of observation.

The story which gives its name to the book, *Le Capitaine Burle*, is perhaps the best, because it has least of this air of artifice. In a military county town, a captain, who lives with his anxious mother and his little, pallid, motherless son, sinks into vicious excesses, and pilfers from the regiment to pay for his vices. It is a great object with the excellent major, who discovers this condition, to save his friend the captain in some way which will prevent an open scandal, and leave the child free for ultimate success in the army. After trying every method, and discovering that the moral nature of the captain is altogether too soft and too far sunken to be redeemed, as the inevitable hour of publicity approaches, the major insults his friend in a café, so as to give him an opportunity of fighting a duel and dying honourably. This is done, and the scandal is evaded, without, however, any good being thereby secured to the family, for the little boy dies of weakness and his grandmother starves. Still, the name of Burle has not been dragged through the mud.

Zola has rarely displayed the quality of humour, but it is present in the story called *La Fête à Coqueville*. Coqueville is the name given to a very remote Norman fishing-village, set in a gorge of rocks, and almost inaccessible except from the sea. Here a sturdy population of some hundred and eighty souls, all sprung from one or other of two rival families, live in the condition of a tiny Verona, torn between contending interests. A ship laden with liqueurs is wrecked on the rocks outside, and one precious cask after another comes riding into Coqueville over the breakers. The villagers, to whom brandy itself has hitherto been the rarest of luxuries, spend a glorious week of perfumed inebriety, sucking splinters that drip with bénédictine, catching noyau in iron cups, and supping up curaçao from the bottom of a boat. Upon this happy shore chartreuse flows like cider, and trappistine is drunk out of a mug. The rarest drinks of the world—Chios mastic and Servian sliwowitz, Jamaica rum and arrack, crême de moka and raki drip among the mackerel nets and deluge the seaweed. In the presence of this extraordinary and fantastic bacchanal all the disputes of the rival families are forgotten, class prejudices are drowned, and the mayor's rich daughter marries the poorest of the fisher-sons of the enemy's camp. It is very amusingly and very picturesquely told, but spoiled a little by Zola's pet sin—the overcrowding of details, the theatrical completeness and orchestral big-drum of the final scene. Too many barrels of liqueur come in, the village becomes too universally drunk, the scene at last becomes too Lydian for credence.

In the two remaining stories of this collection—*Pour une Nuit d'Amour* and *L'Inondation*—the fault of mechanical construction is still more plainly obvious. Each of these narratives begins with a carefully accentuated picture of a serene life : in the first instance, that of a timid lad sequestered in a country town; in the second, that of a prosperous farmer, surrounded by his family and enjoying all the delights of material and moral success. In each case this serenity is but the prelude to events of the most appalling tragedy—a tragedy which does not merely strike or wound, but positively annihilates. The story called *L'Inondation*, which describes the results of a bore on the Garonne, would be as pathetic as it is enthralling, exciting, and effective, if the destruction were not so absolutely complete, if the persons so carefully enumerated at the opening of the piece were not all of them sacrificed, and, as in the once popular

song called " An 'Orrible Tale," each by some different
death of peculiar ingenuity. As to *Pour une Nuit
d'Amour*, it is not needful to do more than say that it
is one of the most repulsive productions ever published
by its author, and a vivid exception to the general
innocuous character of his short stories.

No little interest, to the practical student of literature,
attaches to the fact that in *L'Inondation* Zola is really
re-writing, in a more elaborate form, the fourth section
of his *Jean Gourdon*. Here, as there, a farmer who has
lived in the greatest prosperity, close to a great river, is
stripped of everything—of his house, his wealth, and
his family—by a sudden rising of the waters. It is
unusual for an author thus to re-edit a work, or tell the
same tale a second time at fuller length, but the sequences
of incidents will be found to be closely identical, although
the later is by far the larger and the more populous
story. It is not uninteresting to the technical student
to compare the two pieces, the composition of which
was separated by about ten years.

V

Finally, in 1884, Zola published a fourth collection,
named, after the first of the series, *Naïs Micoulin*.
This volume contained in all six stories, each of considerable extent. I do not propose to dwell at any
length on the contents of this book, partly because they
belong to the finished period of naturalism, and seem
more like castaway fragments of the Rougon-Macquart
epos than like independent creations, but also because
they clash with the picture I have sought to draw of an
optimistic and romantic Zola returning from time to
time to the short story as a shelter from his theories.

Of these tales, one or two are trifling and passably insipid; the Parisian sketches called *Nantas* and *Madame Neigon* have little to be said in favour of their existence. Here Zola seems desirous to prove to us that he could write as good Octave Feuillet, if he chose, as the author of *Monsieur de Camors* himself. In *Les Coquillages de M. Chabre*, which I confess I read when it first appeared, and have now re-read with amusement, we see the heavy Zola endeavouring to sport as gracefully as M. de Maupassant, and in the same style. The impression of buoyant Atlantic seas and hollow caverns is well rendered in this most unedifying story. *Naïs Micoulin*, which gives its name to the book, is a disagreeable tale of seduction and revenge in Provence, narrated with the usual ponderous conscientiousness. In each of the last mentioned the background of landscape is so vivid that we half forgive the faults of the narrative.

The two remaining stories in the book are more remarkable, and one of them, at least, is of positive value. It is curious that in *La Mort d'Olivier Bécailles* and *Jacques Damour* Zola should in the same volume present versions of the Enoch Arden story, the now familiar episode of the man who is supposed to be dead, and comes back to find his wife re-married. Olivier Bécaille is a poor clerk, lately arrived in Paris with his wife; he is in wretched health, and has always been subject to cataleptic seizures. In one of these he falls into a state of syncope so prolonged that they believe him to be dead, and bury him. He manages to break out of his coffin in the cemetery, and is picked up fainting by a philanthropic doctor. He has a long illness, at the end of which he cannot discover what has become of his wife. After a long search, he finds that she has married a very excellent young fellow, a neighbour; and in the

L

face of her happiness, Olivier Bécaille has not the courage
to disturb her. Like Tennyson's " strong, heroic soul,"
he passes out into the silence and the darkness.

The exceedingly powerful story called *Jacques Damour*
treats the same idea, but with far greater mastery, and
in a less conventional manner. Jacques Damour is a
Parisian artisan, who becomes demoralised during the
siege, and joins the Commune. He is captured by the
Versailles army, and sentenced to penal servitude in
New Caledonia, leaving a wife and a little girl behind
him in Paris. After some years, in company with two
or three other convicts, he makes an attempt to escape.
He, in fact, succeeds in escaping, with one companion,
the rest being drowned before they get out of the colony.
One of the dead men being mistaken for him, Jacques
Damour is reported home deceased. When, after
credible adventures, and at the declaration of the
amnesty, he returns to Paris, his wife and daughter have
disappeared. At length he finds the former married to a
prosperous butcher in the Batignolles, and he summons
up courage, egged on by a rascally friend, to go to the
shop in midday and claim his lawful wife. The successive scenes in the shop, and the final one, in which
the ruddy butcher, sure of his advantage over this
squalid and prematurely wasted ex-convict, bids Félicie
take her choice, are superb. Zola has done nothing
more forcible or life-like. The poor old Damour retires,
but he still has a daughter to discover. The finale of the
tale is excessively unfitted for the young person, and no
serious critic could do otherwise than blame it. But, at
the same time, I am hardened enough to admit that I
think it very true to life and not a little humorous, which,
I hope, is not equivalent to a moral commendation. We
may, if we like, wish that Zola had never written *Jacques*

Damour, but nothing can prevent it from being a superbly constructed and supported piece of narrative, marred by unusually few of the mechanical faults of his later work.

The consideration of the optimistic and sometimes even sentimental short stories of Zola helps to reveal to a candid reader the undercurrent of pity which exists even in the most "naturalistic" of his romances. It cannot be too often insisted upon that, although he tried to write books as scientific as anything by Pasteur or Claude Bernard, he simply could not do it. His innate romanticism would break through, and, for all his efforts, it made itself apparent even when he strove with the greatest violence to conceal it. In his *contes* he does not try to fight against his native idealism, and they are, in consequence, perhaps the most genuinely characteristic productions of his pen which exist.

1892.

FERDINAND FABRE

FERDINAND FABRE

On the 11th of February, 1898, carried off by a brief attack of pneumonia, one of the most original of the contemporary writers of France passed away almost unobserved. All his life through, the actions of Ferdinand Fabre were inopportune, and certainly so ambitious an author should not have died in the very central heat of the Zola trial. He was just going to be elected, moreover, into the French Academy. After several misunderstandings and two rebuffs, he was safe at last. He was standing for the chair of Meilhac, and " sûr de son affaire." For a very long while the Academy had looked askance at Fabre, in spite of his genius and the purity of his books. His attitude seemed too much like that of an unfrocked priest; he dealt with the world of religion too intimately for one who stood quite outside. Years ago, Cardinal Perraud is reported to have said, " I may go as far as Loti—but as far as Fabre, never ! " Yet every one gave way at last to the gentle charm of the Cévenol novelist. Taine and Renan had been his supporters; a later generation, MM. Halévy, Claretie, and Jules Lemaître in particular, were now his ardent friends. The Cardinals were appeased, and the author of *L'Abbé Tigrane* was to be an Immortal at last. Ferdinand Fabre would not have been himself if he had not chosen that moment for the date of his decease. All his life through he was isolated, a little awkward, not in the central stream; but for all that his was a talent so marked and so individual that it came scarcely short

151

of genius. Taine said long ago that one man, and one
man only, had in these recent years understood the soul
of the average French priest, and that one man was
Ferdinand Fabre. He cared little for humanity unless
it wore a cassock, but, if it did, his study of its peculiarities was absolutely untiring. His books are galleries of
the portraits of priests, and he is to French fiction what
Zurbaran is to Spanish painting.

I

Ferdinand Fabre was born in 1830 at Bédarieux, in
the Hérault, that department which lies between the
southern masses of the Cévennes Mountains and the
lagoons of the Mediterranean. This is one of the most
exquisite districts in France; just above Bédarieux,
the great moors or *garrigues* begin to rise, and brilliant
little rivers, the Orb and its tributaries, wind and dash
between woodland and meadow, hurrying to the hot
plains and the fiery Gulf of Lyons. But, up there in
the Espinouze, all is crystal-fresh and dewy-cool, a mild
mountain-country positively starred with churches,
since if this is one of the poorest it is certainly one of
the most pious parts of France. This zone of broken
moorland along the north-western edge of the Hérault
is Fabre's province; it belongs to him as the Berry
belongs to George Sand or Dorsetshire to Mr. Hardy.
He is its discoverer, its panegyrist, its satirist. It was
as little known to Frenchmen, when he began to write,
as Patagonia; and in volume after volume he has made
them familiar with its scenery and its population. For
most French readers to-day, the Lower Cévennes are
what Ferdinand Fabre has chosen to represent them.

When the boy was born, his father was a successful
local architect, who had taken advantage of a tide of

prosperity which, on the revival of the cloth-trade, was
sweeping into Bédarieux, to half-rebuild the town.
But the elder Fabre was tempted by his success to enter
into speculations which were unlucky; and, in particular, a certain too ambitious high-road (often to be
mentioned in his son's novels), between Agde on the sea
and Castres on the farther side of the mountains, completed his ruin. In 1842, when the boy was twelve, the
family were on the brink of bankruptcy. His uncle,
the Abbé Fulcran Fabre, priest of the neighbouring
parish of Camplong, offered to take Ferdinand to himself
for awhile. In *Ma Vocation* the novelist has given an
enchanting picture of how his uncle fetched him on foot,
and led him, without a word, through almond planta-
tions thronged with thrushes and over brawling water-
courses, till they reached an open little wood in sight
of the moors, where Ferdinand was allowed to feast upon
mulberries, while Uncle Fulcran touched, for the first
time, on the delicate question whether his little garrulous
nephew had or had not a call to the priesthood. Uncle
Fulcran Fabre is a type which recurs in every novel that
Ferdinand afterwards wrote. Sometimes, as in *Mon
Oncle Célestin*, he has practically the whole book to himself; more often he is a secondary character. But he
was a perpetual model to his nephew, and whenever a
naïf, devoted country priest or an eccentric and holy
professor of ecclesiastical history was needed for fore-
ground or background, the memory of Uncle Fulcran
was always ready.

The " vocation " takes a great place in all the psychological struggles of Ferdinand Fabre's heroes. It
offers, indeed, the difficulty which must inevitably rise
in the breast of every generous and religious youth who
feels drawn to adopt the service of the Catholic Church.

How is he to know whether this enthusiasm which rises in his soul, this rapture, this devotion, is the veritable and enduring fragrance of Lebanon, the all-needful *odor suavitatis ?* This doubt long harassed the breast of Ferdinand Fabre himself. In that poor country of the Cévennes, to have the care of a parish, to be sheltered by a *presbytère*—by a parsonage or manse, as we should say—is to have settled very comfortably the problem of subsistence. The manse will shelter a mother, at need a sister or an aged father; it reconstructs a home for such a shattered family as the Fabres were now. Great, though unconscious, pressure was therefore put upon the lad to make inevitable his " vocation." He was sent to the Little Seminary at St. Pons de Thomières, where he was educated under M. l'Abbé Dubreuil, a man whose ambitions were at once lettered and ecclesiastical, and who, although Director of the famous Académie des Jeux Floraux, eventually rose to be Archbishop of Avignon.

During this time, at the urgent request of his uncle at Camplong, Ferdinand Fabre kept a daily journal. It was started in the hope that cultivating the expression of pious sentiments might make their ebullition spontaneous, but the boy soon began to jot down, instead of pious ejaculations, all the external things he noticed : the birds in the copses, the talk of the neighbours, even at last the oddities and the disputes of the excellent clergymen his schoolmasters. When the Abbé Fulcran died in 1871, his papers were burned and most of Ferdinand's journals with them; but the latest and therefore most valuable *cahier* survived, and is the source from which he extracted that absorbingly interesting fragment of autobiography, *Ma Vocation*. This shows us why, in spite of all the pressure of his people, and in spite of the entreaties of his amiable professors at the Great Seminary of Montpellier, the natural man was too strong in Ferdinand Fabre to permit him to take the final vows. In his nineteenth year, on the night of the 23rd of June 1848, after an agony of prayer, he had a vision in his cell. A great light filled the room; he saw heaven opened, and the Son of God at the right hand of the Father. He approached in worship, but a wind howled him out of heaven, and a sovereign voice cried, " It is not the will of God that thou shouldst be a priest." He rose up, calm though broken-hearted; as soon as morning broke, without hesitation he wrote his decision to his family, and of the " vocation " of Ferdinand Fabre there was an end.

There could be no question of the sincerity of a life so begun, although from the very first there may be traced in it an element of incompatibility, of *gaucherie*. Whatever may be said of the clerical novels of Fabre, they are at least built out of a loving experience. And, in 1889, replying to some accuser, he employed words which must be quoted here, for they are essential to a comprehension of the man and his work. They were addressed to his wife, *dilectæ uxori*, and they take a double pathos from this circumstance. They are the words of the man who had laid his hand to the plough, and had turned away because life was too sweet :—

" Je ne suis pas allé à l'Église de propos délibéré pour la peindre et pour la juger, encore moins pour faire d'elle métier et marchandise ; l'Église est venue à moi, s'est imposée à moi par la force d'une longue fréquentation, par les émotions poignantes de ma jeunesse, par un goût tenace de mon esprit, ouvert de bonne heure à elle, à elle seule, et j'ai écrit tout de long de l'aune, naïvement. . . . Je demeurais confiné dans mon coin étroit,

dans mon 'diocèse,' comme aurait dit Sainte-Beuve.
. . . De là une série de livres sur les desservants, les
curés, les chanoines, les évêques."

But if the Church was to be his theme and his obsession, there was something else in the blood of Ferdinand
Fabre. There was the balsam-laden atmosphere of the
great moorlands of the Cévennes. At first it seemed
as though he were to be torn away from this natural
perfume no less than from the odour of incense. He
was sent, after attempting the study of medicine at
Montpellier, to Paris, where he was articled as clerk to
a lawyer. The oppression of an office was intolerable
to him, and he broke away, trying, as so many thousands
do, to make a living by journalism, by the untrained and
unaccomplished pen. In 1853 he published the inevitable volume of verses, *Les Feuilles de Lierre*. It seemed
at first as if these neglected ivy-leaves would cover the
poor lad's coffin, for, under poverty and privation, his
health completely broke down. He managed to creep
back to Bédarieux, and in the air of the moors he soon
recovered. But how he occupied himself during the
next eight or ten years does not seem to have been
recorded. His life was probably a very idle one; with
a loaf of bread and a cup of wine beneath the bough,
youth passes merrily and cheaply in that delicious
country of the Hérault.

In the sixties he reappeared in Paris, and at the age
of thirty-two, in 1862, he brought out his first novel,
Les Courbezon : Scènes de la Vie Cléricale. George
Eliot's *Scenes of Clerical Life* had appeared a few years
earlier; the new French novelist resembled her less
than he did Anthony Trollope, to whom, with considerable clairvoyance, M. Amédée Pichot immediately compared him. In spite of the limited interests involved

and the rural crudity of the scene—the book was all
about the life of country priests in the Cévennes—
Les Courbezon achieved an instant success.   It was
crowned by the French Academy, it was praised by
George Sand, it was carefully reviewed by Sainte-Beuve,
who called the author " the strongest of the disciples of
Balzac." Ferdinand Fabre had begun his career, and
was from this time forth a steady and sturdy constructor
of prose fiction.   About twenty volumes bear his name
on their title-pages.   In 1883 he succeeded Jules Sandeau
as curator of the Mazarin Library, and in that capacity
inhabited a pleasant suite of rooms in the Institute,
where he died.   There are no other mile-stones in the
placid roadway of his life except the dates of the most
important of his books : *Le Chevrier*, 1867; *L'Abbé
Tigrane*, 1873; *Barnabé*, 1875; *Mon Oncle Célestin*,
1881; *Lucifer*, 1884; and *L'Abbé Roitelet*, 1890. At
the time of his death, I understand, he was at work on
a novel called *Le Bercail*, of which only a fragment was
completed.   Few visitors to Paris saw him; he loved
solitude and was shy.   But he is described as very genial
and smiling, eager to please, with a certain prelatical
unction of manner recalling the Seminary after half a
century of separation.

II

The novels of Ferdinand Fabre have one signal merit :
they are entirely unlike those of any other writer; but
they have one equally signal defect—they are terribly
like one another.   Those who read a book of his for the
first time are usually highly delighted, but they make a
mistake if they immediately read another.   Criticism,
dealing broadly with Ferdinand Fabre, and anxious to
insist on the recognition of his great merits, is wise if

it concedes at once the fact of his monotony. Certain
things and people—most of them to be found within
five miles of his native town—interested him, and he
produced fresh combinations of these. Without ever
entirely repeating himself, he produced, especially in
his later writings, an unfortunate impression of having
told us all that before. Nor was he merely monotonous;
he was unequal. Some of his stories were much better
constructed and even better than others. It is therefore
needless, and would be wearisome, to go through the
list of his twenty books here. I shall merely endeavour
to present to English readers, who are certainly not
duly cognisant of a very charming and sympathetic
novelist, those books of Fabre's which, I believe, will
most thoroughly reward attention.

By universal consent the best of all Fabre's novels is
L'Abbé Tigrane, Candidat à la Papauté. It is, in all the
more solid and durable qualities of composition, unquestionably among the best European novels of the last
thirty years. It is as interesting to-day as it was when
it first appeared. I read it then with rapture, I have
just laid it down again with undiminished admiration.
It is so excellently balanced and moulded that it positively does its author an injury, for the reader cannot
resist asking why, since *L'Abbé Tigrane* is so brilliantly
constructed, are the other novels of Fabre, with all their
agreeable qualities, so manifestly inferior to it? And
to this question there is no reply, except to say that on
one solitary occasion the author of very pleasant, characteristic and notable books, which were not quite
masterpieces, shot up in the air and became a writer
almost of the first class. I hardly know whether it is
worth while to observe that the scene of *L'Abbé Tigrane*,
although analogous to that which Fabre elsewhere

portrayed, was not identical with it, and perhaps this slight detachment from his beloved Cévennes gave the novelist a seeming touch of freedom.

The historical conditions which give poignancy of interest to the ecclesiastical novels of Ferdinand Fabre are the re-assertion in France of the monastic orders proscribed by the Revolution, and the opposition offered to them by the parochial clergy. The battle which rages in these stormy books is that between Roman and Gallican ambition. The names of Lacordaire and Lamennais are scarcely mentioned in the pages of Fabre,[1] but the study of their lives forms an excellent preparation for the enjoyment of stories like *L'Abbé Tigrane* and *Lucifer*. The events which thrilled the Church of France about the year 1840, the subjection of the prelates to Roman authority, the hostility of the Government, the resistance here and there of an ambitious and headstrong Gallican—all this must in some measure be recollected to make the intrinsic purpose of Fabre's novels, which Taine has qualified as indispensable to the historian of modern France, intelligible. If we recollect Archbishop de Quélen and his protection of the Peregrine Brethren; if we think of Lacordaire (on the 12th of February 1841) mounting the pulpit of Notre-Dame in the forbidden white habit of St. Dominic; if we recall the turmoil which preceded the arrival of Monseigneur Affre at Paris, we shall find ourselves prepared by historic experience for the curious ambitions and excitements which animate the clerical novels of Fabre.

The devout little city of Lormières, where the scene

---

[1] I should except the curious anecdote of the asceticism of Lamennais which is told by the arch-priest Rupert in the sixteenth chapter of *Lucifer*.

of *L'Abbé Tigrane* is laid, is a sort of clerical ante-
chamber to Paradise.   It stands in a wild defile of the
Eastern Pyrenees, somewhere between Toulouse and
Perpignan ; it is not the capital of a department, but a
little stronghold of ancient religion, left untouched in its
poverty and its devotion, overlooked in the general
redistribution of dioceses.   The Abbé Rufin Capdepont,
about the year 1866, finds himself Vicar-General of its
Cathedral Church of St. Irénée ; he is a fierce, domineer-
ing man, some fifty years of age, devoured by ambition
and eating his heart out in this forgotten corner of
Christendom.   He is by conviction, but still more by
temper, a Gallican of the Gallicans, and his misery is to
see the principles of the Concordat gradually being
swept away by the tide of the Orders setting in from
Rome.   The present Bishop of Lormières, M. de Roquebrun, is a charming and courtly person, but he is under
the thumb of the Regulars, and gives all the offices which
fall vacant to Dominicans or Lazarists.   He is twenty
years older than Rufin Capdepont, who has determined
to succeed him, but whom every year of delay embitters
and disheartens.

    Rufin Capdepont is built in the mould of the un-
scrupulous conquerors of life.   The son of a peasant
of the Pyrenees and of a Basque-Spanish mother, he is
a creature like a tiger, all sinuosity and sleekness when
things go well, but ready in a moment to show claws and
fangs on the slightest opposition, and to stir with a roar
that cows the forest.   His rude violence, his Gallican-
ism, the hatred he inspires, the absence of spiritual
unction—all these make his chances of promotion
rarer ; on the other side are ranked his magnificent
intellect, his swift judgment, his absolutely imperial
confidence in himself, and his vigilant activity.   When

they remind him of his mean origin, he remembers that Pope John XXII. was humbly born hard by at Cahors, and that Urban IV. was the son of a cobbler at Troyes.

What the episcopate means to an ambitious priest is constantly impressed on his readers by Ferdinand Fabre. Yesterday, a private soldier in an army of one hundred thousand men, the bishop is to-day a general, grandee of the Holy Roman Church, received *ad limina apostolorum* as a sovereign, and by the Pope as " Venerable Brother." As this ineffable prize seems slipping from the grasp of Rufin Capdepont, his violence becomes insupportable. At school his tyranny had gained him the nickname of Tigranes, from his likeness to the Armenian tyrant king of kings; now to all the chapter and diocese of Lormières he is l'Abbé Tigrane, a name to frighten children with. At last, after a wild encounter, his insolence brings on an attack of apoplexy in the bishop, and the hour of success or final failure seems approaching. But the bishop recovers, and in a scene absolutely admirable in execution contrives to turn a public ceremony, carefully prepared by Capdepont to humiliate him, into a splendid triumph. The bishop, still illuminated with the prestige of this *coup*, departs for Rome in the company of his beloved secretary, the Abbé Ternisien, who he designs shall succeed him in the diocese. Capdepont is left behind, wounded, sulky, hardly approachable, a feline monster who has missed his spring.

But from Paris comes a telegram announcing the sudden death of Monsieur de Roquebrun, and Capdepont, as Vicar-General, is in provisional command of the diocese. The body of the bishop is brought back to Lormières, but Capdepont, frenzied with hatred and passion, refuses to admit it to the cathedral. The Abbé

M

Ternisien, however, and the other friends of the last
régime, contrive to open the cathedral at dead of night,
and a furtive but magnificent ceremony is performed,
under the roar of a terrific thunderstorm, in defiance of
the wishes of Capdepont. The report spreads that not
he, but Ternisien, is to be bishop, and the clergy do not
conceal their joy. But the tale is not true; Rome
supports the strong man, the priest with the iron hand,
in spite of his scandalous ferocity and his Gallican
tendencies. In the hour of his sickening suspense,
Capdepont has acted like a brute and a maniac, but
with the dawning of success his tact returns. He
excuses his violent acts as the result of illness; he
humbles himself to the beaten party, he purrs to his
clergy, he rubs himself like a great cat against the
comfortable knees of Rome. He soon rises to be Archbishop, and we leave him walking at night in the garden
of his palace and thinking of the Tiara. "Who knows?"
with a delirious glitter in his eyes, "who knows?"

With *L'Abbé Tigrane* must be read *Lucifer*, which is
the converse of the picture. In Rufin Capdepont we
see the culmination of personal ambition in an ecclesi-
astic who is yet devoted through the inmost fibres of
his being to the interests of the Church. In the story
of Bernard Jourfier we follow the career of a priest who
is without individual ambition, but inspired by intense
convictions which are not in their essence clerical.
Hence Jourfier, with all his virtues, fails, while Capdepont, with all his faults, succeeds, because the latter
possesses, while the former does not possess, the " vocation." Jourfier, who resembles Capdepont in several,
perhaps in too many, traits of character, is led by his
indomitable obstinacy to oppose the full tide of the
monastic orders covering France with their swarms.

We are made to feel the incumbrance of the Congregations, their elaborate systems of espionage, and the insult of their direct appeal to Rome over the heads of the bishops. We realise how intolerable the bondage of the Jesuits must have been to an independent and somewhat savage Gallican cleric of 1845, and what opportunities were to be found for annoying and depressing him if he showed any resistance.

The young Abbé Bernard Jourfier is the grandson and the son of men who took a prominent part in the foundation and maintenance of the First Republic. Although he himself has gone into the Church, he retains an extreme pride in the memory of the Spartans of his family. To resist the pretensions of the Regulars becomes with him a passion and a duty, and for expressing these views, and for repulsing the advances of Jesuits, who see in him the making of a magnificent preacher, Jourfier is humiliated and hurt by being hurried from one miserable *succursale* in the mountains to another, where his manse is a cottage in some rocky *combe* (like the Devonshire " coomb "). At last his chance comes to him; he is given a parish in the lowest and poorest part of the episcopal city of Mireval. Here his splendid gifts as an orator and his zeal for the poor soon make him prominent, though not with the other clergy popular. His appearance—his forehead broad like that of a young bull, his great brown flashing eyes, his square chin, thick neck and incomparable voice— would be eminently attractive if the temper of the man were not so hard and repellent, so calculated to bruise such softer natures as come in his way.

The reputation of Jourfier grows so steadily, that the Chapter is unable to refuse him a canon's stall in the Cathedral of St. Optat. But he is haunted by his mundane devil, the voice which whispers that, with all his austerity, chastity, and elevation of heart, he is not truly called of God to the priesthood. So he flings himself into ecclesiastical history, and publishes in successive volumes a great chronicle of the Church, interpenetrated by Gallican ideas, and breathing from every page a spirit of sturdy independence which, though orthodox, is far from gratifying Rome. This history is rapidly accepted as a masterpiece throughout France, and makes him universally known. Still he wraps himself in his isolation, when the fall of the Empire suddenly calls him from his study, and he has to prevent the citizens of Mireval from wrecking their cathedral and insulting their craven bishop. Gambetta, who knew his father, and values Jourfier himself, procures that he shall be appointed Bishop of Sylvanès. The mitre, so passionately desired by Capdepont, is only a matter of terror and distraction to Jourfier. He is on the point of refusing it, when it is pointed out to him that his episcopal authority will enable him to make a successful stand against the Orders.

This decides him, and he goes to Sylvanès to be consecrated. But he has not yet been preconised by the Pope, and he makes the fatal mistake of lingering in his diocese, harassing the Congregations, who all denounce him to the Pope. At length, in deep melancholy and failing health, he sets out for Rome, and is subjected to all the delays, inconveniences, and petty humiliations which Rome knows how to inflict on those who annoy her. The Pope sees him, but without geniality; he has to endure an interview with the Prefect of the Congregations, Cardinal Finella, in which the pride of Lucifer is crushed like a pebble under a hammer. He is preconised, but in the most scornful

way, on sufferance, because Rome does not find it convenient to embroil herself with the French Republic,
and he returns, a broken man, to Sylvanès. Even his
dearest friends, the amiable and charming trio of Gallican
canons, who have followed him from Mireval, and to
find offices for whom he has roughly displaced Jesuit
fathers, find the bishop's temper intolerable. His
palace is built, like a fortress, on a rocky eminence over
the city, and one wild Christmas night the body of the
tormented bishop is discovered, crushed, at the foot of
the cliff, whether in suicide cast over, or flung by a false
delirious step as he wandered in the rain. This endless
combat with the Church of which he was a member, had
ended, as it was bound to end, in madness and despair.

As a psychological study *Lucifer* is more interesting,
perhaps, than *L'Abbé Tigrane*, because more complex,
but it is far from being so admirably executed. As the
story proceeds, Jourfier's state of soul somewhat evades
the reader. His want of tact in dealing with his diocese
and with the Pope is so excessive that it deprives him
of our sympathy, and internal evidence is not wanting
to show that Fabre, having brought his Gallican professor
of history to the prelacy, did not quite know what to do
with him then. To make him mad and tumble him over
a parapet seems inadequate to the patient reader, who
has been absorbed in the intellectual and spiritual
problems presented. But the early portions of the book
are excellent indeed. Some of the episodes which soften
and humanise the severity of the central interest are
charming; the career of Jourfier's beloved nephew, the
Abbé Jean Montagnol, who is irresistibly drawn towards
the Jesuits, and at last is positively kidnapped by them
from the clutches of his terrible uncle; the gentle old
archpriest Rupert, always in a flutter of timidity, yet

with the loyalty of steel; the Canon Coulazou, who
watches Jourfier with the devotion of a dog through his
long misanthropic trances; these turn *Lucifer* into an
enchanting gallery of serious clerical portraits.

III

But there are other faces in the priestly portrait-
gallery which Ferdinand Fabre has painted, and some
of them more lovable than those of Tigrane and Lucifer.
To any one who desires an easy introduction to the
novelist, no book can be more warmly recommended
than that which bears the title of *L'Abbé Roitelet*, or, as
we might put it, " The Rev. Mr. Wren " (1890).   Here
we find ourselves in a variety of those poverty-stricken
mountain parishes, starving under the granite peaks of
the Cévennes, which Fabre was the first writer of the
imagination to explore; groups of squalid huts, sprinkled
and tumbled about rocky slopes, hanging perilously
over ravines split by tumultuous rivulets that race in
uproar down to the valleys of the Orb or the Tarn.
Here we discover, assiduously but wearily devoted to
the service of these parched communities, the Abbé
Cyprien Coupiac, called Roitelet, or the Wren, because
he is the smallest priest in any diocese of France.   This
tiny little man, a peasant in his simplicity and his shyness, has one ungovernable passion, which got him into
trouble in his student-days at Montpellier, and does
his reputation wrong even among the rocks of the black
Espinouze : that is his infatuation for all kinds of birds.
He is like St. Bonaventure, who loved all flying things
that drink the light, *rorem bibentes atque lumen ;* but he
goes farther, for he loves them to the neglect of his
duties.

Complaints are made of Coupiac's intense devotion to his aviary, and he is rudely moved to a still more distant parish; but even here a flight of what seem to be Pallas's sand-grouse is his ruin. He is summoned before the bishop at Montpellier, and thither goes the little trembling man, a mere wren of humanity, to excuse himself for his quaint and innocent vice. Happily, the bishop is a man of the world, less narrow than his subalterns, and in a most charming scene he comforts the little ornithological penitent, and even brings him down from his terrible exile among the rocks to a small and poor but genial parish in the chestnut woodlands among his own folk, where he can be happy. For a while the Abbé Coupiac is very careful to avoid all *Vogel-weiden* or places where birds do congregate, and when he meets a goldfinch or a wryneck is most particular to look in the opposite direction; but in process of time he succumbs, and his manse becomes an aviary, like its predecessors. A terrible lesson cures the poor little man at last. An eagle is caught alive in his parish, and he cannot resist undertaking to cure its broken wing. He does so, and with such success that he loses his heart to this enormous pet. Alas! the affection is not reciprocated, and one morning, without any warning, the eagle picks out one of the abbé's eyes. With some difficulty Coupiac is safely nursed to health again, but his love of birds is gone.

However, it is his nature, shrinking from rough human faces, to find consolation in his dumb parishioners; he is conscious to pain of that " voisinage et cousinage entre l'homme et les autres animaux " of which Charron, the friend of Montaigne, speaks. So he extends a fatherly, clerical protection over the flocks and herds of Cabre-rolles, and he revives a quaint and obsolescent custom by which, on Christmas night, the Cévenol cattle are brought to the door of their parish church to listen to the service, and afterwards are blessed by the priest. The book ends with a sort of canticle of yule-tide, in which the patient kine, with faint tramplings and lowings, take modestly their appointed part; and these rites at the midnight mass are described as Mr. Thomas Hardy might have described them if Dorchester had been Bédarieux. In the whole of this beautiful little novel Ferdinand Fabre is combating what he paints as a besetting sin of his beloved Cévenols—their indifference and even cruelty to animals and birds, from which the very clergy seem to be not always exempt.

To yet another of his exclusively clerical novels but brief reference must here be made, although it has been a general favourite. In *Mon Oncle Célestin* (1881) we have a study of the entirely single and tender-hearted country priest—a Tertullian in the pulpit, an infant out of it, a creature all compact of spiritual and puerile qualities. His innocent benevolence leads him blind-fold to a deplorable scandal, his inexperience to a terrible quarrel with a rival archæologist, who drives Célestin almost to desperation. His enemies at length push him so far that they determine the bishop to suspend him so that he becomes *révoqué;* but his health had long been undermined, and he is fortunate in dying just before this terrible news can be broken to him. This tragic story is laid in scenes of extraordinary physical beauty; in no book of his has Fabre contrived to paint the sublime and varied landscape of the Cévennes in more delicious colours. In Célestin, who has the charge of a youthful and enthusiastically devoted nephew, Fabre has unquestionably had recourse to his recollections of the life at Camplong when he was a

child, in the company of his sainted uncle, the Abbé
Fulcran.

In the whole company of Ferdinand Fabre's priests
the reader will not find the type which he will perhaps
most confidently await—that, namely, of the cleric who
is untrue to his vows of chastity. There is here no
Abbé Mouret caught in the mesh of physical pleasures,
and atoning for his *faute* in a pinchbeck Garden of
Eden. The impure priest, according to Fabre, is a
dream of the Voltairean imagination. His churchmen
are sternly celibate; their first and most inevitable
duty has been to conquer the flesh at the price of their
blood; as he conceives them, there is no place in their
thoughts at all for the movements of a vain concupi-
scence. The solitary shadow of the Abbé Vignerte, suspended for sins of this class, does indeed flit across the
background of *Lucifer*, but only as a horror and a
portent. In some of these priests, as they grow middle-
aged, there comes that terror of women which M. Anatole
France notes so amusingly in *Le Mannequin d'Osier*.
The austre Abbé Jourfier trembles in all his limbs when
a woman, even an old peasant-wife, calls him to the
confessional. He obeys the call, but he would rather
be told to climb the snowy peak of the highest Cévennes
and stay there.

To make such characters attractive and entertaining
is, manifestly, extremely difficult. Fabre succeeds in
doing it by means of his tact, his exhaustive knowledge
of varieties of the clerical species, and, most of all perhaps, by the intensity of his own curiosity and interest.
His attitude towards his creations becomes, at critical
moments, very amusing. " The reader will hardly
credit what was his horrible reply," Fabre will say, or
" How can we explain such an extreme violence in our

principal personage ? " He forgets that these people
are imaginary, and he calls upon us, with eager complacency, to observe what strange things they are saying
and doing. His vivacious sincerity permits him to put
forth with success novel after novel, from which the
female element is entirely excluded. In his principal
books love is not mentioned, and women take no part
at all. *Mon Oncle Célestin* is hardly an exception, because the female figures introduced are those of a spiteful
virago and a girl of clouded intelligence, who are merely
machines to lift into higher prominence the sufferings
and the lustrous virtues of the Abbé Célestin. Through
the dramatic excitement, the nerve-storm, of *L'Abbé
Tigrane* there never is visible so much as the flutter of
a petticoat; in *Lucifer*, the interesting and pathetic
chapter on the text *Domine, ad adjuvandum me festina*
dismisses the subject in a manner which gives no en-
couragement to levity. Those who wish to laugh with
Ariosto or to snigger with Aretine must not come to
Ferdinand Fabre. He has not faith, he pretends to no
vocation; but that religious life upon which he looks
back in a sort of ceaseless nostalgia confronts him in its
purest and most loyal aspect.

IV

The priest is not absolutely the only subject which
preoccupies Ferdinand Fabre; he is interested in the
truant also. Wild nature is, in his eyes, the great and
most dangerous rival of the Seminary, and has its notable
victories. One of the prettiest books of his later years,
Monsieur Jean (1886), tells how a precocious boy,
brought up in the manse of Camplong—at last Fabre
inextricably confounded autobiography with fiction—

is tempted to go off on an innocent excursion with a
fiery-blooded gipsy girl called Mariette. The whole
novel is occupied by a recital of what they saw and what
they did during their two days' escapade, and offers the
author one of those opportunities which he loves for
dealing almost in an excess of *naïveté* with the incidents
of a pastoral life. Less pretty, and less complete, but
treated with greater force and conviction, is the tale of
Toussaint Galabru (1887), which tells how a good little
boy of twelve years old fell into the grievous sin of going
a-poaching on Sunday morning with two desperate
characters who were more than old enough to know
better. The story itself is nothing. What is delicious
is the reflection of the boy's candid and timid but ad-
venturous soul, and the passage before his eyes of the
innumerable creatures of the woodland. At every step
there is a stir in the oleanders or a flutter among the
chestnut-leaves, and ever and anon, through a break
in the copses, there peep forth against the rich blue
sky the white peaks of the mountains. *Toussaint
Galabru* is the only book known to me in the French
language which might really have been written by
Richard Jefferies, with some revision, perhaps, by Mr.
Thomas Hardy.

One curious book by Ferdinand Fabre demands
mention in a general survey of his work. It stands
quite apart, in one sense, from his customary labours;
in another sense it offers the quintessence of them.
The only story which he has published in which everything is sacrificed to beauty of form is *Le Chevrier* (1867),
which deserves a term commonly misused, and always
dubious; it may be called a " prose-poem." In his
other books the style is sturdy, rustic and plain, with
frequent use of *patois* and a certain thickness or heaviness

of expression.   His phrases are abrupt, not always quite
lucid; there can be no question, although he protested
violently against the attribution, that Fabre studied the
manner of Balzac, not always to his advantage.   But in
Le Chevrier—which is a sort of discouraged *Daphnis and
Chloë* of the Cévennes—he deliberately composed a
work in modulated and elaborate numbers.   It might
be the translation of a poem in Provençal or Spanish;
we seem in reading it to divine the vanished form of
verse.

It is, moreover, written in a highly artificial language,
partly in Cévenol *patois*, partly in French of the sixteenth
century, imitated, it is evident, from the style of Amyot
and Montaigne.   *Le Chevrier* begins, in ordinary French,
by describing how the author goes up into the Larzac,
a bleak little plateau that smells of rosemary and wild
thyme in the gorges of the High Cévennes, for the purpose of shooting hares, and how he takes with him an
elderly goatherd, Eran Erembert, famous for his skill
in sport.   But one day the snow shuts them up in the
farmhouse, and Eran is cajoled into telling his life's
history.   This he does in the aforesaid mixture of *patois*
and Renaissance French, fairly but not invariably sus-
tained.   It is a story of passionate love, ill requited.
Eran has loved a pretty foundling, called Félice, but she
prefers his master's son, a handsome ne'er-do-weel,
called Frédéry, whom she marries.   Eran turns from her
to Françon, a still more beautiful but worthless girl, and
wastes his life with her.   Frédéry dies at last, and Eran
constrains Félice to marry him; but her heart is elsewhere, and she drowns herself.   It is a sad, impassioned
tale, embroidered on every page with love of the High
Cévenol country and knowledge of its pastoral rites and
customs.

The scene is curious, because of its various elements.
The snow, congealing around a neighbouring peak in
the Larzac, falls upon the branches of a date-palm in
the courtyard of the farmhouse at Mirande, and on the
peacocks, humped up and ruffled in its branches. But
through all the picture, with its incongruities of a southern
mountain country, moves the *cabrade*, the docile flock
of goats, with Sacripant, a noble pedigree billy, at their
head, and these animals, closely attending upon Eran
their herd, seem to form a chorus in the classico-rustic
tragedy. And all the country, bare as it is, is eminently
giboyeux ; it stirs and rustles with the incessant movement of those living creatures which Ferdinand Fabre
loves to describe. And here, for once, he gives himself
up to the primitive powers of love; the priest is kept
out of sight, or scarcely mars the rich fermentation of
life with glimpses of his soutane and his crucifix.

Le Chevrier has never enjoyed any success in France,
where its archaic pastoralism was misapprehended from
the first. But it was much admired by Walter Pater,
who once went so far as to talk about translating it.
The novelist of the Cévennes had an early and an ardent
reader in Pater, to whom I owe my own introduction to
Ferdinand Fabre. Unfortunately, the only indication
of this interest which survives, so far as I know, is an
article in the privately printed *Essays from the Guardian*,
where Pater reviews one of Fabre's weakest works, the
novel called *Norine* (1889). He says some delicate
things about this idyllic tale, which he ingeniously call
" a symphony in cherries and goldfinches." But what
one would have welcomed would have been a serious
examination of one of the great celibate novels, *L'Abbé
Tigrane* or *Lucifer*. The former of these, I know,
attracted Pater almost more than any other recent

French work in fiction. He found, as Taine did, a solid
psychological value in these studies of the strictly
ecclesiastical passions—the jealousies, the ambitions,
the violent and masterful movements of] types that
were exclusively clerical. And the struggle which is the
incident of life really important to Fabre, the tension
caused by the divine " vocation " on the one hand and
the cry of physical nature on the other, this was of the
highest interest to Pater also. He was delighted, moreover, with the upland freshness, the shrewd and cleanly
brightness of Fabre's country stories, so infinitely removed from what we indolently conceive that we shall
find in " a French novel."

An English writer, of higher rank than Fabre, was
revealing the Cévennes to English readers just when the
Frenchman was publishing his mountain stories. If
we have been reading *Le Chevrier*, it will be found amusing to take up again the *Through the Cévennes with a
Donkey* of Robert Louis Stevenson. The route which
the Scotchman took was from Le Monastier to Alais,
across the north-eastern portion of the mountain-range,
while Fabre almost exclusively haunts the south-western
slopes in the Hérault. Stevenson brings before us a
bleak and stubborn landscape, far less genial than the
wooded uplands of Bédarieux. But in both pictures
much is alike. The bare moors on the tops of the
Cévennes are the same in each case, and when we read
Stevenson's rhapsody on the view from the high ridge
of the Mimerte, it might well be a page translated from
one of the novels of Ferdinand Fabre. But the closest
parallel with the Frenchman is always Mr. Thomas Hardy,
whom in his rustic chapters he closely resembles even in
style. Yet here again we have the national advantage,
since Fabre has no humour, or exceedingly little.

Fabre is a solitary, stationary figure in the current history of French literature. He is the *gauche* and somewhat suspicious country bumpkin in the urban congregation of the wits. He has not a word to say about " schools " and " tendencies "; he is not an adept in *névrosité d'artiste*. It is odd to think of this rugged Cévenol as a contemporary of Daudet and Goncourt, Sardou and Bourget; he has nothing whatever in common with them. You must be interested in his affairs, for he pretends to no interest in yours. Like Mr. Rudyard Kipling's " Native-Born," Ferdinand Fabre seems to say, " Let a fellow sing of the little things he cares about "; and what these are we have seen. They are found among the winding paths that lead up through the oleander-marshes, through the vineyards, through the chestnuts, to the moorlands and the windy peaks; they are walking beside the patient flocks of goats, when Sacripant is marching at their head; they are the poachers and the reapers, the begging friars and the sportsmen, all the quiet, rude population of those shrouded hamlets of the Hérault. Most of all they are those abbés and canons, those humble, tremulous parish priests and benevolently arrogant prelates, whom he understands more intimately than any other author has done who has ever written. Persuade him to speak to you of these, and you will be enchanted; yet never forget that his themes are limited and his mode of delivery monotonous.

A FIRST SIGHT OF VERLAINE

N

A FIRST SIGHT OF VERLAINE

IN 1893 the thoughts of a certain pilgrim were a good deal occupied by the theories and experiments which a section of the younger French poets were engaged upon. In this country, the Symbolists and Decadents of Paris had been laughed at and parodied, but, with the exception of Mr. Arthur Symons, no English critic had given their *tentatives* any serious attention. I became much interested—not wholly converted, certainly, but considerably impressed—as I studied, not what was said about them by their enemies, but what they wrote themselves. Among them all, there was but one, Mallarmé, whom I knew personally; him I had met, more than twenty years before, carrying the vast folio of his Manet-Poe through the length and breadth of London, disappointed but not discouraged. I learned that there were certain haunts where these later Decadents might be observed in large numbers, drawn together by the gregarious attraction of verse. I determined to haunt that neighbourhood with a butterfly-net, and see what delicate creatures with powdery wings I could catch. And, above all, was it not understood that that vaster lepidopter, that giant hawk-moth, Paul Verlaine, uncoiled his proboscis in the same absinthe-corollas?

Timidity, doubtless, would have brought the scheme to nought, if, unfolding it to Henry Harland, who knows his Paris like the palm of his hand, he had not, with enthusiastic kindness, offered to become my cicerone. He was far from sharing my interest in the Symbolo-decadent movement, and the ideas of the " poètes abscons comme la lune " left him a little cold yet he entered at once into the sport of the idea. To race up and down the Boulevard St. Michel, catching live poets in shoals, what a charming game ! So, with a beating heart and under this gallant guidance, I started on a beautiful April morning to try my luck as an entomologist. This is not the occasion to speak of the butterflies which we successfully captured during this and the following days and nights; the expedition was a great success. But, all the time, the hope of capturing that really substantial moth, Verlaine, was uppermost, and this is how it was realised.

As every one knows, the broad Boulevard St. Michel runs almost due south from the Palais de Justice to the Gardens of the Luxembourg. Through the greater part of its course, it is principally (so it strikes one) composed of restaurants and brasseries, rather dull in the daytime, excessively blazing and gay at night. To the critical entomologist the eastern side of this street is known as the chief, indeed almost the only habitat of *poeta symbolans*, which, however, occurs here in vast numbers. Each of the leaders of a school has his particular café, where he is to be found at an hour and in a chair known to the *habitués* of the place. So Dryden sat at Will's and Addison at Button's, when chocolate and ratafia, I suppose, took the place of absinthe. M. Jean Moréas sits in great circumstance at the Restaurant d'Harcourt—or he did three years ago—and there I enjoyed much surprising and stimulating conversation. But Verlaine—where was he ? At his café, the François-Premier, we were told that he had not been seen for four days. " There is a letter for him—he must be ill," said Madame; and we felt what the tiger-hunter feels when the tiger has gone to visit a friend in another valley. But to persist is to succeed.

The last of three days devoted to this fascinating sport had arrived. I had seen Symbolists and Decadents to my heart's content. I had learned that Victor Hugo was not a poet at all, and that M. Gustave Kahn was a splendid bard; I had heard that neither Victor Hugo nor M. Gustave Kahn had a spark of talent, but that M. Charles Morice was the real Simon Pure. I had heard a great many conflicting opinions stated without hesitation and with a delightful violence; I had heard a great many verses recited which I did not understand because I was a foreigner, and could not have understood if I had been a Frenchman. I had quaffed a number of highly indigestible drinks, and had enjoyed myself very much. But I had not seen Verlaine, and poor Henry Harland was in despair. We invited some of the poets to dine with us that night (this is the etiquette of the " Bou' Mich' ") at the Restaurant d'Harcourt, and a very entertaining meal we had. M. Moréas was in the chair, and a poetess with a charming name decorated us all with sprays of the *narcissus poeticus*. I suppose that the company was what is called " a little mixed," but I am sure it was very lyrical. I had the honour of giving my arm to a most amiable lady, the Queen of Golconda, whose precise rank among the crowned heads of Europe is, I am afraid, but vaguely determined. The dinner was simple, but distinctly good; the chairman was in magnificent form, *un vrai chef d'école*, and between each of the courses somebody intoned his own verses at the top of his voice. The windows were wide open on to the Boulevard, but there was no public expression of surprise.

It was all excessively amusing, but deep down in my
consciousness, tolling like a little bell, there continued
to sound the words, "We haven't seen Verlaine." I
confessed as much at last to the sovereign of Golconda,
and she was graciously pleased to say that she would
make a great effort. She was kind enough, I believe,
to send out a sort of search-party. Meanwhile, we
adjourned to another café, to drink other things, and our
company grew like a rolling snowball. I was losing all
hope, and we were descending the Boulevard, our faces
set for home; the Queen of Golconda was hanging heavily
on my arm, and having formed a flattering misconception as to my age, was warning me against the
temptations of Paris, when two more poets, a male
and a female, most amiably hurried to meet us with the
intoxicating news that Verlaine had been seen to dart
into a little place called the Café Soleil d'Or. Thither
we accordingly hied, buoyed up by hope, and our party,
now comprising a dozen persons (all poets), rushed into
an almost empty drinking-shop. But no Verlaine was
to be seen. Moréas then collected us round a table,
and fresh grenadines were ordered.

Where I sat, by the elbow of Moréas, I was opposite
an open door, absolutely dark, leading down, by oblique
stairs, to a cellar. As I idly watched this square of black-
ness I suddenly saw some ghostly shape fluttering at the
bottom of it. It took the form of a strange bald head,
bobbing close to the ground. Although it was so dim
and vague, an idea crossed my mind. Not daring to
speak, I touched Moréas, and so drew his attention
to it. "Pas un mot, pas un geste, Monsieur!" he
whispered, and then, instructed in the guile of his race,
insidias Danaûm, the eminent author of *Les Cantilènes*
rose, making a vague detour towards the street, and then

plunged at the cellar door. There was a prolonged scuffle and a rolling downstairs; then Moréas reappeared triumphant; behind him something flopped up out of the darkness like an owl,—a timid shambling figure in a soft black hat, with jerking hands, and it peeped with intention to disappear again. But there were cries of "Venez donc, Maître," and by-and-by Verlaine was persuaded to emerge definitely and to sit by me.

I had been prepared for strange eccentricities of garb, but he was very decently dressed; he referred at once to the fact, and explained that this was the suit which had been bought for him to lecture in, in Belgium. He was particularly proud of a real white shirt; "C'est ma chemise de conférence," he said, and shot out the cuffs of it with pardonable pride. He was full of his experiences of Belgium, and in particular he said some very pretty things about Bruges and its *béguinages*, and how much he should like to spend the rest of his life there. Yet it seemed less the mediæval buildings which had attracted him than a museum of old lace. He spoke with a veiled utterance, difficult for me to follow. Not for an instant would he take off his hat, so that I could not see the Socratic dome of forehead which figures in all the caricatures. I thought his countenance very Chinese, and I may perhaps say here that when he was in London in 1894 I called him a Chinese philosopher. He replied: "Chinois—comme vous voulez, mais philosophe—non pas!"

On this first occasion (April 2, 1893), recitations were called for, and Verlaine repeated his *Clair de Lune*:—

> "Votre âme est un paysage choisi
> Que vont charmant masques et bergamasques
> Jouant du luth et dansant et quasi
> Tristes sous leurs déguisements fantasques,"

and presently, with a strange indifference to all incongruities of scene and company, part of his wonderful *Mon Dieu m'a dit :*—

> " J'ai répondu : ' Seigneur, vous avez dit mon âme.
> C'est vrai que je vous cherche et ne vous trouve pas.
> Mais vous aimer !   Voyez comme je suis en bas,
> Vous dont l'amour toujours monte comme la flamme:
>
> ' Vous, la source de paix que toute soif réclame,
> Hélas !   Voyez un peu tous mes tristes combats !
> Oserai-je adorer la trace de vos pas,
> Sur ces genoux saignants d'ur rampement infâme ? ' "

He recited in a low voice, without gesticulation, very delicately. Then Moréas, in exactly the opposite manner, with roarings of a bull and with modulated sawings of the air with his hand, intoned an eclogue addressed by himself to Verlaine as " Tityre."   And so the exciting evening closed, the passionate shepherd in question presently disappearing again down those mysterious stairs.   And we, out into the soft April night and the budding smell of the trees.

1896.

THE IRONY OF M. ANATOLE FRANCE

THE IRONY OF M. ANATOLE FRANCE

IF we are asked, What is the most entertaining intelligence at this moment working in the world of letters ? I do not see that we can escape from replying, That of M. Anatole France. Nor is it merely that he is sprightly and amusing in himself; he is much more than that. He indicates a direction of European feeling; he expresses a mood of European thought. Excessively weary of all the moral effort that was applied to literature in the eighties, all the searchings into theories and 'proclaimings of gospels, all the fuss and strain of Ibsen and Tolstoi and Zola, that the better kind of reader should make a *volte-face* was inevitable. This general consequence might have been foreseen, but hardly that M. Anatole France, in his quiet beginnings, was preparing to take the position of a leader in letters. He, obviously, has dreamed of no such thing; he has merely gone on developing and emancipating his individuality. He has taken advantage of his growing popularity to be more and more courageously himself; and doubtless he is surprised, as we are, to find that he has noiselessly expanded into one of the leading intellectual forces of our day.

After a period of enthusiasm, we expect a great suspicion of enthusiasts to set in. M. Anatole France is what they used to call a Pyrrhonist in the seventeenth century—a sceptic, one who doubts whether it is worth while to struggle insanely against the trend of things. The man who continues to cross the road leisurely, although the cyclists' bells are ringing, is a Pyrrhonist —and in a very special sense, for the ancient philosopher who gives his name to the class made himself conspicuous by refusing to get out of the way of careering chariots. After a burst of moral excitement, a storm of fads and fanaticism, there is bound to set in calm weather and the reign of indifferentism. The ever-subtle Pascal noticed this, and remarked on the importance to scepticism of working on a basis of ethical sensitiveness. " Rien fortifie plus le pyrrhonisme," he says, " que ce qu'il y en a qui ne sont pas pyrrhoniens." The talent of M. Anatole France is like a beautiful pallid flower that has grown out of a root fed on rich juices of moral strenuousness. He would not be so delicately balanced, so sportive, so elegantly and wilfully unattached to any moral system, if he had not been preceded by masters of such a gloomy earnestness.

LE MANNEQUIN D'OSIER

After many efforts, more or less imperfectly successful, M. France seems at last to have discovered a medium absolutely favourable to his genius. He has pursued his ideal of graceful scepticism from period to period. He has sought to discover it in the life of late antiquity (*Thais*), in the ironic *naïveté* of the Middle Ages (*Balthasar* and *Le Puits de Sainte Claire*), in the humours of eighteenth-century deism (*La Rôtisserie de la Reine Pédauque* and *M. Jérôme Coignard*), in the criticism of contemporary books (*La Vie Littéraire*), in pure philosophical paradox (*Le Jardin d'Épicure*). Only once, in my opinion, has he ceased to be loyal to that *sagesse et élégance* which are his instinctive aim; only once—in that crude

Le Lys Rouge, which is so unworthy of his genius in
everything but style. With this exception, through
fifteen delightful volumes he has been conscientiously
searching for his appropriate medium, and, surely, he
has found it at last. He has found it in that unnamed
town of the north of France, where he listens to the
echoes and reverberations of the life of to-day, and
repeats them naïvely and maliciously to us out of his
mocking, resonant lips.

The two books which M. Anatole France published
in 1897 belong to the new category. Perhaps it was
not every reader of *L'Orme du Mail* who noticed the
words "*Histoire Contemporaine*" at the top of the
title-page. But they are repeated on that of *Le Mannequin d'Osier*, and they evidently have a significance.
Is this M. Anatole France's mode of indicating to us
that he is starting on some such colossal enterprise as a
Comédie Humaine, or a series like *Les Rougon Macquart?*
Nothing quite so alarming as this, probably, but doubtless a series of some sort is intended; and, already, it is
well to warn the impetuous reader not to open *Le
Mannequin d'Osier* till he has mastered *L'Orme du Mail*,
at the risk of failing to comprehend the situation. The
one of these books is a direct continuation of the other.

There was no plot in *L'Orme du Mail*. We were
introduced, or rather invisibly suspended within, a
provincial city of France of to-day, where, under all
species of decorous exteriors, intrigues were being
pushed forward, domestic dramas conducted, the
hollowness of intellectual pretensions concealed and
even—for M. Anatole France knows the value of the
savage note in his exquisite concert—brutal crimes
committed. With a skill all his own, he interested us
in the typical individualities in this anthill of a town,

and he knows how to produce his effects with so light
and yet so firm a hand, that he never for a moment
wearied us, or allowed us to forget his purpose.   He has
become no less persuaded than was Montaigne himself
of the fact that man is in his essence " ondoyant et
divers," and he will teach us to see these incongruities,
no longer in some fabulous Jérôme Coignard, but in
the very forms of humanity which elbow us daily in
the street.   He will do this with the expenditure of that
humour   which   alone   makes   the   Pyrrhonist   attitude
tolerable, and he will scatter the perfume of his gaiety
in gusts so delicate and pure that it shall pervade his
books from end to end, yet never for a moment betrays
the author into farce or caricature.   He will, moreover,
lift his dialogue on to a plane of culture much higher
than is customary even in French novels, where the
standard of allusion and topic in conversation has
always been more instructed than in English stories of a
similar class.   He will examine, with all his array of wit
and tolerance and paradoxical scepticism, how the minds
of average men and women are affected by the current
questions of the hour.

Readers of *L'Orme du Mail* were prepared for the
entertainment which was bound to follow.   They were
familiar with the battle royal for the vacant mitre which
was silently raging between M. l'Abbé Lantaigne and M.
l'Abbé Guitrel; they sympathised with the difficulties of
the préfet, M. Worms-Clavelin, so little anxious to make
himself disagreeable, and so good-natured and clever
underneath his irradicable vulgarity; they had listened
with eagerness to the afternoon conversations in the
bookshop of M. Paillot; they had hung over the back
of the seat in the shadow of the great elm-tree on the
Mall, to overhear the endless amiable wranglings of

M. Lantaigne and the Latin professor, M. Bergeret, the
only persons in the whole town who " s'interessaient
aux idées générales." They had thrilled over the
murder of Madame Houssieu, and laughed at the
sophistications of M. de Terremondre, the antiquary.
L'Orme du Mail ended like a volume of *Tristram Shandy*,
nowhere in particular. We laid it down with the
sentence, " Noémi est de force à faire un évêque; "
saying to ourselves, " Will she do it ? " And now that
we have read *Le Mannequin d'Osier*, we know as little
as ever what she can do.

But we know many other things, and we are not
quite happy. *Le Mannequin d'Osier* is not so gay a
book as its predecessor, and the Pyrrhonism of M.
Anatole France seems to have deepened upon him. The
air of insouciance which hung over the sun-lighted Mall
has faded away. M. Bergeret sits there no longer, or
but very seldom, arguing with M. l'Abbé Lantaigne; the
clouds are closing down on the fierce Abbé himself, and
he will never be Bishop of Tourcoing. In the new book,
M. Bergeret, who took a secondary place in *L'Orme du
Mail*, comes into predominance. His sorrows and
squalor, the misfortunes of his domestic life, his consciousness of his own triviality of character and mediocrity of brain—those are subjected to cruel analysis.
The difference between *L'Orme du Mail* and *Le Mannequin d'Osier* is that between the tone of Sterne and of
Swift. The comparison of Madame Bergeret, by her
husband, to an obsolete and inaccurate Latin lexicon
is extremely in the manner of *A Tale of a Tub*, and the
horribly cynical and entertaining discussion as to the
criminal responsibility of the young butcher Lecœur—
who has murdered an old woman in circumstances of
the least attenuated hideousness, but who gains the

sympathy of the prison chaplain—is exactly in the temper of the " Examination of Certain Abuses."   It is curious to find this Swift-like tone proceeding out of the Shandean spirit which has of late marked the humour of M. Anatole France.   He is so little occupied with English ideas that he is certainly unconscious of the remarkable resemblance between his reflections as to the nationalisation of certain forms of private property at the Revolution—" en quelque sorte un retour à l'ancien régime," and a famous page of Carlyle.

Around that dressmaker's dummy of Madame Bergeret, which gives its name to the book, there gather innumerable ideas, whimsical, melancholy, contradictory, ingenious, profound.   The peculiar obscurity and helplessness of poor M. Bergeret, compiling a *Virgilius Nauticus* with his desk cramped by an enormous plaster cylinder in front of it, and the terrible dummy behind it, exacerbated by his indigence and his mediocrity, by the infidelities of Madame Bergeret and the instability of his favourite pupils, his abject passivity, like that of a delicate, sentient thing, possessing neither tongue, nor hands, nor feet—all this forms in the end a sinister picture.   Is M. Anatole France mocking his own kith and kin ?   Is the most brilliant man of letters that the modern system of education in France has produced holding that very system up to ridicule ?   We might warn him to take care that the fate of Orpheus does not overtake him, were not his tact and rapidity equal to his penetration.   We are quite sure that, like M. Bergeret when M. Roux recited his incomprehensible poem in *vers libres*, M. Anatole France will always know the right moment to be silent " for fear of affronting the Unknown Beauty."

HISTOIRE COMIQUE

The intelligent part of the English public has been successfully dragooned into the idea that M. Anatole France is the most ingenious of the younger writers of Europe. It is extraordinary, but very fortunate, that the firm expression of an opinion on the part of a few expert persons whose views are founded on principle and reason still exercises a very great authority on the better class of readers. When it ceases to do so the reign of chaos will have set in. However, it is for the present admitted in this country that M. Anatole France, not merely is not as the Georges Ohnets are, but that he is a great master of imagination and style. Yet, one can but wonder how many of his dutiful English admirers really enjoy his books—how many, that is to say, go deeper down than the epigrams and the picturesqueness; how many perceive, in colloquial phrase, what it is he is " driving at," and, having perceived, still admire and enjoy. It is not so difficult to understand that there are English people who appreciate the writings of Ibsen and of Tolstoi, and even, to sink fathoms below these, of D'Annunzio, because although all these are exotic in their relation to our national habits of mind, they are direct. But Anatole France—do his English admirers realise what a heinous crime he commits ?— for all his lucidity and gentleness and charm, Anatole France is primarily, he is almost exclusively, an ironist.

In the literary decalogue of the English reader the severest prohibition is " Thou shalt not commit irony ! " This is the unpardonable offence. Whatever sentiments a writer wishes to enforce, he has a chance of toleration in this country, if he takes care to make his language exactly tally with his intention. But once let him

o

adopt a contrary method, and endeavour to inculcate his meaning in words of a different sense, and his auditors fly from him. No one who has endeavoured for the last hundred years to use irony in England as an imaginative medium has escaped failure. However popular he has been until that moment, his admirers then slip away from him, silently, as Tennyson's did when he wrote the later sections of *Maud*, and still more strikingly as Matthew Arnold's did when he published *Friendship's Garland*. The result of the employment of irony in this country is that people steal noiselessly away from the ironist as if he had been guilty in their presence of a social incongruity. Is it because the great example of irony in our language is the cruel dissimulation of Swift ? Is it that our nation was wounded so deeply by that sarcastic pen that it has suspected ever since, in every ironic humorist, " the smiler with the knife " ?

But the irony of M. Anatole France, like that of Renan, and to a much higher degree, is, on the contrary, beneficent. It is a tender and consolatory raillery, based upon compassion. His greatest delight is found in observing the inconsistencies, the illusions of human life, but never for the purpose of wounding us in them, or with them. His genius is essentially benevolent and pitiful. This must not, however, blind us to the fact that he is an ironist, and perhaps the most original in his own sphere who has ever existed. Unless we see this plainly, we are not prepared to comprehend him at all, and if our temperaments are so Anglo-Saxon as to be impervious to this form of approach, we shall do best to cease to pretend that we appreciate M. Anatole France. To come to a case in point, the very title of the *Histoire Comique* is a dissimulation. The idea of calling this tale of anguish and disillusion a " funny story " would certainly baffle us, if we did not, quite by chance, in the course of a conversation, come upon the explanation. Constantin Marc, discussing the suicide of the actor Chevalier, " le trouvait comique, c'est-à-dire appartenant aux comédiens." And this gives the keynote to the title and to the tale; it is a story about men and women who deal with the phenomenal sides of things, and who act life instead of experiencing it. It is a book in which the personages, with the greatest calmness, do and say the most terrible things, and the irony consists in the mingled gravity and levity with which they do and say them.

The design of the author, as always—as most of all in that most exquisite of his books, *Le Jardin d'Épicure* —is to warn mankind against being too knowing and too elaborate. Be simple, he says, and be content to be deceived, or you cannot be happy. Doctor Trublet, in the *Histoire Comique*, the wise physician who attends the theatre, and whom the actresses call Socrates, exclaims, " Je tiens boutique de mensonages. Je soulage, je console. Peut-on consoler et soulager sans mentir ? " This is a characteristic Anatolian paradox, and no one who has followed the author's teaching will find any difficulty in comprehending it. Over and over again he has preached that intelligence is vanity, that the more we know about life the less we can endure the anguish of its impact. He says somewhere—is it not in *Le Lys Rouge ?*—that the soul of man feeds on chimeras. Take this fabulous nourishment from us, and you spread the banquet of science before us in vain. We starve on the insufficiency of a diet which has been deprived of all our absurd traditional errors, " nos idées bêtes, augustes et salutaires." It is strange that all the subtlety of this marvellous brain should have found its

way back to the axiom, Unless ye become as little children,
ye cannot enter into the kingdom of heaven.

These reflections may bewilder those who take up the
Histoire Comique as a work of mere entertainment.
They may even be scandalised by the story; and indeed
to find it edifying at all, it is needful to be prepared for
edification.   Novelists are like the three doctors whom,
at a critical moment, Mme. Douce recommends to be
called in.   They were all clever doctors, but Mme.
Douce could not find the address of the first, the second
had a bad character, and the third was dead.   M.
Anatole France belongs to the first category, but we
must take care that we know his address.   In the
Histoire Comique he has quitted his series called *Histoire
Contemporaine*, and, we regret, M. Bergerat.   Nor has
he returned, as we admit we hoped he had done, to the
Rôtisserie de la Reine Pédauque, and the enchanting
humours of his eighteenth century. He has written a novel
of to-day, of the same class as *Le Lys Rouge*.   He has
taken the *coulisses* of a great theatre as the scene of the
very simple intrigue of his story, which is, as always
with M. Anatole France, more of a chronicle than a
novel, and extremely simple in construction.

He has chosen the theatre for his scene, one may
conjecture, because of the advantage it offers to a narrator who wishes to distinguish sharply between emotions
and acts.   It troubles M. Anatole France that people
are never natural.   They scarcely ever say a thing
because they think it.   They say it because it seems
the proper thing to say, and it is extremely rare to find
any one who is perfectly natural.   In this book Félicie
Nanteuil congratulates herself that her lover, Robert
de Ligny, is natural; but that is her illusion; he is not.
This contrast between what people feel and think and

what they say is projected in the highest relief upon the theatre. A violent symbol of this is shown in the great scene where the actress, fresh from the funeral of the man whose jealousy has destroyed her happiness for ever, is obliged, at a rehearsal, to repeat over and over the phrase, " Mon cousin, je suis éveillée toute joyeuse ce matin."

It would perhaps be difficult to point to a single book which M. Anatole France has published in which his theory that only two things, beauty and goodness, are of any importance in life, seems at first sight to be less prominent than in his *Histoire Comique*. But it prevails here, too, we shall find, if we are not hasty in judgment. And if we do not care to examine the philosophy of the story, and to reconcile its paradoxes with ethical truth, we can at least enjoy the sobriety, the precision, the elasticity of its faultless style. If the reader prefers to do so, he may take *Histoire Comique* simply as a melancholy and somewhat sensuous illustration of the unreasonable madness of love, and of the insufficiency of art, with all its discipline, to regulate the turbulent spirit of youth.

1903.

PIERRE LOTI

PIERRE LOTI

IT is one of the advantages of foreign criticism that it can stand a little aloof from the movement of a literature, and be unaffected by the passing fluctuations of fashion. It is not obliged to take into consideration the political or social accidents which may affect the reputation of an author at home. The sensitive and dreamy traveller whose name stands at the head of this page was, for ten years after his first appearance with that delicious fantasia which he called *Raharu*, but which the public insisted on knowing as *Le Mariage de Loti*, the spoiled favourite of the Parisian press. His writings of this first period have been frequently examined in England, by no one, however, so delicately and exhaustively as by Mr. Henry James. In 1891 " Pierre Loti " (whose real name, of course, is Captain Louis Marie Julien Viaud) was elected a member of the French Academy. His candidature began in mischief, as we read in the *Journal* of Goncourt, and in jest it ended. His *discours de réception* may have been a very diverting document, but it could not be considered a wise one. The merry sailor had his joke, and lost his public—that is to say, not to exaggerate, he alienated the graver part of it. Since that time there has been a marked disposition in French criticism to reduce Pierre Loti's pretensions, to insist upon " showing him his place." If the attention paid him before was excessive, so has been the neglect which has since been his portion. Neither the one nor the other has been perfectly sane;

neither one nor the other should prevent a foreign critic
from endeavouring, from the vantage-ground of distance, to discover the place in contemporary literature
held by an artist whose range is limited, but who
possesses exquisite sensibilities and a rare faculty of
notation. In the following pages I have successively
examined the main publications of Pierre Loti since the
crisis in his literary fortunes.

LE DÉSERT

This is the first work of importance which Pierre Loti
has published since he was made an Academician, for
Fantôme d'Orient exceeded the permission given to its
author to be sentimental and languishing, while *Matelot*,
in spite of certain tender pages, was distinctly below
his mark. The disturbance caused by his surprising
entry into the Mazarin Palace must now have passed
away, for, in his new book he is eminently himself
again. This, at all events, is *du meilleur Loti*, and the
patient readers of fifteen previous volumes know what
that means. There is no more curious phenomenon in
the existing world of letters than the fascination of Loti.
Here is a man and a writer of a thousand faults, and we
forgive them all. He is a gallant sailor, and he recounts
to us his timidities and his effeminacies; we do not care.
He is absolutely without what we call " taste "; he
exploits the weakness of his mother and the death-bed
of his aunt; it makes no difference to us. Irritated
travellers of the precise cast say that he is inaccurrate;
no matter. Moralists throw up their hands and their
eyes at Aziyadé and Chrysanthème and Suleima; well,
for the moment, we are tired of being moral. The fact
is, that for those who have passed under the spell of
Loti, he is irresistible. He wields the authority of the

charmer, of the magician, and he leads us whither he chooses. The critical spirit is powerless against a pen so delicately sensitive, so capable of playing with masterly effect on all the finer stops of our emotions.

Even the sempiternal youth of Loti, however, is waning away, and we are sensible in *Le Désert* that the vitality of the writer is not what it was when he made his first escapades in Senegambia, in Montenegro, in Tahiti. Doubtless, the austerity of the theme excludes indiscretion; there is little room for scandal in the monastery of Mount Sinai or in the desert of Tih. But the secret of the sovereign charm of Loti has always been the exactitude with which his writing has transcribed his finest and most fleeting emotions. He has held up his pages like wax tablets and has pressed them to his heart. This deep sincerity, not really obscured to any degree by his transparent affectations, has given his successive books their poignancy. And he has always known how to combine this sincerity with tact, no living writer understanding more artfully how to arrange and to suggest, to heighten mystery or to arrest an indolent attention. Hence it would not be like him to conceal the advances of middle age, or to attempt to deceive us. We find in *Le Désert* a Loti who is as faithful to his forty-five years as the author of *Le Roman d'un Spahi* was to his five-and-twenty. The curiosity in mankind, and in particular in himself, seems to have grown less acute; the outlook on the world is clearer and firmer, less agitated and less hysterical. The central charm, the exquisite manner of expressing perfectly lucid impressions, remains absolutely unmodified.

The book is the record of an expedition which occupied just four weeks. Armed with a safe-conduct from the

powerful Seïd, Omar El Senoussi El Hosni, at the end
of February, 1894, and in company of a noble friend
whose name does not occur in his pages, although
it constantly occupied the newspapers of Paris, Pierre
Loti started from Cairo on his way to Palestine. His
great design was to pass through the heart of Idumæa,
by the route of Petra, it having been ten years since
any European had crossed that portion of the desert.
The sheik of Petra, it appears, is in revolt against both
Turkey and Egypt, and has closed a route which in
Stanley's day was open and comparatively easy. Loti
was unable, as will be seen, to achieve his purpose, but
a unique fortune befell him. In the meanwhile, he
started by Suez, landing on the other side of the gulf,
ascended Sinai, descended again eastward, reached the
sea, and marched beside it up to the head of the bay,
halting in that strange little town of Akabah, which
represents the Eziongaber of Scripture and the Ælama
of the Crusaders. From this point he should have
started for Petra; but as that proved quite impossible,
the expedition held a little to the west and proceeded
north through the singular and rarely visited desert of
Tih, the land of the Midianites and the Amalekites.
On Good Friday they crossed the frontier of Palestine,
and three days later dismounted in one of the most
ancient and most mysterious cities in the world, Gaza
of the Philistines, a land of ruins and of dust, a cluster
of aged minarets and domes girdled by palm-trees.
The book closes with the words, " To-morrow, at break
of day, we shall start for Jerusalem."

The sentiment of the desert has never been so finely
rendered before. Without emphasis, in his calm, pro-
gressive manner, Loti contrives to plunge us gradually
in the colour and silence and desolation of the wilder-

ness. His talent for bringing up before the eye delicate and complicated schemes of aërial colour was never more admirably exercised. He makes us realise that we have left behind us the littleness and squalor of humanity, lost in the hushed immensity of the land-scape. There are no crises in his narrative; it proceeds slowly onward, and, by a strange natural magic in the narrator, we sweep onward with him. The absence of salient features concentrates our attention on the vast outlines of the scene. As they left the shores of the Gulf of Suez, the travellers quitted their European dress, and with it they seemed to have left the western world behind. Every night, as they camped in dark-ness, the granite peaks still incandescent about them, the air full of warm aromatic perfumes, they descended into a life without a future and without a past, into a dim land somewhere behind the sun and the moon.

This is the class of impression which Pierre Loti is particularly fortunate in rendering. We turn from his pages to those of a traveller who was, in his own class, an admirable writer, a quick and just observer. Forty years before Loti set forth, Canon (afterwards Dean) Stanley attempted almost exactly the same adventure, and his *Sinai and Palestine* is still a classic. It is very instructive to see how the same scenes struck two such distinct minds, both so intelligent and subtle, but the one a philosopher, the other an artist. One of the most singular spots on the earth's surface must be the desolate shore of the still more desolate Gulf of Akabah. This is how Stanley regarded it :—

" What a sea ! what a shore ! From the dim silvery mountains on the further Arabian coast, over the blue waters of the sea, melting into colourless clearness as they roll up the shelly beach—that beach red with the

red sand, or red granite gravel, that pours down from
the cliffs above—those cliffs sometimes deep red, sometimes yellow and purple, and above them all the blue
cloudless sky of Arabia. Of the red sand and rocks I
have spoken; but, besides these, fragments of red coral
are for ever being thrown up from the shores below, and
it is these coralline forests which form the true ' weeds '
of this fantastic sea. But, above all, never did I see
such shells. Far as your eye can reach you can see
the beach whitening with them, like bleaching bones."

This is eloquent, and Stanley is seldom so much
moved. But how much broader is the palette on Loti's
thumb, and how much more vivid is his fragment of
the same landscape :—

" L'ensemble des choses est rose, mais il est comme
barré en son milieu par une longue bande infinie, presque
noire à force d'être intensément bleue, et qu'il faudrait
peindre avec du bleu de Prusse pur légèrement zébré
de vert émeraude. Cette bande, c'est la mer, l'invrai-
semblable mer d'Akabah; elle coupe le désert en deux,
nettement, crûment; elle en fait deux parts, deux zones
d'une couleur d'hortensia, d'un rose exquis de nuage
de soir, où, par opposition avec ces eaux aux couleurs
trop violentes et aux contours trop durs, tout semble
vaporeux, indécis à force de miroiter et d'éblouir, où
tout étincelle de nacre, de granit et de mica, où tout
tremble de chaleur et de mirage."

The analysis of such a passage as this, and it is not
exceptionally remarkable, tends to show the reader what
a singular, perhaps what an unprecedented gift Loti has
for recording, with absolute precision, the shades and
details of a visual effect. His travels in the desert, where
there is scarcely anything but elementary forms of light

and colour to be seen, have given him an unparalleled opportunity for the exercise of a talent which is less frequent than we are apt to suppose, and which no recent French writer has possessed in equal measure. There are pages of *Le Désert* with which there is nothing in European literature, of their limited class, to compare, except certain of the atmospheric pictures in Fromentin's two books and in *Modern Painters*. How bad this sort of thing can be in clumsy hands, the gaudy sunsets of William Black remind us. We turn in horror from the thought, and re-read the descriptions in *Le Désert* of morning and evening from the ramparts of the monastery on Mount Sinaï, of the enchanted oasis of Oued-el-Aïn, of the cemetery of Akabah at midnight. These, and a score more pictures, seem to pass in the very reality of vision before our eyes, as the author quietly rolls them out of the magic lantern of his journal.

The lover of adventure will find nothing to excite him in Loti's panorama. The Bedouins were amiable and exacting, the expedition never lost its way, such dangers as threatened it proved merely to be mirages. If the travellers met a panther in a cave, it merely opened half a yellow eye; if robbers hovered in the distance, they never came within rifle shot. Sir Henry Rider Haggard would make our flesh creep in a single paragraph more than the amiable French pilgrim does in his whole volume. In the deep and sonorous desert Loti went to seek, not a sword, but peace. One central impression remains with the reader, of a great empty red land, a silent Edom, red as when Diodorus Siculus described it two thousand years ago, unchanging in its dry and resonant sterility. Loti's book is simply the record of a peaceful promenade, on the backs of swaying dromedaries, across a broad corner of this vague and rose-coloured infinity.

1895.

JÉRUSALEM

In the midst of that persistent and maddening search for novelty which is the malady, and at the same time the absurdity, of our feverish age, there is present in most of us an instinct of a diametrically opposite nature. If no quarter of a century has ever flung itself against the brazen door of the future with so crazy a determination to break into its secrets, to know, at all hazards, what to-morrow is to be like, it is equally certain that no previous epoch has observed with so deep an attention the relics of the extreme past, nor listened with an ear bent so low for a whisper from the childhood of the world. The bustle of modern life cannot destroy our primal sense of the impressiveness of mystery, and nothing within our range of ideas is so mysterious as the life which those led who imprinted on the face of our earth indelible marks of their force two or even three thousand years ago. Of all the human forces which interest and perplex, those of the founders of religion overpower the imagination most. If we can discover on this earth a city which has been the cradle, not of one mode of faith, but of many modes, we may be sure that around the crumbling and defaced walls of that city a peculiar enchantment must depend. There is but one such place in the world, and no processes of civilisation, no removal of barriers, no telegraphs or railways, can part the idea of Jerusalem from its extraordinary charm of sacrosanct remoteness. The peculiar sentiment of Zion is well expressed for us in the volume which Pierre Loti has dedicated to it, a book which none of those who propose to visit the Holy Land should fail to pack away in their trunks. M. Loti is the charmer *par excellence* among living writers. To him in higher degree than to any one else is given the power of making us see the object he describes, and of flooding the vision in the true, or at all events the effective, emotional atmosphere. He has no humour, or at least he does not allow it to intrude into his work. To take up a book on the Holy Land, and to find it jocose—what an appalling thing that would be ! We fancy that Jerusalem is one of the few cities which Mark Twain has never described. May he long be prevented from visiting it ! A sense of humour is an excellent thing in its place ; but the ancient and mysterious cradles of religion are not its proper fields of exercise. Mr. Jerome's Three Men do very well in a Boat ; but it would require the temper of an archimandrite to sojourn with them in Jerusalem. M. Loti is never funny ; but he is pre-eminently sensitive, acute, and sympathetic.

With most of us the idea of Jerusalem was founded in childhood. We retain the impression of a clean, brilliantly white city, with flat roofs and a few scattered domes, perched on the crag of a mountain, while precipices yawn below it and a broken desert spreads around. To enhance the whiteness of the shining town, the sky had usually been surcharged with tempest by the artist. We formed the notion that if we could climb to its neatly-fashioned gates and escape the terrors of the dark gulfs below, something very exquisite—above all, very fresh, trim, and lustrous—would reward us inside those strange ramparts. It is thus that Jerusalem appears to-day to hundreds of thousands of spiritual pilgrims. The hymns we sing, and the sermons we

P

listen to support this illusion. They confound the New Jerusalem with the old, and they suggest the serenity and beauty of broad white streets and saintly calm. Nothing could be falser to fact. The real Jerusalem is what Lord Chesterfield calls, in another sense, "a heterogeneous jumble of caducity." It is a city that has turned reddish with the concentrated dust of centuries. Under this coating of dust there lurk fragments of all the civilisations which have swept over it, one after the other, one in the steps of the other.

This is the solemnising (even the terrifying) aspect of Jerusalem. Its composite monuments, in their melancholy abandonment, speak of the horrors of its historic past. Nowhere can this past be heard to speak more plainly than in the wonderful kiosk, covered with turquoise-coloured faïence, which stands close to the Mosque of Omar in the Haram-esh-Cherif. M. Loti describes its double row of marble columns as a museum of all the *débris* of the ages. Here are Greek and Roman capitals, fragments of Byzantine and of Hebrew architecture; and among these comparatively historic specimens there are others of a wild and unknown style, at the sight of which the imagination goes back to some forgotten art of the primitive Jebusites, the very nature of which is lost in the obscurity of remote time. It is the peculiarity of Jerusalem that, whilst nothing has been completely preserved, nothing has been wholly lost. Jealous religions have fought with one another for the possession of this rocky sanctuary which they all have claimed. None has entirely succeeded, and gradually all have settled down to an uneasy toleration, each scraping away the dust and fashioning an altar for itself among cyclopean stones which were ancient in the days of Solomon, inside fortifications which Herod may have built over the place of martyrdom of some primitive and fabulous saint.

At the very foot of the Valley of Jehoshaphat, where the path has crossed the Kedron and is just about to mount again towards Gethsemane, there is an extraordinary example of this sordid and multifarious sanctity. A melancholy mausoleum is seen, in the midst of which an ancient iron door admits to the Tomb of the Virgin, a church of the fourth century, which, for more than a thousand years, has been the theatre of incessant ecclesiastical battle. At the present moment the Western Churches are excluded from this singular conventicle; but the Greeks, the Armenians, the Syrians, the Abyssinians, the Copts, and even the Mahometans, make themselves at home in it. The visitor enters, and is met by darkness and a smell of damp and mildew. A staircase, dimly perceived before him, leads down into the bowels of the earth, and presently introduces him to a church, which is more like a grotto than a human construction, and continues to sink lower as he proceeds. This strange cavern is dimly lighted by hundreds of gold and silver lamps, of extreme antiquity, hung from the low roof in wreaths and garlands. Within this agitating place, which is full of dark corners and ends of breakneck stairs that climb to nothing, five or six religions, each halting the rest, carry on simultaneously their ancient rituals, and everywhere there ascend discord of incoherent prayer and distracted singing, with candles waving and incense burning, processions in mediæval brocades that disturb kneeling pilgrims in the green turban of Mecca; a chaos of conflicting religions humming and hurrying in the darkness of this damp and barbarous cavern. Nothing could give a stronger impression of the bewildered genius of Jerusalem.

It was the privilege of M. Loti to be admitted to the arcane treasuries of the Armenian Church in Jerusalem, a privilege which, we understand him to say, no previous traveller has enjoyed. Under the special patronage of His Beatitude the Patriarch, and after a strange diplomatic entertainment of coffee, cigarettes, and a conserve of rose-leaves, the French writer was permitted to visit one of the oldest and most curious churches in Jerusalem. Its walls and all its massive pillars are covered with the lovely azure porcelain which is the triumph of ancient Arabic art. The thrones of the Patriarchs are wrought in mosaics of mother-of-pearl of an almost prehistoric workmanship. From the roof hang golden lamps and ostrich-eggs mounted in silver, while the marble floors are concealed from view under thick Turkey carpets of extreme antiquity, faded into exquisite harmonies of yellow, blue, and rose-colour. It was in front of the high altar, in the midst of all this profusion of superb, archaic decoration, that pale priests, with clear-cut profiles and black silky beards, brought out to M. Loti one by one the pieces of their incomparable and unknown Treasure,—a missal presented nearly seven hundred years ago by a Queen of Cilicia, mitres heavy with emeralds and pearls, tiaras of gold and rubies, fairy-like textures of pale crimson, embroidered with lavish foliage of pearl-work, in which the flowers are emeralds and each fruit is a topaz. Then, by little doors of mother-of-pearl, under ancient hangings of velvet, through sacristies lined with delicate porcelain, the visitor was hurried from chapel to chapel, each stranger and more archaic than the last, while his conductor, as though speaking of the latest historical event which had come to his knowledge, loudly lamented the cruelties of that sacrilegious king Khosroes II. and the ravages he had committed in Jerusalem.

This is an excellent specimen of the surprises that the sacred city reserves for pious visitors. It is a mass of decrepit fragments, a dust-heap of the religions of centuries upon centuries, preserving here and there, under the mask of its affliction and its humiliation, folded away in its mysterious sanctuaries, remnants of the beauty of the past so complete, so isolated, and so poignant, that the imagination finds it almost painful to contemplate them. " Jerusalem, if thou hadst known, even thou, at least in this thy day, the things which belong unto thy peace ! But now they are hid from thine eyes."

1895.

La Galilée

The trilogy of travel is now concluded with *La Galilée*. The completed work certainly forms the most picturesque description of the Holy Land and its surroundings which has yet been given to the world. We close this third volume with a sense of having really seen the places which had been a sort of sacred mystery to us from earliest childhood. Loti is a master of enchantment, and so cunningly combines the arts of harmony and colour in writing that he carries us, as though we were St. Thomas, whither we would not. In other words, by the strange and scarcely analyzable charm of his style, he bewitches us beyond our better judgment. But a reaction comes, and we are obliged to admit that in the case of *La Galilée* it has come somewhat soon.

It was only while reading this third volume that we became conscious that Pierre Loti was doing rather a mechanical thing. In *Le Désert* we were ready to believe that nothing but the fascination of wild places took him across the wilderness and up into that grotesque shrine

of Christianity that lurks among the fierce pinnacles of
Mount Sinai. In *Jérusalem*, led away by the pathos
of the scene and the poignant grace of the pilgrim's
reflections, we still persuaded ourselves to see in him
one who withdrew from the turmoil of the West that he
might worship among the dead upon Mount Moriah.
But in *La Galilée* the illusion disappears. Loti crosses
Palestine, embarks upon the Sea of Gennesaret, ascends
Mount Hermon, winds down into the rose-oasis of
Damascus, no longer as the insouciant and aristocratic
wanderer, " le Byron de nos jours," but as a tourist
like ourselves, wrapped in a burnous, it is true, and not
personally conducted by Messrs. Cook & Sons, yet not
the less surely an alien, manufacturing copy for the
press. He is revealed as the " special correspondent,"
bound, every night, however weary he may be, to " pan
out " sufficient description to fill a certain space on the
third page of the " Figaro."

There is nothing dishonourable in being a special
correspondent, nor is there a journalist living who might
not envy Pierre Loti the suppleness and fluid felicity of
his paragraphs. But this is not the light in which we
have learned to know him. He has very carefully taught
us to regard him as one to whom literature is indifferent,
who never looks at a newspaper, whose impressions of
men and manners are formed in lands whither his duties
as a sailor have casually brought him, who writes of them
out of the fullness of his heart, in easy exquisite numbers
cast forth as the bird casts its song. We have had an
idea that Loti never looks at a proof, that some comrade
picks up the loose leaves as they flutter in the forecastle,
and sends them surreptitiously to kind M. Calmann
Lévy. When he is elected to the French Academy, he
is the last to know it, and wonders, as he is rowed back

from some Algerian harbour, what his men are shouting
about on board his ship. All this is the legend of Loti,
and we have nourished and cherished it, but it will not
bear the fierce light that beats upon *La Galilée*. We
cannot pretend any longer; we cannot force ourselves
to think of a romantic pilgrim of the sea, flung ashore
at Aleppo and wandering vaguely up into the spurs of
Carmel. Certainly not! This is a Monsieur Loti who
is travelling in the pay of an enterprising Parisian
newspaper, who does his work very conscientiously,
but who is sometimes not a little bored with it.

The reader, who finds out that he has been played
with, grows captious and unjust. The result of discovering that Pierre Loti, notwithstanding the burnous
and the Arab carpets, is nothing better than a glorified
commis voyageur, has made us crusty. We are displeased
that he should travel so fast, and be willing to scamper
through the whole of " ce pays sacré de Gâlil " in six
weeks. It is really no matter of ours whether he lingers
or not, and yet we resent that he should push on as
monotonously as any of the Cookites do, about whom
he is so sarcastic. Our disgust invades us even when
we read the famous descriptions; we feel, not that they
impressed themselves irresistibly upon him, but that
he went out for the purpose of making them, and made
them as fast as he could. He becomes, to our affronted
fancy, a sort of huge and infinitely elaborate photographic machine, making exquisite kodaks as his guides
hurry him along. All this, we admit, is very unfair, but
it exemplifies the danger of admitting the public too
far into the works of the musical box. We find ourselves glancing back at our old favourites with horrid
new suspicions. Was he paid so much a line to make
love to his plaintive bride in Tahiti? Did some news-

paper engage him to pursue Aziyadé so madly through the length and breadth of Stamboul ? Was the Press kept waiting while Tante Claire was dying ? These are hideous questions, and we thrust them from us, but Pierre Loti should really be made to realise that the romantic attachment which his readers bear him is a tender plant. He holds them because he is so wayworn and desolate, but if he read his Shelley he would learn that " desolation is a delicate thing."

We would not be supposed to deny that *La Galilée* is full of pages which Loti only could write, pictures which he alone could paint. Here is a marvellous vignette of that sombre and sepulchral city of Nablous, so rarely visited by Christians, so isolated in its notorious bigotry, which an outrage on a small Protestant mission has just brought prominently before us. Here is Nazareth in twilight, with the moon flooding the boundless gulf of grasses that stretches from its rocky feet. Very impressive is the picture of the dead city of Tiberias, along whose solemn and deserted quays, once thronged with shipping, no vessel has been moored for centuries, looking down at the reflection of its crenelated walls in the tideless waters of Gennesaret. Beautiful, too, and " du meilleur Loti " is the description of the descent from the grey terraces of Hermon, to that miraculous oasis in the Idumean desert where Damascus lifts its rose-coloured minarets and domes out of pale-green orchards of poplars and pomegranates, beneath whose boughs the rivulets run sparkling over a carpet of iris and anemone. It is in forming impressions such as these, where no detail escapes the narrator's eye, and not a word is said too little or too much, that Pierre Loti asserts that supremacy as a master of description of which no carelessness and no inconsistency can deprive him. He has little pretension to being an intellectual force in literature, but as a proficient in this species of sensuous legerdemain he has had no rival, and is not likely soon to be surpassed.

1896.

FIGURES ET CHOSES QUI PASSAIENT

It has long been the custom of Pierre Loti to gather together at intervals those short pieces of his prose which have not found their place in any consecutive fiction or record of travel. In the case of most authors, even of the better class, such chips from the workshop would excite but a very languid interest, or might be judged wholly impertinent. All that Loti does, however, on whatever scale, is done with so much care and is so characteristic of him, that his admirers find some of their richest feasts in these his baskets of broken meat. The genuine Lotist is a fanatic, who can give no other reason for the faith that is in him than this, that the mere voice of this particular writer is an irresistible enchantment. It is not the story, or the chain of valuable thoughts, or the important information supplied by Pierre Loti that enthrals his admirers. It is the music of the voice, the incomparable magic of the mode in which the mournful, sensuous, exquisite observations are delivered. He is a Pied Piper, and as for his admirers, poor rats, as he pipes, they follow, follow. He who writes these lines is always among the bewitched.

The convinced Lotist, then, will not be discouraged to hear that *Figures et Choses qui passaient*, which is the twentieth tune (or volume) which this piper has played to us, is made up entirely of bits and airs that seem to have lost their way from other works. On the contrary,

it will amuse and stimulate him to notice that *Passage
d'Enfant* suggests a lost chapter of *Le Livre de la Pitié
et de la Mort ;* that *Instant de Recueillement* reads like a
rejected preface to the novel called *Ramuntcho ;* that
Passage de Sultan is a sort of appendix to *Fantôme
d'Orient ;* and that *Passage de Carmencita* forms a quite
unexpected prelude to *Le Mariage de Loti.*   But this
at least may be said, that this *beau gabier* of literature,
the fantastic and wayward sailor so signally unlike the
kind of mariner (with a pigtail, and hitching up white
ducks), who still continues to be our haunting maritime
convention—this complicated and morbid *Alcade de la
Mer* who walks so uncompromisingly the quarter-deck
of the French Academy, has never published a book
which more tyrannically presupposes an acquaintance
with all his previous works.   But he knows our frailty;
and I will make a confession which may go to the heart
of other Lotists.   There is one piece in *Figures et Choses*
which certainly ought never to have been written.   I
hope to screw up my courage, presently, to reprove it
by name; it is horrible, unseemly.   But I have read
every word of it, slowly, with gusto, as we read our
Loti, balancing the sentences, drawing the phrases over
the palate.   It is a vice, this Lotism; and I am not sure
that there ought not to be a society to put it down.
Yet if I were persuaded to sign a pledge never to read
another page of Loti, I know that I should immediately
break it.

Yet Loti does everything which, according to the
rules, he should not do.   *Passage d'Enfant,* with which
this volume opens, is a study such as no Englishman
can conceive himself proposing to write.   The author
is in Paris, about some official business.   He receives
a letter and a telegram to say that a little boy of two

years old, the child of a pair of his domestic servants at Rochefort, has suddenly died of croup. The resulting emotion is so capricious, so intimate, so poignant, that one would hardly be able to tell it, were it one's own experience, to one's most familiar friend. Pierre Loti tells it to the world in full detail, without concealment of names or places or conditions, and with an absolute perfection of narrative. He weaves it into a sort of diatribe against "the stupid cruelty of death." He flies back to his home, he visits the little newly-made grave, he mingles his tears with those of the child's father, he recalls a score of pretty tricks and babblings. There seems to us English people a certain lack here of decent proportion or self-command. Yet these are local matters, and the standard of taste varies so much at different times in different countries that one hesitates to dogmatise. And besides, the whole thing is steeped in that distinguished melancholy beauty which redeems and explains everything.

A large section of this new volume deals with the customs and landscape of that extreme corner of south-western France which the author has made his own during the years in which he has been stationed at the mouth of the Bidassoa. All these studies of the "Euskal-Erria," the primitive Basque Country, are instinct with the most graceful qualities of Pierre Loti's spirit. He has an exquisite instinct for the preservation of whatever is antique and beautiful, a superstitious conservatism pushed almost to an affectation. As he grows older, this characteristic increases with him. He has become an impassioned admirer of cathedrals; he is moved, almost to an act of worship, by sumptuous and compli-cated churches; he bows a dubiously adoring knee at Loyola and at Burgos. He is very eager to take part in processions, he is active among crowds of penitents, he omits no item in the sensual parts of ritual, and is swayed almost to intoxication on the ebb and flood of mysterious and archaic incantations. The reader of his *Jérusalem* will recall how earnestly and how vainly Pierre Loti sought for a religious idea, or a genuine inspiration of any spiritual kind, among the shrines and waters of Palestine. Once more this unction is denied him. Doomed for ever to deal with the external side of things, the exquisite envelope of life, Loti, as time goes by, seems knocking with a more and more hopeless agitation at the door of the mystical world. But that which is revealed to children will never be exposed to him. It ought to be enough for Loti that he surpasses all the rest of his fellow-men in the perfection of his tactile apparatus. That which is neither to be seen, nor touched, nor smelled, nor heard, lies outside his province.

But, within his province, what a magician he is! *Vacances de Pâques*, apparently a cancelled chapter from *Le Roman d'un Enfant*, tells us how a certain Easter holiday was spent in Loti's childhood, and how the days flew one after another, in the same cold rain, under the same black sky. The subject, mainly dealing with a neglected imposition and the dilatory labours of an idle schoolboy, seems as unpromising as possible, but the author's skill redeems it, and this little essay contains one page on the excessive colour of bright flowers under a grey or broken sky which ranks among the best that he has written. Pierre Loti is always excellent on this subject; one recollects the tiny blossoms that enamelled the floor of his tent in *Au Maroc*. In the present volume, while he is waiting on the hill-side to join the procession winding far up the Pyrenees to

Roncevaux, he notes the long rosy spindles of the
foxgloves, lashed with rain, the laden campanulas, the
astonishing and almost grotesque saxifrages torn and
ravaged by the hail.   And here and there a monotonous
flush of red flowers—rosy moss-campions, rosy gera-
niums, rosy mallows—and from the broken stalks the
petals flung in pink ribands across the delicate deep
green mosses.

An example of the peculiar subtlety of Loti's symbolism is afforded by the curious little study here called
Papillon de Mite.   In that corner of his house in Rochefort of which he has often told us, where all the treasures
are stored up that he has brought home from his travels,
the author watches a clothes-moth disengage itself from
a splendid Chinese robe of red velvet, and dance in a
sunbeam.   Rapidly, rapidly, in the delirium of existence, this atom waves its wings of silken dust, describing
its little gay, fantastic curves of flight.   Loti strikes it
carelessly to the ground, and then begins to wonder
what it is that it reminds him of.   Where had he once
seen before in his life something " papillonnement gris
pareil " which had caused him a like but a less transient
melancholy ?   And he recollects—it was long ago, at
Constantinople, on the wooden bridge that connects
Stamboul and Pera.   A woman who had lost both her
legs was begging, while a little, grey, impassive child,
with shrivelled hands, lay at her side.   Presently the
mother called the child to come and have its small
garment put on, when all at once it leaped from her
hands and escaped, dancing about in the cold wind, and
flapping the sleeves of its burnous-like wings.   And it
was of this poor child, soon exhausted, soon grey and
immobile again, but for an instant intoxicated with the
simple ecstasy of existence and motion, that Loti was

reminded by the curves and flutterings of the clothes-moth. This is a wonderfully characteristic example of the methods of the author, of his refined sensibility, vivid memory for details, and fondness for poignant and subtle impressions of association.

In *Profanation*—the study which I have dared to speak of with reprobation—I feel sure that he carries too far his theory that we may say anything if only we say it exquisitely enough and in the interests of pity. Loti's ideas of " taste," of reticence, are not ours; he does not address an Anglo-Saxon audience. But the cases in which he offends against even our conventions are very few in *Figures et Choses*. I have left myself no space to speak of the vivid pictures of sports among the primeval Basque population—studies, one might conjecture them to be, for the book that afterwards became *Ramuntcho*. I can but refer, with strong commendation, to the amazing description of the sacred dance of the Souletins. The last one hundred pages of this enchanting volume are occupied by *Trois Journées de Guerre*, an exceedingly minute and picturesque report of the storming of the city of Hué in the Annam War of 1883. Unless I am mistaken, these notes were originally sent home to some Parisian newspaper, where their publication gave great offence at the French Admiralty or War Office. Why it should do so, it is not easy after fifteen years of suppression to conceive. These *Trois Journées de Guerre en Annam* form one of the most admirably solid of all Pierre Loti's minor writings. They ought to be read in conjunction with the book called *Propos d'Exil*.

    1897.

RAMUNTCHO

In *Ramuntcho* Pierre Loti returns to the class of work which originally made him famous. It is eleven years since he published *Pêcheur d'Islande*, the latest of his genuine novels, for we refuse to include among these the distressing sketch called *Matelot*. During this decade he has written much, and some of it, such as *Fantôme d'Orient*, has taken a form half-way between fact and fiction; the rest has been purely descriptive, culminating, or rather going to seed, in the rather empty volume called *La Galilée*. It is probable that Loti—who for a person who never reads anything (as he told the French Academy) is remarkably shrewd in feeling the pulse of literature—has become conscious that he must recover some lost steps of his position. After a considerable pause, then, he comes forward with a book which is not only one of the most attractive that he has ever written, but belongs to the class which the public particularly enjoys. In *Ramuntcho* the tribe of the Lotists recover the Loti that they like best, the Loti of *Pêcheur d'Islande* and *Le Roman d'un Spahi*. Such a book as this, very carefully written in his best style by the most sensitive writter now living, is an event, and one on which to congratulate ourselves.

The scene of *Ramuntcho* is the extreme south-western corner of France, between the Bay of Biscay and the Pyrenees, where the remanants of an ancient race speak their mysterious and unrelated Basque language, and live a life apart from the interests and habits of their fellow-countrymen. We are reminded of the Breton scenes in *Mon Frère Yves*, with their flashes of sunshine breaking through long spells of rain and mist; and Ramuntcho, the hero of the book, is, indeed, a sort of

Yves—less intelligent, less developed, carried less far into manhood, but with the same dumb self-reliance, the same unadulterated physical force, the same pathetic resignation as the scion of a wasting, isolated race. The landscape of the Basque country interpenetrates the whole fabric of the story; we never escape from it for a moment. We move among grey hamlets, infinitely old, which are perched among great chestnuts, high up upon the terraces of mountain sides. On one hand the Bay of Biscay, with its troubled waters, never ceases to moan; on the other, the tumultuous labyrinth of the Pyrenees, with its sinuous paths and winding streams, stretches interminably, obscure and threatening. In each of the sparse mountain villages two monuments of great antiquity hold the local life together; one is the massive and archaic church, often as solid as a fortress; the other is the fives-court, in which for generations past all the young men of the parish have tempered their muscles of steel, and become adepts in this national game of *la pelote*.

Those who are familiar with the way in which the imagination of M. Loti works will have no difficulty in guessing the line he takes with such a landscape as this. Its inaccessibility to modern innovations, its secular decay, the gravity and dignity of its inhabitants, their poverty and independence, their respect for physical beauty, their hardy activity—all these are qualities naturally fascinating to M. Loti, and he adds to a combination of these the peculiar melancholy, the sense of the inexorable " fallings from us, vanishings," of which he is so singular a master. Never has he been more pathetic, more deeply plunged in the consciousness that, as the Persian poet puts it,

> " The Stars are setting, and the Caravan
> Starts for the Dawn of Nothing."

Never has he expended a greater wealth of melody and colour, never fused his effects into tones of rarer delicacy, than in this tale of smuggling, *pelote*-playing and courtship in a mountain village of the Basques.

No injustice is done to the author of such a novel as this by giving an outline of his plot, for the mere story is primitive and simple; it is in the telling that the art consists. The hamlet of Etchézar is the home of Franchita, a lonely woman, who, with one little son, Raymond or (in Basque) Ramuntcho, stole back thither some fifteen years before the tale opens, having been deserted by the man, an unnamed person of quality from Paris, whose mistress she had been in Biarritz. Ramuntcho grows up with a mixed temperament; partly he is a Basque, stolid, impenetrable, intensely local, but partly also he is conscious of cosmopolitan instincts, faint blasts of longing, like those which come to Arne in Björnson's beautiful story, for the world outside, the *au-delà*, or, as Ramuntcho vaguely puts it, "les choses *d'ailleurs*." In the village of Etchézar, which mainly supports itself by smuggling, the widow Dolores is a prominent personage, with her intensely respectable past, her store of money, and the two beautiful children, her son Arrochkoa and her daughter Gracieuse. But she hates and despises the unfortunate Franchita, and scorns Ramuntcho. The latter youth, arriving at the maturity of seventeen years, and in close amity with Arrochkoa, is admitted into the secret fellowship of a most desperate and successful band of smugglers, who, under the guidance of Itchoua, a much older man, harry the frontier of Spain.

The excursions of the smugglers give M. Loti opportunities for his matchless power in visual writing. The great scene in which, under the intoxication of the

Q

magical south wind, the band of desperadoes cross the shining estuary of the Bidassoa at sunrise, is superb. But still more striking are the pictures of home life in the village, the ceremonies and entertainments on All Saints' Day, scenes the theatres of which are the church and the *pelote*-court. In the national game—the Basque fives *in excelsis*—Ramuntcho becomes, as he approaches the age of eighteen, extremely skilful; he and Arrochkoa, indeed, are the two champion players of the whole district, and are thus drawn into closer mutual friendship. And under the smile with which Gracieuse rewards his prowess at the game, an old affection for the sister of his friend is blown into a passion, which is returned, and would be avowed, but for the jealousy of old Dolores. The lovers are driven to innocent clandestine meetings on the stone bench under Dolores' house, or, upon moonlight nights, within the dense shadow of the chestnut trees. If there is any theme in which M. Loti delights, and to the delineation of which he brings his most delicate and sympathetic gifts, it is the progress of the passion of love in adolescence. Ramuntcho comes to Gracieuse from his perilous skirmishings with the Spanish Custom-house officers, and from long vigils which have brought him close to the very pulse of nature. I cannot refrain from quoting, in this connexion, one passage intimately characteristic of its author:—

" Voici venir les longs crépuscules pâles de juin. . . . Pour Ramuntcho, c'est l'époque où la contrebande devient un métier presque sans peine, avec des heures charmantes : marcher vers les sommets, à travers les nuages printaniers; franchir les ravins, errer dans des régions de sources et de figuiers sauvages; dormir, pour attendre l'heure convenue avec les carabiniers complices, sur des tapis de menthes et d'œillets. La bonne senteur

des plantes imprégnait ses habits, sa veste jamais mise
qui ne lui servait que d'oreiller ou de couverture ; et
Gracieuse quelquefois lui disait le soir : ' Je sais la contrebande que vous avez faite la nuit dernière, car tu
sens les menthes de la montagne au-dessus de Mendiazpi,'
ou bien : ' Tu sens les absinthes du marais de Subernoa.' "

This happy condition of things is brought to an end
by the necessity on which Ramuntcho finds himself of
opting for Spanish or French citizenship. If he chooses
the latter, he must prepare for three years' absence on
military duty before he can marry Gracieuse. He determines, however, that to accept his fate is the manly
thing to do ; but hardly has he so decided, when an
unexpected letter comes from an uncle Ignacio, in
Uruguay, offering to adopt him if he will go out to
America. The proposal comes too late, and he starts
for his military service. Then the tragedy begins. He
returns after his three years' absence to find his mother
dying, and his Gracieuse vanished. The bitter old
Dolores, after vainly thrusting a rich suitor upon her
daughter, has driven her to take the veil, and she is now
a nun in a little remote mountain-convent close to the
Spanish frontier. Ramuntcho takes up the old wild life
as a smuggler, but he cannot get the idea of Gracieuse
out of his mind ; and at last, encouraged by Arrochkoa,
he determines to make a raid on the convent, snatch
Gracieuse from her devotions, and fly with her to Argen-
tina. The two young men make an elaborate plan for a
nocturnal rape of their Iberian Sabine. But when they
arrive at the peaceful, noiseless nunnery, and are
hospitably received by the holy women, their ardour
dies away. Gracieuse gives no sign of any wish to fly ;
she merely says, when she hears that Ramuntcho is
leaving the country, that they will all pray the Virgin

that he may have a happy voyage. Intimidated by the
sanctity of the life which it seemed so easy to break
into as they talked about it late at nights over their
chacoli, but which now seems impregnable, the lads go
peaceably away, Arrochkoa sullenly to his nocturnal
foray on the frontier, Ramuntcho with a broken heart
to Bordeaux and Buenos Ayres. And so, with that
tribute to the mutability of fortune which Loti loves,
and with a touch of positive pietism which we meet
with in his work almost for the first time—there was a
hint of it in *Jérusalem*—this beautiful and melancholy
book closes. We feel as we put down the volume more
convinced than ever of the unique character of its
author's talent, so evasive and limited, and yet within
its own boundaries of so exquisite a perfection. It is a
talent in which intellect has little part, but in which
melody and perfume and colour combine with extraordinary vivacity to produce an impression of extreme
and perhaps not quite healthy sensibility.

1897.

LES DERNIERS JOURS DE PÉKIN

It was a fortunate chance which sent to China, in the
late autumn of 1900, the man in whom, perhaps more
delicately than in any other living person, are com-
bined the gifts of the seeing eye and the expressive pen.
The result is a book which, so far as mere visual present-
ment goes, may safely be said to outweigh the whole
bulk of what else was sent home from the extreme East,
in letters and articles to every part of the world, during
that terrible period of storm and stress. Pierre Loti
arrived when the fighting was over, when the Imperial
family had fled, and when the mysteries of the hitherto

inviolable capital of China had just first been opened to
the Powers. He reaped the earliest harvest of strange
and magnificent impressions, and he saw, with that
incomparably clear vision of his, what no European had
seen till then, and much that no human being will ever
see again. Moreover, the great artist, who had seemed
in *Jérusalem*, and still more in *La Galilée*, to have
tired his pen a little, and to have lost something of his
firm clairvoyance, has enjoyed a rest of several years.
His style proclaims the advantage of this reserve of
vigour. Loti is entirely himself again; never before,
not even in the matchless *Fleurs d'Exil*, has he presented his talent in a form more evenly brilliant, more
splendidly characteristic in its rich simplicity, than
in *Les Derniers Jours de Pékin*.

Pierre Loti arrived at Ning-Haï, on the Yellow Sea,
in a French man-of-war, on October 3, and a week later
he started on a mission to Peking. His journey thither
was marked by no very striking events, except by his
passage through the vast and deserted city of Tong-
Tchéou, full of silence and corpses, and paved with
broken porcelain. The horrors of this place might fill
a niche in some eastern Inferno; and they offer Loti his
first opportunity to exercise in China his marvellous
gift for the reproduction of phenomena. We pass with
him under the black and gigantic ramparts of Tong-
Tchéou, and thread its dreadful streets under the harsh
and penetrating light of Chinese autumn. The cold-
ness, the dark colour, the awful silence, the importunate
and crushing odour of death, these he renders as only
a master can. The little party pursues its course, and
on October 18, quite suddenly, in a grim solitude, where
nothing had been visible a few seconds before, a huge
crenelated rampart hangs high above their heads, the

disconcerting and grimacing outer wall of the Tartar city of Peking.

We cannot follow the author through his intellectual adventures, on a scene the most mysterious and the most tragic in the modern world, where, it is true, the agony of movement had ceased, but where, in the suspense and hush, the mental excitement was perhaps even greater than it had been during the siege. Everywhere was brooding the evidence of massacre, everywhere the horror of catastrophe, in what had so lately been the most magnificent city in the world, and what was now merely the most decrepit. The author, by virtue of his errand and his fame, had the extreme good fortune to be passed from the ruined French Embassy, in and in, through the Yellow City and the Pink City, to the very Holy of Holies, the ultimate and mysterious shrine, never before exhibited or even described to a Western eye, where, above the fabulous Lake of Lotus, the Empress and the Emperor had their group of secluded palaces. He was lodged in a gallery, walled entirely with glass and rice-paper, where marvellous ebony sculptures dropped in lacework from the ceiling, and where Imperial golden-yellow carpets, incredibly soft and sumptuous, rolled their dragons along the floor. Here the Empress, until a month or two before, had played the goddess among her great ladies in an indolent magnificence of flowers and satins and music.

But, perhaps, more incalculable still was the little dark chamber, furnished with a deep austerity of taste, and faintly pervaded with an odour of tea, of withered roses and of old silks, where, on a low bed, the dark blue coverlid thrown hastily aside, no change had been made since the pale and timid Emperor, whose innermost lair this was, had risen, in a paroxysm of terror, to fly for his life into the darkness, into the unknown spaces, guided only by that fierce and wonderful woman, of whose personal greatness everything that reaches us through the dimness of report merely seems to intensify our perception.

It is impossible here to do more than indicate the fullness of the descriptive passages which throng this volume. All the scenes, by day and night, in the Pink City, with its ramparts the colour of dried blood; all the pictures of temples and pagodas, half-lost in groves of immemorial cedars, and stained, in their exquisite and precious beauty, by dust, and corruption, and neglect; all the visits to sinister mandarins; all the chiaroscuro of night, scented and twinkling, falling upon this foul and fairylike nightmare—all must be read in the author's own language. How concise that is, how unaffected, how competent to transfer to us the image strongly imprinted upon Loti's own delicately ductile vision, one extract must suffice to exemplify. It is the conclusion of the account he gives of his visit to the triple Temple of the Lamas, where all had been in contrast, in its colour of ochre and rust, with the rose-colour and golden yellow of purely Chinese state ornament :—

" Ce dernier temple—le plus caduc peut-être, le plus déjeté, et le plus vermoulu—ne présente que la répétition obsédante des deux autres—sauf pourtant l'idole du centre qui, au lieu d'être assise et de taille humaine, surgit debout, géante, imprévue et presque effroyable. Les plafonds d'or, coupés pour la laisser passer, lui arrivent à mi-jambe, et elle monte toute droite sous une espèce de clocher doré, qui la tient par trop étroitement emboîtée. Pour voir son visage, il faut s'approcher tout contre les autels, et lever la tête au milieu des brûle-parfums et des rigides fleurs; on dirait alors une momie de Titan erigée dans sa gaine, et son regard baissé, au premier abord, cause quelque crainte. Mais, en la fixant, on subit d'elle un maléfice plutôt charmeur; on se sent hypnotisé et retenu là par son sourire, qui tombe d'en haut si détaché et si tranquille, sur tout son entourage de splendeur expirante, d'or, et de poussière, de froid, de crépuscule, de ruines, et de silence."

Pierre Loti's brief visit was paid just when the tide was turning. Even while he stayed in his fairy palace he noted the rapid recovery of Peking. The corpses were being buried out of sight, the ruins repaired, the raw edges of useless and barbarous destruction healed over. And now, after so short an absence, the mysterious Empress and her flock of mandarins are back once more, to restore as best they may their sparkling terraces of alabaster and their walls of sanguine lac. Once more the secrets of the Pink City will fold their soft curtains around them, and that inscrutable existence of ceremonious luxury resume its ancient course. Will any living Western man see again what Loti and his comrades saw in the winter of 1900 ? In one sense it is impossible that he should, since the adorable palace of the Empress, occupied by Field-Marshal von Waldersee, was burned down by accident in April 1901. But even what survives is only too likely to be hidden again for ever from European eyes, unless, indeed, another massacre of Christians throws it open to our righteous Vandalism.

1902.

SOME RECENT BOOKS OF
M. PAUL BOURGET

SOME RECENT BOOKS OF M. PAUL BOURGET

Voyageuses

THE talent of M. Paul Bourget has but rarely consented to submit itself to that precision of form and rapidity of narrative which are necessary for the conduct of a short story. His novels, indeed, have been becoming longer and longer, and the latest, *Un Crime d'Amour*, had, we are bound to confess, such an abundance of reflections and so little plot that it seemed to take us back to the days of Marivaux and Richardson. It was, therefore, a pleasant surprise to open M. Bourget's new volume, and discover that it is a collection of six independent stories, not one of them lengthy. The title, *Voyageuses*, is explained by a brief preface. These are tales of female travellers, whom the author has met (or feigns to have met) in the course of those restless perambulations of the world which he describes to us, every now and then, in his graceful " sensations." M. Bourget appears to us in *Voyageuses* in his very happiest vein, with least of his mannerism and most of his lucid gift of penetrating through action to motive.

The first of these stories is also the most subtle and pleasing. " Antigone " is the name the author gives to a Frenchwoman whom he meets in Corfu. She is the sister of a deputy who has been attainted in the Panama scandal, and who still tries to be dignified in exile. This ignoble person affects complete innocence, and has deceived a noble Ionian burgher, Napoléon Zaffoni, into a belief in him, so that Zaffoni entrusts to him the MS. of a book, the work of his lifetime, on the history and constitution of the Ionian Islands. From this the deputy grossly plagiarises, and would be cast forth even from Corfu were he not protected by the fervent good faith of his sister, who, in spite of all his rogueries, persists in believing in him. His character is presently whitewashed in Paris, and he returns to the Chamber of Deputies triumphant, owing all to the long-suffering old maid whom he probably robs and upon whom he certainly tramples.

We pass over to America in the somewhat fantastic tale called " Deux Ménages." The author has been told in Paris that he *must* make the acquaintance of Mrs. Tennyson R. Harris, who is " such " a bright, cultured woman with a " lovely " home at Newport. Unfortunately there is a husband, a common millionaire, without any conversation ; but one need take no notice of him. M. Bourget visits Mrs. Tennyson R. Harris, but finds her pretentious, scandalous and empty, and her lovely home a crazy shop of knick-knacks. But, on the other hand, he becomes deeply interested in the husband, a silent, down-trodden man, horribly over-worked and beginning to suffer from " nerve-trouble." He is ordered south for rest, and invites the author to come with him. At Thomasville, a fashionable watering-place in Georgia, they have a curious experience, which M. Bourget must be left to tell in his own words.

We are next in Ireland, in the exquisite story called " Neptunevale." Two young Parisians of fashion, the one as empty-headed as the other, but, beneath their frivolity, deeply and mutually enamoured, receive soon after their marriage a singular legacy. It is nothing less than a small property on the west coast of Ireland, where an uncle of the hero's, having persisted against the wish of his family in marrying a governess, retired half a century ago in dogged determination of exile. The young people do not know what to do with this little white Irish elephant, except to sell it for as much cash as it would fetch. But they have a curiosity to see it first, and, utterly ignorant, they persuade M. Bourget, who "knows the language," to come over with them. Neptunevale—for that is the name of their uncle's home—lies on the coast of county Galway; they have to get out at Oranmore station and drive to it. The arrival at the strange house, the reception of the French visitors by the old Irish servants, the way that the Celtic sentiment invades and engulfs the new-comers, so that at last they are afraid to sell the place at all, but find it exercising a curious fascination over them, an attraction half of terror and half of love—all this is described with extreme skill and delicacy. Nor can we fail to remark, with some degree of surprise as well as of admiration, how exactly M. Bourget, who can have but a slight and superficial knowledge of Ireland, has caught the note of Irish mysticism. There is a scene in which an old mad woman and a little boy sacrifice a cock, with horrid rites, to some dim Celtic deity, which is calculated to give Mr. Yeats himself a shiver.

Much more conventional is "Charité de Femme," a story which I should be inclined to describe as in-significant, were it not that it contains an incident, very naturally and unexpectedly introduced, which illuminates it, as with a flash of lightning. The scene of this tale, moreover, is laid in the islands off the coast of Provence, a territory which seemed to belong till lately to Guy de

Maupassant, and has since been annexed by M. Melchior de Vogüé. There is a vague sense in which we conceive that certain districts are the property of particular novelists, and resent the intrusion of others, unless the newcomers bring with them some very marked freshness of the point of view. This is wanting in " Charité de Femme." More striking is " Odile," which is composed, in point of fact, of two distinct episodes. In a Parisian drawing-room the author meets a strange Marquise d'Estinac, very distinguished, shy and mysterious, who invites him to take a drive with her in her carriage, for the purpose, as he afterwards divines, of enabling her to conquer an otherwise irresistible tendency to suicide. He learns that she is extremely fond of her husband, who neglects her for a *belle mondaine*, Madame Justel. While the author is still bewildered at a circumstance which is unparalleled in his career—for the companion of his drive refused to speak to him or look at him—he abruptly hears of the sudden and mysterious death of Madame d'Estinac. A couple of years afterwards, being at Maloja, he meets in the hotel there the Marquis, who has in the meantime married Madame Justel. A third person is of the party, Mademoiselle Odile d'Estinac, a girl of fourteen, the exact counterpart of her unfortunate mother. M. Bourget soon perceives that between this proud, reserved child and her new stepmother the relations are more than strained. He is witness to the insulting tyranny of the one, the isolation and despair of the other; and the body of Odile is presently discovered in the tarn below the hotel.

The longest and the most elaborated of these stories is the last, and it does not properly belong to them, for " La Pia " is no *voyageuse*, but a dweller, against her will, in the tents of Shem. This beautiful and extraordinary tale of a masterpiece stolen from the remote basilica of San Spirito in Val d'Elsa is one of the most effective examples we have met with of M. Bourget's method. It would be unfair to describe it fully, for while the five previous stories, of which we have given the brief outlines, depend exclusively for their effect on their execution, here the surprises of the plot have their adventitious value. The English readers of this volume will be inclined to see in it a curious tribute to an artist of our own race. It is hardly possible to believe that M. Bourget, who has always shown himself sensitive, as perhaps no other French writer of equal value, to exotic influences, has been an inattentive reader of Mr. Henry James's latest volumes, and, in particular, of *Embarrassments* and *Terminations*. He remains, of course, essentially himself; but, as Guy de Maupassant in *Notre Cœur* was evidently trying his hand at an essay in the Bourget manner, so in " Antigone " and " La Pia " M. Bourget is discovered, so it seems at least to us, no less indubitably trying what he can produce with the pencils and two-inch square of ivory that are the property of Mr. Henry James.

1897.

LA DUCHESSE BLEUE

The violence of public movements in France in 1897 was so great as to produce an unusual scarcity in literary productions. In such a barren season, therefore, the fecundity of M. Paul Bourget is remarkable. *La Duchesse Bleue* is the third volume which he has published this year, and it is one of the most solid and elaborate of his novels. But it is not quite new, although it is now given to the public for the first time in book form. Five years ago, if I remember right, the " Journal " applied to

M. Bourget in great haste for a new novel, and he wrote, somewhat in a hurry and for that special purpose, a story called *Trois Âmes d'Artistes.* He was dissatisfied with it, and left it there in the lost columns of a daily newspaper, from which he has now redeemed it, taking the opportunity to revise, adapt and indeed rewrite it as *La Duchesse Bleue.* We are not sure that this is ever a very fortunate method of producing a book, and, although the novel before us bears trace of extraordinary care and fastidious correction, it lacks that spontaneity which comes with work which has been run on right lines from its very inception. *La Duchesse Bleue*, let me admit at once, is not M. Bourget's masterpiece.

But it possesses a dedication, which is something of a literary event. The dedications of M. Bourget have always been a curious feature of his work. They are often, as in the present case, essays of some length and seriousness; they frequently develop a theory or a philosophy of the ingenious writer's. On principle, we are adverse to such prefatory disquisitions. If an author, long after the date of original publication, likes to gossip to us about the mode in which the plot and place commended themselves to him, we are well pleased to listen. But to open a new novel, and to find that a critical or metaphysical essay divides us from the tale, is not, to our mind, a happy discovery. It tends to destroy the illusion; it is, in its distinguished way, of the same order of obstacle as " this is a fact " of the very clumsy narrator. We begin by passing under a cold shower of scepticism; the effort to believe in the story is vastly increased. The dedicatory prefaces of M. Bourget are peculiarly disillusioning. He talks in them so much about the craftsman and the artist, so much about methods and forms; in short, he takes the music-box to pieces before us so resolutely, that we start with a sense of artificiality. Even in these complex days, we like to pretend that we are sitting in a ring around the story-teller, under the hawthorn-tree, and that when he says, " There was, once upon a time," once upon a time there was.

In the case before us we are, as usual, of opinion that the " dedication " is no help to the reader in giving him faith in the incidents about to be related to him, but it forms in itself an agreeable and suggestive piece of literature. It is addressed to Madame Matilde Serao, the Neapolitan novelist, whose astonishing *Il paese di Cuccagna*, by the way, has been excellently translated out of the Italian by Madame Paul Bourget. M. Bourget has been reading this brilliant book, and he has felt, once more, what a chasm divides the crowded and animated scenes of Madame Serao from his own limited studies of psychological problems. Accordingly he writes a long letter to explain this to Madame Serao, and to remind her that in the house of the novel there are many chambers. The great central hall, no doubt, is that occupied by herself and Balzac, Zola and Tolstoi —and, we may add, by Fielding and Dickens—where an eager creative energy sets on their feet, and spurs to concerted action personages of every kind, in hundreds at a time. This prodigious power to crowd the canvas with figures belongs to Madame Serao alone among the living novelists of Italy. One has only to recollect how entirely it is wanting to Gabriele d'Annunzio. It is a gift not to be despised ; it suggests a virility of intellect and a breadth of sympathy which are rewarded by a direct influence over a wide circle of readers. The success of such novels, in the hands of a great artist, is not problematical, because they possess, obviously and

R

beyond contradiction, what M. Bourget calls " le coloris de la vie en mouvement."

If, however, this kind of scene-painting were the only species of fiction permitted, there are many novelists who could never earn their daily bread, and M. Bourget is one of them. Accordingly his flattering address to Madame Serao is merely the prelude to an ingenious apology for the painting of sentiments and emotions in the novel which analyses minute and fugitive impressions. This demands a closeness of texture and a strenuous uniformity of technical effort which are in themselves advantages, but which are with difficulty exercised in the huge world-romance. In the course of his essay M. Bourget pauses to express his warm admiration of Mr. Henry James, whom he takes as the first living exponent of this peculiarly intense and vivid manner of contemplating, as through a microscope, the movement of intellectual life. We cannot but record this fact with complaisance, since, in reviewing *Voyageuses* last year, we remarked that, if it were possible to imagine that a prominent French writer could undergo the influence of an Anglo-Saxon contemporary, the transition which the style and attitude of M. Bourget are now undergoing would point to a deliberate study of Mr. James's manner. M. Bourget, in the dedication to *La Duchesse Bleue*, practically confesses that we were correct in what seemed our almost daring conjecture. He names Mr. James's volume called *Terminations* as the model which he has placed before himself in his recent treatment of problems of artistic psychology.

The original name of the story before us was *Trois Âmes d'Artistes*, as we have already said. M. Bourget explains that, on reflection, he thought this too ambitious a title. It was at least descriptive, whereas

La Duchesse Bleue suggests nothing; it proves upon examination to be the nickname of a part in a play in which the heroine made a success. M. Bourget has portrayed in this book three artistic temperaments set side by side. These are respectively those of a novelist and dramatist, an actress and a painter, and he has shown these three persons to us in a mutual crisis of tragical passion. Jacques Moran, the dramatist, has a play being acted, for the principal *rôle* in which a charming little actress, with a Botticelli face, Camille Favier, makes a great success; the painter is Vincent la Croix, who tells the story. Moran is adored by Camille, but deserts her for a woman of fashion, Madame de Bonnivet, while Vincent, worked upon by his generous indignation at this treatment, fails to perceive through three hundred pages that he himself loves Camille, and might be loved in return. The plot is no more complicated than this, and we confess that it requires some respect for M. Bourget and some enthusiasm for the processes of the psychological novel to carry us through so long a book attached to so slender a thread of plot.

Moran and Camille are entirely successful in life, Vincent la Croix is a failure in everything he touches, and the object of *La Duchesse Bleue* seems to be to distinguish between the one race of artists which translates marvellously without itself experiencing, and the other race which experiences without being able to translate. For a phrase to say on the boards, for a sentence to write in a book, the former class would sell their father or their mother.

The moral of *La Duchesse Bleue*, in a nutshell, is that if we wish to keep our hearts tender and fresh, we must be content to be ourselves mediocre and obscure. The thesis is a not unfamiliar one. It occurred to the fiery spirit of Elizabeth Browning while she watched the great god Pan, down by the reeds in the river, "draw out the pith like the heart of a man." In the hypothesis of the French novelist, a love, a hatred, a joy, a sorrow, is to the really successful artist nothing more than so much manured earth out of which he can force the flower of his talent, that blossom of delicacy and passion, to perfect which he will not hesitate for a moment to kill in himself every true delicacy and every living emotion. It is not a pleasant theory, and the ugliness of it may help us who form the vast majority of men and women to bear with fortitude the mortifying fact that we were not born to be geniuses. But we think that M. Bourget makes a mistake in attributing this peculiarly inhuman hardness of heart exclusively to the artist of the highest class. We are afraid that our experience has led us to observe the vanity—which is really at the root of this moral deformity—in those who have nothing of genius in their nature except its fretfulness and its ferocity.

1898.

COMPLICATIONS SENTIMENTALES

In reading M. Bourget's collection of short stories called *Voyageuses*, we observed that he had quitted for a moment that perfumed atmosphere of the salon and the boudoir which he loves, and that he had consented to take us with him out into the fresh air. It was but an episode; in *Complications Sentimentales* we find ourselves once more in the scented world of Parisian elegance, among those well-bred people of wealth, without occupation, whose intrigues and passions M. Bourget has taught himself to analyse with such extraordinary precision. His new book consists of three

tales, or short novels, one of which at least, " L'Écran,"
might easily be expanded into the form of a complete
work. These three stories deal with three critical
conditions of the mind and temper of a woman. The
first and second end in a moral tragedy : the third ends
well, after excursions and alarms, and may be called a
tragi-comedy of the soul. All three analyse symptoms
of that disease which M. Bourget believes to be so
widely disseminated in the feminine society of the
day, " la trahison de la femme," deception under the
guise of a bland and maiden candour. The heroines of
the three stories are all liars : but while two of them
are minxes, the third is a dupe. Admirers of that
clever novel, *Mensonges*, will find themselves quite in
their element when they read *Complications Sentimentales*.

One of these three stories, " L'Écran," is in its way
a masterpiece. M. Bourget has never written anything
which better exemplifies his peculiar qualities, the
insinuating and persistent force of his style, his pre-
occupation with delicate subtleties and undulations
of feeling, the skill with which he renders the most
fleeting shades of mental sensation. In " L'Écran,"
moreover, he avoids to a remarkable degree that defect
of movement which has seriously damaged several of
his most elaborate books : which, for instance, makes
Une Idylle Tragique scarcely readable. His danger,
like that of Mr. Henry James, whom he resembles on
more sides than one, is to delay ín interminable psychological reflections until our attention has betrayed us,
and we have lost the thread of the story. This error,
or defect, would seem to have presented itself as a peril
to the mind of M. Bourget : for in his latest stories he
is manifestly on his guard against it, and " L'Écran,"

in particular, is a really excellent example of a tale told to excite and amuse even those who are quite indifferent to the lesson it conveys, and to the exquisite art of its delivery.

In the month of June the Lautrecs and the Sarlièves, two aristocratic *ménages* of Paris, come over to England to enjoy the London season, into the whirlpool of which they descend.   But at almost the same moment arrives the Vicomte Bertrand d'Aydie, who is understood to nurse an absolutely hopeless and respectful passion for the sainted Marquise Alyette de Lautrec.   This devotion is much " chaffed " in clubs and smilingly alluded to in drawing-rooms as pure waste of time, since the purity and dignity of Madame de Lautrec are above the possibility of suspicion.   But Madame de Lautrec's dearest friend happens to be the Vicomtesse Emmeline de Sarlième—a gay and amiable butterfly, of whom no one thinks seriously at all.   Bertrand and Emmeline have, however, for some time past, carried on with complete immunity a *liaison*, under the shadow of their friendship for Alyette, *l'écran*, the screen.   Bertrand encourages the idea that he is throwing away a desperate passion on the icy heart of Alyette, when he is really planning with Emmeline rendezvous, which owe their facility to the presence of Alyette.   The reader does not know M. Bourget if he is not by this time conscious that here are united all the elements for one of his most ingenious ethical problems.   The visit of the quintette to London precipitates the inevitable catastrophe. M. Bourget's sketch of our society is wonderfully skilful and entertaining, and Londoners will recognise some familiar faces, scarcely disguised under the travesty of false names.

1899.

Outre-Mer

The author of *Outre-Mer* takes himself, as the phrase goes, rather seriously. He passes in New York and in Paris as a kind of new De Tocqueville. It is no detraction of his gifts, nor of the charm of his amusing volumes, to say that they are not quite so important to an English as to a French or to an American audience. They are important in France, because M. Bourget is a highly accomplished public favourite, whose methods attract attention whatever subject he may deal with, and whose mind has here been given to the study of a kind of life not familiar to Frenchmen. They are important in America, because America is greatly moved by European opinion, and must be flattered at so close an examination of her institutions by an eminent French writer. But in England our contact with the United States is closer and more habitual than that between those States and France, while our vanity is not more stimulated by M. Bourget's study of America than by M. Loti's pictures of Jerusalem. To put it boldly, we know more and care less than the two main classes who will form the audience of *Outre-Mer*.

Taking, then, this calmer standpoint, the feats of M. Bourget's sympathetic appreciation, and the deficiencies in his equipment, leave us, on the whole, rather indifferent. No book of this author has been so much talked of beforehand, or so ardently expected, as *Outre-Mer*, and we do not suppose that its two main bodies of readers will be at all disappointed. But no philosophical Englishman will consider it the best of M. Bourget's books. He will, for example, be infinitely less pleased with it than he was with *Sensations d'Italie*, a much less popular work. The fact is that in reading what the elegant psychologist has to say about America, " on y regrette," as he himself would say, " la douce et lente Europe." The reason of this is, that in dealing with certain superficial features of a vast and crude new civilisation, M. Bourget is a razor cutting a hone. The razor is amazingly sharp and bright, but it is not doing its proper business. M. Bourget is a subtle and minute analyst, whose gift it is to distinguish between delicate orders of thought which are yet closely allied, to determine between new elements and old ones in survival, to provoke, with profundity and penetration, long developments of reverie. He is at home in old societies and waning cities; he is a master in the evocation of new lights on outworn themes. He is full of the nostalgia of the past, and he dreams about the dead while he moves among the living. It is obvious that such a writer is out of place in the study of a country that has no past, no history, no basis of death, a country where a man looks upon his grandfather as a historical character, and upon a house a hundred years old as a historical monument. What M. Bourget has done is extraordinarily clever and brilliant, but he was not the man to be set to do it.

The conditions under which the work progressed were, though specious, not less unfavourable to its perfection. These notes, by a famous Frenchman, on the social life of America to-day, were prepared to appear first of all in an enterprising New York journal. That M. Bourget should accept such a test proclaims his courage, and that he should, in the main, have endured the ordeal, his accuracy and care. It is none the less a shock to find the book dedicated, in a very clever prefatory epistle, to Mr. James Gordon Bennett, and to realise that before its impressions could be given to the world they had to pass through the mill of the *New York Herald*. The result is a book which is beautifully written, and which, above all, gives the impression of being sincerely written —a book which contains many brilliant flashes of intuition, many just and liberal opinions, and some pictures of high merit, but which, somehow, fails to be philosophical, and is apt to slip between the stools of vain conjecture and mere reporter's work. A great deal which will be read with most entertainment in *Outre-Mer*—the description of Chicago, for instance, and the visit to the night-side of New York—is really fitted to appear in a daily newspaper, and then to be forgotten. It is very full and conscientious, but it is the production of a sublimated reporter, and there is precious little De Tocqueville about it.

This, however, may be considered hypercritical. M. Bourget spent eight or nine months in the United States, with no other occupation than the collection of the notes from which these volumes are selected. He had all possible facilities given to him, and he worked in a fair and generous spirit. He was genuinely interested in America, interested more intelligently, no doubt, than any other recent Frenchman has been. It would have been strange if he had not written a book which repaid perusal. The faults of M. Bourget's style have always been over-elaboration and excess of detail. Here he has been tempted to indulge these frailties, and we cannot say that he is not occasionally tedious when he lingers upon facts and conditions obvious to all Englishmen who visit America. Hence, we like his book best where it gives us the results of the application of his subtle intellect to less familiar matters. All he has to say about the vitality of the Catholic Church in the United States is worthy of close attention. His interviews with Cardinal Gibbon and Archbishop Ireland are of material interest, and his notes on the socialistic tendencies of American Catholicism singularly valuable. No pages here are more graphic than those which record a visit to a Roman church in New York, and the sermon which the author listened to there. He was struck, as all visitors to America must be, with the absence of reverie, of the spiritual and experimental spirit, in the teaching and tendency of the Church of Rome in America, and with its practical energy, its businesslike activity and vehemence. In a few words M. Bourget renders with admirable skill that air of antiquity and Catholic piety which make Baltimore more like a city of Southern Europe than any other in the United States. In observation of this kind M. Bourget can always be trusted.

As befits the inquiry of a Latin psychologist, the question of woman takes a very prominent part in the investigation of M. Bourget. On this subject what he has to say and what he has to admit ignorance of are equally interesting. He has to confess himself baffled by that extraordinary outcome of Western civilisation, the American girl, but he revenges himself by the notation of innumerable instances of her peculiarities and idiosyncrasies. On the whole, though she puzzles him, he is greatly delighted with her. We remember hearing of the visit paid to Newport by a young French poet of the Symbolists, who was well acquainted with the American language, but whose manners were all adjusted to the model of the Boulevard St. Michel. He made a dozen serious blunders, all of which were benignly forgiven, before he settled down to some due recognition of the cold, free, stimulating and sphinx-like creature that woman is on the shores of America. M. Bourget

is too much a man of the world, and has been too carefully trained, to err in this way, but his wonder is no less
pronounced. He comes to the curious " résultat que le
désir de la femme est demeuré au second rang dans les
préoccupations de ces hommes." He considers, as
other observers have done, that this condition of things
can be but transitory, and that the strange apotheosis
of the American girl, with all that it presupposes in the
way of reticence of manners, is but a passing phase.
He falls into an eloquent description of the American
idol, the sexless woman of the United States, and closes
it with a passage which is one of the most remarkable in
his volumes :—

" Cette femme peut ne pas être aimée. Elle n'a pas
besoin d'être aimée. Ce n'est ni la volupté ni la ten-
dresse qu'elle symbolise. Elle est comme un objet
d'art vivant, une savante et dernière composition
humaine qui atteste que le Yankee, ce désespéré d'hier,
ce vaincu du vieux monde, a su tirer de ce sauvage
univers où il fut jeté par le sort toute une civilisation
nouvelle, incarnée dans cette femme-là, son luxe et son
orgueil. Tout s'éclaire de cette civilisation au regard
de ces yeux profonds, . . . tout ce qui est l'Idéalisme
de ce pays sans Idéal, ce qui sera sa perte peut-être,
mais qui jusqu'ici demeure sa grandeur : la foi absolue,
unique, systématique et indomptable dans la *Volonté*."

With the West the author does not seem to have any
personal acquaintance. In his chapter on " Cowboys "
he tells some marvellous stories. We know not what
to think of the vivacious anecdote of the men who,
weary to see some eminent emanation of the East,
planned the kidnapping of Madame Sarah Bernhardt
as she passed Green River on her way to the Pacific.
The great actress had taken an earlier express, and was

saved from her embarrassing captors. M. Bourget
occupies nearly fifty pages with a " Confession of a Cow-
boy," the source of which is very vaguely stated. All
this, we must acknowledge, seems rather poor to us,
and must have been collected at worse than second-
hand. Those chapters, on the contrary, which deal
with the South, are particularly fresh and charming.
There is no sort of connection between the close of the
second volume, which deals with an excursion through
Georgia and Florida, and the rest of the book, yet no
one will wish this species of appendix omitted. The
author gives an exceedingly picturesque and humorous
picture of life in a Georgian watering-place, which he
calls Phillipeville, where somebody or other is lynched
every year. M. Bourget, as in duty bound, tells a spirited
story of a " lynchage." He describes, too, in his very
best style, the execution of a rebellious but repentant
mulatto.

When our author proceeded still further South, he
had not the good fortune to see such striking sights, or
to meet with so singular a population. But at Jackson-
ville, Florida, he was able, as nowhere else, to study the
negro at home, and at St. Augustine he discovered to
his delight a sort of Cannes or Monte Carlo of America,
with its gardens of oranges and jasmine, its green oaks and
its oleanders. He rejoiced, after his long inland wander-
ings, to see the ocean breaking on the reefs of Anastasia.
Upon the whole, whether in the North or the South,
M. Bourget has been pleased with the United States.
He has recognised the two great defects of that country :
its incoherence, and its brutality. He has recognised a
factitious element in its cultivation, corruption in its
politics, and a general excess in its activity. He delights
in three typical American words, and discovers " puff,"

" boom," and " bluff " at every turn. He comes back
to Europe at last with that emotion of gratitude which
every European feels, however warmly he has been
welcomed in America, and in however favourable a light
American life has been shown to him. Yet he is conscious of its high virtues, its noble possibilities, and on
the whole his picture of the great Republic, so carefully
and modestly prepared, so conscientiously composed, is
in a high degree a flattering and attractive one.

1895.

L'ÉTAPE

We are so little accustomed in England to the polemical novel, or, indeed, to the novel of ideas in any
form, that it is difficult for us to realise the condition
of mind which has led M. Bourget to fling himself into
the arena of French politics with a romance which must
give extreme offence to the majority of its possible
readers, and which runs violently counter to the traditional complacency of French democratic life. It is
probable that M. Bourget no longer cares very much
whether he offends or pleases, and, doubtless, the more
he scourges the many, the more he endears himself to
the comparatively few. Here, in England, we are
called upon—if only English people would comprehend
the fact—to contemplate and not to criticise the intellectual and moral idiosyncrasies of our neighbours. If
we could but learn the lesson that a curious attention,
an inquisitive observation into foreign modes of thought
becomes us very well, but that we are not asked for
our opinion, it would vastly facilitate our relations. In
calling attention to M. Bourget's extremely interesting
and powerful novel, I expressly deprecate the impertin-
ence of our " taking a side " in the matter of its aim.

We have our own national failings to attend to; let us, for goodness' sake, avoid the folly of hauling our neighbours up to a tribunal of Anglo-Saxon political virtue. It should be enough for us that the phenomena which in France produce a Monneron on the one side and a Ferrand on the other are very interesting. Let us observe them as closely as we can, but not hazard a decision.

The title of M. Bourget's book would offer me a great difficulty if I were called upon to translate it, and I am not sure that a Frenchman will immediately understand what is symbolised by it. An *étape* is a stage, a station; *on brûle l'étape* by rushing through, without, as it were, stopping to change horses. Is, then, the theme of this book the stage, the day's march, as it were, which its over-educated peasant takes in passing over to Conservatism? Does the Monnerons' fault consist in their having " burned " their *étape* in their too great hurry to cut a figure in society? It is not until the final page 516 that we meet with the word and the image, even as we have to reach the last paragraph of Stendhal's masterpiece before we hear of the Chartreuse de Parme. Enough, then, that the subject of this *Étape* is the story of a family of peasants from the Ardèche, one of whom has received an education in excess of his fitness for it; has become, in other words, a functionary and a *bourgeois* without the necessary preparation. It might be rash to suppose that so practised an author as M. Bourget would condescend to be influenced by a much younger writer, or else I should say that throughout this book I am constrained to perceive the spirit of M. Maurice Barrès. The attitude of the writer of *L'Étape* has, at all events, become astonishingly identical with that of the author of *Les Déracinés*, and to have read

that extraordinary work will prepare a reader in many
ways for the study of the novel before us. In both the
one and the other it would, perhaps, be more critical to
say that we see fructifying and spreading the pessimist
influence of Taine.

The uncomfortable and paradoxical condition of
modern society in France is attributed by these writers
of the school of Taine to the obstinate cultivation of
political chimeras which have outlived the excitement
of the Revolution. The keynote to the attitude of
modern democracy is conceived by M. Bourget to be
hostility to the origins and history of the country. The
good hero of the story, M. Ferrand (who is inclined, like
all good heroes, to be a little oracular), reminds the
young socialist of a passage in Plato's *Timæus* where we
are told that a most ancient priest of the temple of Sais
warned Solon that the weakness of the Greeks was their
possessing no ancient doctrine transmitted by their
ancestors, no education passed down from age to age by
venerable teachers. It is this lack of authoritative
continuity which M. Bourget deplores; his view of
1789 is that it snapped the thread that bound society
to the past, that it vulgarised, uprooted, shattered,
and destroyed things which were essential to national
prosperity and to individual happiness. He thinks that
one of these links still exists and can be strengthened
indefinitely—namely, the Catholic religion. Therefore,
according to M. Bourget, the first thing a Frenchman has
to do is to abandon his ideology and his collectivism,
which lead only to anarchical and incoherent forms of
misery, and to humble himself before the Church, by
the aid of which alone a wholesome society can be rebuilt
on the ruins of a hundred years of revolutionary madness.

One is bound, however, to point out that if Taine's

teaching can be interpreted in a reactionary sense, there is nothing in his writings which seems to justify its being distorted for political and clerical purposes. I have endeavoured to summarise as fairly as possible what seem to be M. Bourget's views about " the lack of authoritative continuity." But Taine is careful, in *L'Ancien Régime*, precisely to insist that all the Revolution did was to transfer the exercise of absolute power from the King to a central body of men in Paris. Here was no breach of continuity; it was merely a new form of precisely the same thing. M. Bourget, and those who act with him, seem to overlook completely the kernel of Taine's argument, namely, that the Revolution was not a spontaneous growth, but the outcome of three centuries of antecedent events. The latest reactionaries, I must confess, appear to me to introduce an element of wilful obscurity into a position which Taine left admirably clear and plain.

Considered purely as a story, *L'Étape* is told with all M. Bourget's accustomed solidity and refinement. It has, moreover, a vigorous evolution which captivates the attention, and prevents the elaboration of the author's analysis from ever becoming dull. The action passes in university society, and practically within the families of two classical professors at the Sorbonne. M. Ferrand, the Catholic, who is all serenity and joy, has a gentle, lovely daughter, Brigitte. She is courted by Jean, the eldest son of M. Monneron, who has the misfortune to be a Republican and a Dreyfusard, and everything, in fact, which is sinister and fatal in the eyes of M. Bourget. Brigitte will not marry Jean Monneron unless he consents to become a Catholic, and the intrigue of the novel proceeds, with alarming abruptness, during the days in which Jean is making up his mind to take the leap. Terrible things happen to the agitated members of the Monneron family—things which lead them to forgery and attempted murder—and all on account of their deplorable political opinions, while the happy and virtuous Ferrands sit up aloft, in the purity of their reaction, and, ultimately, as it happens, take care of the life of poor Jean. Told baldly thus, or rather not told at all, but summarised, the plot seems preposterous; and it cannot, I think, be denied that it is in some degree mechanical. Is not this a fault to which those novelists in France who throw in their lot with the disciples of Balzac are peculiarly liable?

Plot, however, in our trivial sense, is the least matter about which M. Bourget troubles himself. He is occupied with two things : the presentation of his thesis —we may almost say his propaganda—and the conduct of his personages when face to face in moments of ex-alted spiritual excitement. In the past, he has some-times shirked the clash of these crises, as if shrinking a little from the mere physical disturbance of them. But he does not do so in *L'Étape*, which will be found "awfully thrilling," even by the Hildas of the circulating libraries. In the study of the " Union Tolstoi," which is a sort of Toynbee Hall, founded in the heart of Paris by Crémieu-Dax (a curious reminiscence, whether conscious or not, of our own Leonard Montefiore), M. Bourget is led away by the blindness of his exclusive fanaticism. A lighter touch, a little of the playfulness of humour, would have rendered more probable and human this humanitarian club of Jews and Protestants and Anarchists and faddists, united in nothing but in their enmity to the ancient government and faith of France. And the ruin of the " Union Tolstoi " is shown to be so inevitable, that we are left to wonder how it could ever have seemed to flourish.

S

The portraits in the book, however, are neither mechanical nor hard. The old Monneron, gentle, learned, and humane, but bound hand and foot by his network of political prejudices; the impudent Antoine; Julie, the type of the girl emancipated on Anglo-American lines, and doomed to violent catastrophe; the enthusiastic and yet patient, fanatical and yet tender millionaire socialist, Solomon Crémieu-Dax; in a lesser degree the unfortunate Abbé Chanut, who believes that the democracy can be reconciled to the Church—all these are admirable specimens of M. Bourget's art of portraiture. The novel is profoundly interesting, although hardly addressed to those who run while they read; but it must not be taken as a text-book of the state of France without a good deal of counteracting Republican literature. Yet it is a document of remarkable value and a charming work of art.

1902.

M. RENÉ BAZIN

M. RENÉ BAZIN

When I was young I had the pleasure of knowing a prominent Plymouth Brother, an intelligent and fanatical old gentleman, into whose house there strayed an attractive volume, which he forbade his grown-up son and daughter to peruse. A day or two later, his children, suddenly entering his library, found him deep in the study of the said dangerous book, and gently upbraided him with doing what he had expressly told them not to do. He replied, with calm good-humour, "Ah! but you see I have a much stronger spiritual digestion than you have!" This question of the "spiritual digestion" is one which must always trouble those who are asked to recommend one or another species of reading to an order of undefined readers. Who shall decide what books are and what books are not proper to be read? There are some people who can pasture unpoisoned upon the memoirs of Casanova, and others who are disturbed by *The Idyls of the King*. They tell me that in Minneapolis *Othello* is considered objectionable; our own great-aunts thought *Jane Eyre* no book for girls. In the vast complicated garden of literature it is always difficult to say where the toxicologist comes in, and what distinguishes him from the purveyor of a salutary moral tonic. In recent French romance, everybody must acknowledge, it is practically impossible to lay down a hard and fast rule.

The object of this chapter, however, is not to decide

how far the daring apologist can go in the recommendation of new French novel-writers, but to offer to the notice of shy English readers a particularly " nice " one. But, before attempting to introduce M. René Bazin, I would reflect a moment on the very curious condition of the French novel in general at the present time. No one who observes the entire field of current French literature without prejudice will deny that the novel is passing through a period which must prove highly perilous to its future, a period at once of transition and of experiment. The school of realism or naturalism, which was founded upon the practice of Balzac in direct opposition to the practices of George Sand and of Dumas *père*, achieved, about twenty years ago, one of those violent victories which are more dangerous to a cause than defeat itself. It was in 1880 that M. Zola published that volume of polemical criticism which had so far-reaching an effect in France and elsewhere, and which was strangely ignored in England—*Le Roman Expérimental*. This was just the point of time at which the Rougon-Macquart series of socio-pathological romances was receiving its maximum of hostile attention. M. Zola's book of criticism was a plausible, audacious, magnificently casuistical plea, not merely for the acceptance of the realistic method, but for the exclusion of every other method from the processes of fiction. It had its tremendous effect; during the space of some five years the " romanciers naturalistes," with M. Zola at their head, had it all their own way. Then came, in 1885, *La Terre*, an object-lesson in the abuse of the naturalistic formula, and people began to open their eyes to its drawbacks. And then we all dissolved in laughter over the protest of the " Cinq Purs," and the defection of a whole group of disciples. M. Zola, like

the weary Titan that he was, went on, but the prestige
of naturalism was undermined.

But, meanwhile, the old forms of procedure in romance
had been dishonoured. It was not enough that the weak
places in the realistic armour should be pierced by the
arrows of a humaner criticism; the older warriors whom
Goliath had overthrown had to be set on their legs again.
And it is not to be denied that some of them were found
to be dreadfully the worse for wear. No one who had
read Flaubert and the Goncourts, no one who had been
introduced to Tolstoi and Dostoieffsky, could any
longer endure the trick of Cherbuliez. It was like going
back to William Black after Stevenson and Mr. Barrie.
Even Ferdinand Fabre, the Thomas Hardy of the
Cévennes, seemed to have lost his savour. The novels
of Octave Feuillet were classics, but no one yearned for
fresh imitations of *Monsieur de Camors*. Pierre Loti
turned more and more exclusively to adventures of the
ego in tropical scenery. Alphonse Daudet, after a melancholy eclipse of his fresh early genius, passed away.
Even before the death of Edmond, the influence of the
Goncourts, although still potent, spread into other fields
of intellectual effort, and became negligible so far as the
novel, pure and simple, was concerned. What was most
noteworthy in the French *belles-lettres* of ten years ago
was the brilliant galaxy of critics that swam into our
ken. In men like MM. Lemaître, Anatole France,
Brunetière and Gaston Paris, the intelligent reader
found purveyors of entertainment which was as charming
as fiction, and much more solid and stimulating. Why
read dull novels when one could be so much better
amused by a new volume of *La Vie Littéraire*?

In pure criticism there is now again a certain depression in French literature. The most brilliant of

the group I have just mentioned has turned from the adventures of books to the analysis of life. But the author of *L'Anneau d'Améthyste* is hardly to be counted among the novelists. His philosophical satires, sparkling with wit and malice, incomparable in their beauty of expression, are doubtless the most exquisite productions proceeding to-day from the pen of a Frenchman, but *L'Orme du Mail* is no more a novel than *Friendship's Garland* is. Among the talents which were directly challenged by the theories of the naturalistic school, the one which seems to have escaped least battered from the fray is that of M. Paul Bourget. He stands apart, like Mr. Henry James—the European writer with whom he is in closest relation. But even over this delicious writer a certain change is passing. He becomes less and less a novelist, and more and more a writer of *nouvelles* or short stories. *La Duchesse Bleue* was not a *roman*, it was a *nouvelle* writ large, and in the volume of consummate studies of applied psychology (*Un Homme d'Affaires*), which reaches me as I write these lines, I find a M. Paul Bourget more than ever removed from the battle-field of common fiction, more than ever isolated in his exquisite attenuation of the enigmas of the human heart. On the broader field, M. Marcel Prévost and M. Paul Hervieu support the Balzac tradition after their strenuous and intelligent fashion. It is these two writers who continue for us the manufacture of the " French novel " pure and simple. Do they console us for Flaubert and Maupassant and Goncourt ? Me, I am afraid, they do as yet but faintly console.

Elsewhere, in the French fiction with which the century is closing, we see little but experiment, and that experiment largely takes the form of *pastiche*.

One thing has certainly been learned by the brief
tyranny of realism, namely, that the mere exterior phenomena of experience, briefly observed, do not exhaust
the significance of life. It is not to be denied that a
worthy intellectual effort, a desire to make thought
take its place again in æsthetic literature, marks the
tentatives, often very unsatisfactory in themselves and
unrelated to one another, which are produced by the
younger novelists in France. These books address, it
must never be forgotten, an audience far more cultivated,
far less hide-bound in its prejudices, than does the
output of the popular English novelist. It is difficult
to conceive of a British Huysmans translating, with
the utmost disregard for plot, the voluptuous languors
of religion; it is even more difficult to conceive of a
British Maurice Barrès engaged, in the form of fiction,
in the glorification of a theory of individualism. It is
proper that we should do honour to the man who writes
and to the public that reads, with zeal and curiosity,
these attempts to deal with spiritual problems in the
form of fiction. But it is surely not unfair to ask whether
the experiment so courageously attempted is perfectly
successful? It is not improper to suggest that neither
La Cathédrale nor *Les Déracinés* is exactly to be styled
an ideal novel.

More completely fulfilling the classic purpose of the
romance, the narrative, are some of the experimental
works in fiction which I have indicated as belonging to
the section of *pastiche*. In this class I will name but
three, the *Aphrodite* of M. Pierre Louÿs, *La Nichina* of
M. Hugues Rebell, and *La Route d'Émeraude* of M.
Eugène Demolder. These, no doubt, have been the most
successful, and the most deservedly successful, of a sort
of novel in these last years in France, books in which

the life of past ages has been resuscitated with a full sense of the danger which lurks in pedantry and in a didactic dryness. With these may be included the extraordinary pre-historic novels of the brothers Rosny. This kind of story suffers from two dangers. Firstly, nothing so soon loses its pleasurable surprise, and becomes a tiresome trick, as *pastiche*. Already, in the case of more than one of the young writers just mentioned, fatigue of fancy has obviously set in. The other peril is a heritage from the Naturalists, and makes the discussion of recent French fiction extremely difficult in England, namely, the determination to gain a sharp, vivid effect by treating, with surgical coolness, the maladies of society. Hence—to skate as lightly as possible over this thin ice—the difficulty of daring to recommend to English readers a single book in recent French fiction. We have spoken of a strong spiritual digestion; but most of the romances of the latest school require the digestion of a Commissioner in Lunacy or of the matron in a Lock hospital.

Therefore—and not to be always pointing to the Quaker-coloured stories of M. Édouard Rod—the joy and surprise of being able to recommend, without the possibility of a blush, the latest of all the novelists of France. It has been necessary, in the briefest language, to sketch the existing situation in French fiction, in order to make appreciable the purity, the freshness, the simplicity of M. René Bazin. It is only within the last season or two that he has come prominently to the front, although he has been writing quietly for about fifteen years. It would be absurd to exaggerate. M. Bazin is not, and will not be here presented as being, a great force in literature. If it were the part of criticism to deal in negatives, it would be easy to mention a great many things which M. Bazin is not. Among others, he is not a profound psychologist; people who like the novels of M. Élémir Bourges, and are able to understand them, will, unquestionably, pronounce *Les Noellet* and *La Sarcelle Bleue* very insipid. But it is possible that the French novelists of these last five years have been trying to be a great deal too clever, that they have starved the large reading public with the extravagant intellectuality of their stories. Whether that be so or not, it is at least pleasant to have one man writing, in excellent French, refined, cheerful, and sentimental novels of the most ultra-modest kind, books that every girl may read, that every guardian of youth may safely leave about in any room of the house. I do not say—I am a thousand miles from thinking—that this is everything; but I protest—even in face of the indignant Bar of Bruges—that this is much.

Little seems to have been told about the very quiet career of M. René Bazin, who is evidently an enemy to self-advertisement. He was born at Angers in 1853, and was educated at the little seminary of Montgazon. Of his purely literary career all that is known appears to be that in 1886 he published a romance, *Ma Tante Giron*, to which I shall presently return, which fell almost unnoticed from the press. It found its way, however, to one highly appropriate reader, M. Ludovic Halévy, to whom its author was entirely unknown. M. Halévy was so much struck with the cleanliness and the freshness of this new writer that he recommended the editor of the *Journal des Débats* to secure him as a contributor. To the amazement of M. Bazin, he was invited, by a total stranger, to join the staff of the *Débats*. He did so, and for that newspaper he has written almost exclusively ever since, and there his suc-

cessive novels and books of travel have first appeared.
It is said that M. Halévy tried, without success, to induce
the French Academy to give one of its prizes to *Ma
Tante Giron*. That attempt failed, but no doubt it was
to the same admirer that was due the crowning of M.
René Bazin's second story, *Une Tache d'Encre*. One
can hardly doubt that the time is not far distant when
M. Bazin will himself be in a position to secure the
prizes of the Academy for still younger aspirants. This
account of M. Bazin is meagre; but although it is all
that I know of his blameless career, I feel sure that it
is, as Froude once said on a parallel occasion, " nothing
to what the angels know."

When we turn to M. Bazin's earliest novel, *Ma Tante
Giron*, it is not difficult to divine what it was that
attracted to this stranger the amiable author of *L'Abbé
Constantin* and *Monsieur et Madame Cardinal*. It is
a sprightly story of provincial life, a dish, as was wickedly
said of one of M. Halévy's own books, consisting of
nothing but angels served up with a white sauce of virtue.
The action is laid in a remote corner of Western France,
the Craonais, half in Vendée, half in Brittany. There
are fine old sporting characters, who bring down hares
at fabulous distances to the reproach of younger shots;
there are excellent curés, the souls of generosity and
unworldliness, with a touch of eccentricity to keep them
human. There is an admirable young man, the Baron
Jacques, who falls desperately in love with the beautiful
and modest Mademoiselle de Seigny, and has just worked
himself up to the point of proposing, when he unfortunately hears that she has become the greatest heiress in
the country-side. Then, of course, his honourable
scruples overweigh his passion, and he takes to a capri-
ous flight. Mademoiselle de Seigny, who loves him,

will marry no one else, and both are horribly unhappy, until Aunt Giron, who is the comic providence of the tale, rides over to the Baron's retreat, and brings him back, a blushing captive, to the feet of the young lady. All comes well, of course, and the curtain falls to the sound of wedding bells, while Aunt Giron, brushing away a tear, exclaims, " La joie des autres, comme cela fait du bien ! "

But *Ma Tante Giron* is really the least bit too ingenuous for the best of good little girls. Hence we are not surprised to find M. Bazin's next novel at the same time less provincial and less artless. It is very rare for a second book to show so remarkable an advance upon a first as *Une Tache d'Encre* does upon its predecessor. This is a story which may be recommended to any reader, of whatever age or sex, who wishes for a gay, good-humoured and well-constructed tale, in which the whole tone and temper shall be blameless, and in which no great strain shall be put upon the intellectual attention. It is excellently carpentered; it is as neatly turned-out a piece of fiction-furniture as any one could wish to see. It has, moreover, beyond its sentimental plot, a definite subject. In *Une Tache d'Encre* the perennial hostility between Paris and the country-town, particularly between Paris and the professional countryman, is used, with excellent effect, to hang an innocent and recurrent humour upon. Fabian Mouillard, an orphan, has been educated by an uncle, who is a family lawyer at Bourges. He has been brought up in the veneration of the office, with the fixed idea that he must eventually carry on the profession, in the same place, among the same clients; he is a sort of Dauphin of the *basoche*, and it has never been suggested to him that he can escape from being his uncle's successor. But

Fabian comes up to Paris, that dangerous city, hatred and fear of which have been most carefully instilled into him. He still continues, however, to be as good as gold, when a blot of ink changes the whole current of his life. He is engaged in composing a thesis on the Junian Latins, a kind of slaves whose status in ancient Rome offers curious difficulties to the student of jurisprudence. To inform himself of history in this matter he attends the National Library, and there, one afternoon, he is so unlucky (or so lucky) as to flip a drop of ink by accident on to a folio which is in process of being consulted by M. Flamaran, of the Academy of Moral and Political Sciences. M. Flamaran is a very peppery old pedant, and he is so angry that Fabian feels obliged to call upon him, at his private house, with a further apology. The fond reader will be prepared to learn that M. Flamaran, who is a widower, lives with a very charming daughter, and that she keeps house for him.

The course of true love then runs tolerably smoothly. The virtuous youth without a profession timidly woos the modest maiden without a mamma, and all would go well were it not for the fierce old solicitor at Bourges. M. Flamaran will give his daughter if Fabian will live in Paris; but the uncle will accept no niece unless the young couple will settle in the country. The eccentric violence of M. Mouillard gives the author occasion for a plentiful exercise of that conventional wit about lawyers which never fails to amuse French people, which animates the farces of the Renaissance, and which finds its *locus classicus* in the one great comedy of Racine. There follows a visit to Italy, very gracefully described; then a visit to Bourges, very pathetical and proper; and, of course, the end of it all is that the uncle capitulates in snuff and tears, and comes up to Paris

to end his days with Fabian and his admirable wife.
A final conversation lifts the veil of the future, and
we learn that the tact and household virtues of the
bride are to make the whole of Fabian's career a
honeymoon.

The same smoothness of execution, the same grace
and adroitness of narrative, which render *Une Tache
d'Encre* as pleasant reading as any one of Mr. W. E.
Norris's best society stories, are discovered in *La Sarcelle
Bleue*, in which, moreover, the element of humour is
not absent. As a typical interpreter of decent French
sentiment, at points where it is markedly in contrast
with English habits of thought, this is an interesting
and even an instructive novel. We are introduced, in
a country-house of Anjou, to an old officer, M. Guillaume Maldonne, and his wife, and their young daughter,
Thérèse. With these excellent people lives Robert de
Kérédol, an old bachelor, also a retired officer, the life-
long friend of Maldonne. The latter is an enthusiastic
ornithologist, and keeper of the museum of natural
history in the adjoining country-town. His ambition
is to possess a complete collection of the birds of the
district, and the arrival of Robert de Kérédol is due to
a letter inviting him to come to Anjou and bring his
gun. He has just been wounded in Africa, and the
invitation is opportune. He arrives, and so prolongs
his visit that he becomes a member of the household :—

" Robert recovered, and was soon in a fit state to go
out with his friend. And then there began for both of
them the most astonishing and the most fascinating of
Odysseys. Each felt something of the old life return
to him; adventure, the emotion of the chase, the need
to be on the alert, shots that hit or missed, distant
excursions, nights beneath the stars. All private

estates, princely domains, closed parks, opened their gates to these hunters of a new type. What mattered it to the proprietor most jealous of his rights if a rare woodpecker or butcher-bird was slaughtered ? Welcomed everywhere, fêted everywhere, they ran from one end of the department to the other, through the copses, the meadows, the vineyards, the marshlands. Robert did not shoot, but he had an extraordinary gift for divining that a bird had passed, for discovering its traces or its nest, for saying casually, ' Guillaume, I feel that there are woodcock in the thickets under that clump of birches; the mist is violet, there is an odour of dead leaves about it.' Or, when the silver Spring, along the edges of the Loire, wakens all the little world of clustered buds, he was wonderful in perceiving, motionless on a point of the shore, a ruff with bristling plumage, or even, posed between two alder catkins, the almost imperceptible blue linnet."

It follows that this novel is the romance of ornithology, and in its pleasantest pages we follow the fugitive " humeur d'oiseau." To the local collection at last but one treasure is lacking. The Blue Teal (perhaps a relative of the Blue Linnet) is known to be claimed among the avifauna of Anjou, but Maldonne and Kérédol can never come within earshot of a specimen. Such is the state of affairs when the book opens. Without perceiving the fact, the exquisite child Thérèse Maldonne has become a woman, and Robert de Kérédol, who thinks that his affection for her is still that of an adopted uncle, wakens to the perception that he desires her for his wife. Docile in her inexperience and in her maidenly reserve, Thérèse accustoms her mind to this idea, but at the deathbed of a village child, her protégé, she meets an ardent and virtuous young gentleman of her own age, Claude Revel, and there is love almost at first sight between them.

In France, however, and especially in the provinces, the advances of Cupid must be made with extreme decorum. Revel is not acquainted with M. Maldonne, and how is he to be introduced ? He is no zoologist, but he hears of the old collector's passion for rare birds, and shooting a squirrel, he presents himself with its corpse at the Museum. He is admitted, indeed, but with some scorn; and is instructed, in a high tone, that a squirrel is not a bird, nor even a rarity. He receives this information with a touching lowliness of heart, and expresses a thirst to know more. The zoologist pronounces him marvellously ignorant, indeed, but ripe for knowledge, and deigns to take an interest in him. By degrees, as a rising young ornithologist, he is introduced into the family circle, where Kérédol instantly conceives a blind and rude jealousy of him. Thérèse, on the contrary, is charmed, but he gets no closer to her parents. It is explained to him at last by Thérèse that his only chance is to present himself as a suitor, with a specimen of the Blue Teal in his hands. Then we follow him on cold mornings, before daybreak, in a punt on the reedy reaches of the Loire; and the gods are good to him, he pots a teal of the most cerulean blueness. Even as he brings it in, Kérédol, an incautious Iago, snatches it from him, and spoils it. But now the scales fall from everybody's eyes; Kérédol writes a long letter of farewell, and disappears, while Thérèse, after some coy raptures, is ceremoniously betrothed to the enchanted Claude Revel. It is not suggested that he goes out any longer, searching for blue teal, of a cold and misty morning. *La Sarcelle Bleue* is a very charming story, only spoiled a little, as it seems to me, by the unsports-

T

manlike violence of Robert de Kérédol's jealousy, which is hardly in keeping with his reputation as a soldier and a gentleman.

As he has advanced in experience, M. René Bazin has shown an increasing ambition to deal with larger problems than are involved in such innocent love intrigues as those which we have just briefly analysed. But in doing so he has, with remarkable persistency, refrained from any realisation of what are called the seamy sides of life. In *De Toute son Âme* he attempted to deal with the aspects of class-feeling in a large provincial town, and in doing so was as cautious as Mrs. Gaskell or as Anthony Trollope. This story, indeed, has a very curious resemblance in its plan to a class of novel familiar to English readers of half a century ago, and hardly known outside England. One has a difficulty in persuading oneself that it has not been written in direct rivalry with such books as *Mary Barton* and *John Halifax, Gentleman.* It is a deliberate effort to present the struggle of industrial life, and the contrasts of capital and labour, in a light purely pathetic and sentimental. To readers who remember how this class of theme is usually treated in France—with so much more force and colour, perhaps, but with a complete disregard of the illusions of the heart—the mere effort is interesting. In the case of *De Toute son Âme* the motive is superior to the execution. M. Bazin, greatly daring, does not wholly succeed. The Latin temper is too strong for him, the absence of tradition betrays him; in this novel, ably constructed as it is, there is a certain insipid tone of sentimentality such as is common enough in English novels of the same class, but such as the best masters amongst us have avoided.

True to his strenuous provinciality, M. Bazin does

not take Paris as his scene, but Nantes. That city and
the lucid stretches of the vast Loire, now approaching
the sea, offer subjects for a series of accurate and picturesque drop-scenes. The plot of the book itself centres
in a great factory, in the *ateliers* and the *usines* of the rich
firm of Lemarié, one of the most wealthy and prosperous
industrials of Nantes. Here one of the artisans is
Uncle Eloï, a simple and honest labourer of the better
class, who has made himself the guardian of his orphan
nephew and niece, Antoine and Henriette Madiot.
These two young people are two types—the former of
the idle, sly, and vicious ne'er-do-well, the latter of all
that is most industrious, high-minded and decently
ambitious. But Henriette is really the illegitimate
daughter of the proprietor of the works, M. Lemarié,
and his son Victor is attracted, he knows not why, by
a fraternal instinct, to the admirable Henriette. She
is loved by a countryman, the tall and handsome
Étienne, reserved and silent. The works in Nantes
are burned down, by the spite of Antoine, who has
turned anarchist. Lemarié, the selfish capitalist, is
killed by a stroke of apoplexy on hearing the news. His
widow, a woman of deep religion, gives the rest of her
life to good works, and is aided in her distributions by
Henriette, who finds so much to do for others, in the
accumulation of her labours for their welfare, that her
own happiness can find no place, and the silent Étienne
goes back to his country home in his barge. *De Toute
son Âme* is a well-constructed book, full of noble thoughts;
and the sale of some twenty large editions proves that it
has appealed with success to a wide public in France.
But we are accustomed in England, the home of sensibility, to guard, with humour and with a fear of the
absurd, against being swept away on the full tide of senti-

ment, and perhaps this sort of subject is better treated by a Teutonic than by a Latin mind. At all events, *De Toute son Âme*, the most English of M. Bazin's novels, is likely to be the one least appreciated in England.

A very characteristic specimen of M. Bazin's deliberate rejection of all the conventional spices with which the French love to heighten the flavour of their fiction, is found in the novel called *Madame Corentine*, a sort of hymn to the glory of devoted and unruffled matrimony. This tale opens in the island of Jersey, where Madame Corentine L'Héréec is discovered keeping a bric-à-brac shop in St. Heliers, in company with her thirteen-year-old daughter, Simone. Madame L'Héréec is living separated from her husband, but M. Bazin would not be true to his *parti pris* if he even suggested that there had been any impropriety of moral conduct on either side. On the contrary, husband and wife are excellent alike, only, unhappily, there has been a fatal incompatibility of temper, exacerbated by the husband's vixen mother. Corentine was a charming girl of Perros in Brittany; M. L'Héréec, a citizen of the neighbouring town of Lannion. Now he remains in Lannion, and she has taken refuge in Jersey; no communication passes between them. But the child Simone longs to see her father, and she sends him a written word by a Breton sailor. Old Capt. Guen, Corentine's widowed father, writes to beg her to come to Perros, where her younger sister, Marie Anne, has married the skipper of a fishing-vessel. Pressed by Simone, the mother consents to go, although dreading the approach to her husband. She arrives to find her sister's husband, Sullian, drowned at sea, and the father mourns over two daughters, one of whom is a widow and the other separated from her man. But Sullian comes back to life, and through the instru-

mentality of little Simone, the L'Héréecs are brought
together, even the wicked old mother-in-law getting her
fangs successively drawn. The curtain falls on a scene
of perfect happiness, a general " Bless ye, my children "
of melodrama.

There is a great deal of charming description in this
book, both the Jersey and the Lannion and Perros
scenes being painted in delightful colours. A great part
of the novel is occupied with the pathos of the harvest
of the sea, the agony of Breton women who lose their
husbands, brothers and sons in the fisheries. Here
M. Bazin comes into direct competition with a greater
magician, with Pierre Loti in his exquisite and famous
Pêcheur d'Islande. This is a comparison which is inevitably made, and it is one which the younger novelist,
with all his merits, is not strong enough to sustain. On
the other hand, the central subject of the novel, the
development of character in the frivolous and artless
but essentially good-hearted Corentine, is very good,
and Simone is one of the best of M. Bazin's favourite
" girlish shapes that slip the bud in lines of unspoiled
symmetry." It is not possible for me to dwell here on
Les Noellet, a long novel about provincial society in the
Angevin district of the Vendée, nor on *Humble Amour,*
a series of six short stories, all (except *Les Trois Peines
d'un Rossignol,* a fantastic dream of Naples) dealing with
Breton life, because I must push on to a consideration
of a much more important work.

The most successful, and I think the best, of M. René
Bazin's books, is the latest. When *La Terre qui Meurt*
was published in 1899, there were not a few critics who
said that here at last was a really great novel. There
is no doubt, at all events, that the novelist has found
a subject worthy of the highest talent. That subject

briefly is the draining of the village by the city. He
takes, in *La Terre qui Meurt*, the agricultural class, and
shows how the towns, with their offices, cafés, railway
stations and shops, are tempting it away from the
farms, and how, under the pressure of imported produce,
the land itself, the ancient, free prerogative of France,
the inalienable and faithful soil, is dying of a slow disease.
To illustrate this heroic and melancholy theme, M. Bazin
takes the history of a farm in that flat district occupying
the north-west of the department of the Vendée, between
the sandy shore of the Atlantic and the low hills of the
Bocage, which is called Le Marais. This is a curious
fragment of France, traversed by canals, a little Holland
in its endless horizons, broken up by marshes and pools,
burned hard in summer, floated over by icy fogs in
winter, a country which, from time immemorial, has
been proud of its great farms, and where the traditions
of the soil have been more conservative than anywhere
else. Of this tract of land, the famous Marais Vendéen,
with its occasional hill-town looking out from a chalky
island over a wild sea of corn and vines and dwarf
orchards to the veritable ocean far away in the west,
M. Bazin gives an enchanting picture. It may be
amusing to note that his landscape is as exact as a
guide-book, and that Sallertaine, Challans, St. Gilles,
and the rest are all real places. If the reader should
ever take the sea-baths at Sables d'Olonne, he may
drive northward and visit for himself " la terre qui
meurt " in all its melancholy beauty.

The scene of the novel is an ancient farm, called La
Fromentière (even this, by the way, is almost a real
name, since it is the channel of Fromentine which
divides all this rich marsh-land from the populous island
of Noirmoutiers). This farmstead and the fields around

it have belonged from time immemorial to the family
of Lumineau. Close by there is a château, which has
always been in the possession of one noble family, that
of the Marquis de la Fromentière. The aristocrats at
the castle have preserved a sort of feudal relation to
the farmers, as they to the labourers, the democratisation
of society in France having but faintly extended to these
outlying provinces. But hard times have come. All
these people live on the land, and the land can no longer
support them. The land cannot adapt itself to new
methods, new traditions; it is the most unaltering thing
in the world, and when pressure comes from without
and from within, demanding new ideas, exciting new
ambitions, the land can neither resist nor change, it
can only die.

Consequently, when *La Terre qui Meurt* opens, the
Marquis and his family have long ceased to inhabit their
château. They have passed away to Paris, out of sight
of the peasants who respected and loved them, leaving
the park untended and the house empty. Toussaint
Lumineau, the farmer, who owns La Fromentière, is a
splendid specimen of the old, heroic type of French
farmer, a man patriarchal in appearance, having in his
blood, scarcely altered by the passage of time, the prejudices, the faiths, and the persistencies of his ancient
race. No one of his progenitors has ever dreamed of
leaving the land. The sons have cultivated it by the
side of the fathers; the daughters have married into
the families of neighbouring farms, and have borne sons
and daughters for the eternal service of the soil. The
land was strong enough and rich enough; it could
support them all. But now the virtue has passed out
of the land. It is being killed by trains from Russia
and by ships from America; the phylloxera has smitten

its vineyards, the shifting of markets has disturbed the easy distribution of its products. And the land never adapts itself to circumstances, never takes a new lease of life, never " turns over a new life." If you trifle with its ancient, immutable conditions, there is but one thing that the land can do—it can die.

The whole of *La Terre qui Meurt* shows how, without violence or agony, this sad condition proceeds at La Fromentière. Within the memory of Toussaint Lumineau the farm has been prosperous and wealthy. With a wife of the old, capable class, with three strong sons and two wholesome daughters, all went well in the household. But, gradually, one by one, the props are removed, and the roof of his house rests more and more heavily on the old man's own obstinate persistence. What will happen when that, too, is removed ? For the eldest son, a Hercules, has been lamed for life by a waggon which passed over his legs; the second son and the elder daughter, bored to extinction by the farm life, steal away, the one to a wretched post at a railway station, the other to be servant in a small restaurant, both infinitely preferring the mean life in a country town to the splendid solitude of the ancestral homestead. Toussaint is left with his third son, André, a first-rate farmer, and with his younger daughter, Rousille. In each of these the genuine love of the soil survives.

But André has been a soldier in Africa, and has tasted of the sweetness of the world. He pines for society and a richer earth, more sunlight and a wider chance; and, at length, with a breaking heart, not daring to confide in his proud old father, he, too, steals away, not to abandon the tillage of the earth, but to practise it on a far broader scale in the fertile plains of the Argentine.

The eldest son, the cripple, dies, and the old Toussaint
is left, abandoned by all save his younger daughter, in
whom the heroic virtue of the soil revives, and who
becomes mistress of the farm and the hope of the future.
And happiness comes to her, for Jean Nesmy, the
labourer from the Bocage, whom her father has despised,
but whom she has always loved, contrives to marry
Rousille at the end of the story. But the Marquis is by
this time completely ruined, and the estates are presently
to be sold. The farms, which have been in his family
for centuries, will pass into other hands. What will be
the result of this upon the life at La Fromentière ? That
remains to be seen; that will be experienced, with all
else that an economic revolution brings in its wake, by
the children of Rousille.

A field in which M. René Bazin has been fertile almost
from the first has been the publication in the *Débats*
and afterwards in book-form, of short, picturesque studies
of foreign landscape, manners and accomplishment.
He began with *À l'Aventure*, a volume of sketches of
modern Italian life, which he expanded a few years later
in *Les Italiens d'Aujourd'hui*. Perhaps the best of all
these volumes is that called *Sicile*, a record of a tour
along the shores of the Mediterranean, to Malta, through
the length and breadth of Sicily, northward along
Calabria and so to Naples. In no book of M. Bazin's
are his lucid, cheerful philosophy and his power of eager
observation more eminently illustrated than in *Sicile*.
A tour which he made in Spain during the months of
September and October, 1894, was recorded in a volume
entitled *Terre d'Espagne*. Of late he has expended the
same qualities of sight and style on the country parts
of France, the western portion of which he knows with
the closest intimacy. He has collected these impres-

sions—sketches, short tales, imaginary conversations--
in two volumes, *En Province*, 1896, and *Croquis de France*,
1899. In 1898 he accompanied, or rather pursued, the
Emperor of Germany on his famous journey to Jerusalem,
and we have the result in *Croquis d'Orient*. In short,
M. Bazin, who has undertaken all these excursions in the
interests of the great newspaper with which he is identified, is at the present moment one of the most active
literary travellers in France, and his records have
exactly the same discreet, safe and conciliatory qualities
which mark his novels. Wherever M. Bazin is, and
whatever he writes, he is always eminently *sage*.

We return to the point from which we started. Whatever honours the future may have in store for the author
of *La Terre qui Meurt*, it is not to be believed that he
will ever develop into an author dangerous to morals.
His stories and sketches might have been read, had
chronology permitted, by Mrs. Barbauld to Miss Hannah
More. Mrs. Chapone, so difficult to satisfy, would have
rejoiced to see them in the hands of those cloistered
virgins, her long-suffering daughters. And there is
not, to my knowledge, one other contemporary French
author of the imagination who could endure that
stringent test. M. Bazin's novels appeal to persons
of a distinctly valetudinarian moral digestion. With
all this, they are not dull, or tiresome, or priggish. They
preach no sermon, except a broad and wholesome amia-
bility; they are possessed by no provoking propaganda
of virtue. Simply, M. Bazin sees the beauty of domestic
life in France, is fascinated by the charm of the national
gaiety and courtesy, and does not attempt to look below
the surface.

We may find something to praise, as well as perhaps
something to smile at, in this chaste and surprising

optimism. In a very old-fashioned book, that nobody
reads now, Alfred de Musset's *Confession d'un Enfant
du Siècle*, there is a phrase which curiously prefigures
the ordinary French novelist of to-day "Voyez,"
says the hero of that work, "voyez comme ils parlent
de tout : toujours les termes les plus crus, les plus
grossiers, les plus abjects; ceux-là seulement leur
paraissent *vrais;* tout le reste n'est que parade, convention et préjugés. Qu'ils racontent une anecdote,
qu'ils rendent compte de ce qu'ils ont éprouvé,—toujours le mot sale et physique, toujours la lettre, toujours la mort." What an exact prediction; and it is
to the honour of M. Bazin that all the faults of judgment
and proportion which are here so vigorously stigmatised
are avoided by his pure and comfortable talent.

1901.

M. MAURICE BARRÈS

M. MAURICE BARRÈS

Les Amitiés Françaises

It was in 1883 that M. Maurice Barrès first attracted attention with that curious little volume, *Taches d'Encre*. Since then he has taken as many forms as Proteus; he has been a lion, and then a snake, and then a raging fire. He has gone down into the arena of politics, and has fought with beasts at Ephesus. He made little impression upon the beasts, and they made none on him, so he came up again. It was once possible to smile at M. Barrès, with his *Culte du Moi* and his odd dithyrambics. It is not only the bewildered Philistine who does not always know what this truculent and yet insinuating prophet is precisely saying. But, at the worst, he is saying something. M. Maurice Barrès is a Voice, and one which it is impossible to set aside. It moans like the wind, and thunders like the sea, and warbles like a thrush, but in the intensest of its contradictions, of its wilful inconsistencies, it is always essentially the same. It would be a mistake to judge M. Barrès as an artist; he is an oratorical philosopher, and one whose influence on young men in France has been very great and is growing. There have been sides of his talent that sprang directly from Taine; later on he developed a curious likeness to Matthew Arnold. But, unless one makes a monstrous mistake, M. Barrès is an unusually clear instance of a genius in process of growth, and one that will soon remind the dullest of us of nobody but himself.

Portions of *Les Amitiés Françaises* are slightly obscure, but the darkest of them is the title-page. " French Friendships " is an odd ticket for a book in which what we commonly call " friendship " is not once mentioned. M. Barrès—who blazoned that which most of us would have timidly called " Notes of a Holiday Tour in Spain " as *Du Sang, de la Volupté et de la Mort*—has the courage of Ruskin in his titles. The sub-title of the work before us is " Notes on how a little Lorrain may acquire those feelings which give value to life." We begin to see that we have to do with a link in the author's chain of books on the development of natural energy, and in reality we must go back to a very early work of his, which his admirers still remember, *Un Homme Libre*, to find an analogy to *Les Amitiés Françaises*. We are here not dealing with the friendship of Frenchman with Frenchman, horizontally, but with what may, perpendicularly, tend to unite in sympathy successive generations of the sons of France. The volume is a treatise on education. The author's own little son, Philippe, is six years old, and it is time that he should be trained in the noble, ardent, and chivalrous tradition of his country. Children are little Davids who dance and sing before the Ark before they know why the Ark is venerable. M. Barrès seeks to grasp this tendency, to mould it into a positive enchantment, and to make it the central impulse of a whole scheme of primary education.

Like De Quincey, whom he sometimes resembles as a writer to an extraordinary degree, M. Maurice Barrès suffers from a certain ignorance of the source of his own charm. His weakness is to parade strong thoughts, to be for ever straining after energy. His strength lies in his delicious music, in the originality and tenderness of his ideas, in the ardour and beauty of his sensibility. In

some of his books the two elements clash in a sort of
moral chaos—exciting enough to the reader, but vain
and unsatisfactory; as, for example, in the puerile and
charming book called *Le Jardin de Bérénice* (1891).   He
always, however, writes to express a set of ideas, and
these it is generally easy to follow, whether he chooses
to accompany them on the cymbals or on the soft re-
corder.   In *Les Amitiés Françaises* the latter prevails;
but there are very harsh notes of the former.   M. Barrès
forgets nothing and forgives nothing.   As he walks with
Philippe over the battle-fields of Lorraine the black blood
stirs his pulses.   It is not for us foreigners to judge a
sentiment so natural, yet we may be forgiven for finding
it painful.   M. Barrès's glowing expressions of patriotism
would seem more comfortable, to say the least, if they
were not presented to us as the expression of so bitter a
sentiment of necessity.

M. Maurice Barrès never forgets that he is a Lorrain,
born in the heart of the province which was torn in half
in 1870.   From his earliest years the little Philippe
must walk in the tradition of what the soil of Lorraine
means to French boys and men.   He is taken up to the
heights of Vaudémont and made to listen to the silence
which envelops his ancestors.   He is taken to Domrémy
and told about the maiden who fought for France nearly
five hundred years ago.   He is taken to Niederbronn,
where a mass is being said for those who fell in the
battle of Fröschweiler.   In this way he is trained to
adopt a solemn and enthusiastic reverence for hereditary
emotions, his ductile intelligence being ceaselessly
occupied in contemplating the past history of his
country *in hymnis et canticis*.   So that we begin to see
that by " amitiés " the author means traditional affini-
ties, not with living persons mainly, but with the soil,

U

with the dust in heroic tombs, with supernatural legend, with the absorbing glory of past time. A touch of autobiography, which escapes the author, sums up, as well as a long treatise could, his personal position :—

" Cela m'advint . . . à regarder notre Lorraine où j'eus mon enfance, où reposent mes tombeaux, où je voudrais par delà ma mort ennoblir des âmes un peu serves. Ailleurs, je suis un étranger qui dit avec incertitude quelque strophe fragmentaire, mais, au pays de la Moselle, je me connais comme un geste du terroir, comme un instant de son éternité, comme l'un des secrets que notre race, à chaque saison, laisse émerger en fleur, et si j'éprouve assez d'amour, c'est moi qui deviendrai son cœur. Viens donc, Philippe, sur la vie, comme nous avons fait tous. Les plus sûres amitiés guident tes pas et sur tes yeux mettent d'abord leurs douces mains."

We must all wish that Philippe may grow up to be everything that his ingenious father desires him to be. Some of us, alas ! cannot hope to be present at the blossoming of this educational aloe. But M. Barrès must not be disappointed if the result is not so completely and directly successful as he hopes. Gifts such as he delights in have a provoking way of skipping a generation, and, besides, as Alphonse Karr wittily put it, " Dieu paie—mais il ne paie pas tous les samedis." Philippe's grandson may become a famous general, or his niece the mother of a great philosopher. In any case, M. Maurice Barrès will have done a gallant and a picturesque thing in insisting upon the autochthonal virtues of the soil of France. He sows his beautiful, winged words, and somewhere or other they will find their harvest. So it must appear, as I suppose, to Frenchmen. How a book like the *Amitiés Françaises*

may appear to us Englishmen is, I am afraid, a matter
of indifference to M. Maurice Barrès. It should not be
a matter of indifference to us that it contains pages of
transcendental melody for the like of which we have to
go back to that other nationalistic utterance, the *Suspiria
de Profundis* of Thomas de Quincey.

1903.

LE VOYAGE DE SPARTE

The position of M. Maurice Barrès continues to be
unique. Although he has not long passed his fortieth
year, it is quite certain that his influence is the most
potent now moving in the intellectual world of France.
In Paris, where the rivalries of the spirit are so keen,
and where ridicule and censure blow so incessantly upon
every bud which pushes higher than the thick hedge
of mediocrity, M. Barrès has contrived to expand and
flourish, in spite of vehement blasts of criticism. There
is something in him which appeals, with an extraordinary directness, to the instinct of those who are
hungry for sympathy and help. Men who are ambitious
and still young, and not quite happy, simply cannot
resist the appeal of M. Barrès. Even those who are no
longer young, who have the misfortune to be a generation older than M. Barrès, are subjected to the impelling
charm of his melancholy, poignant fluting. It is fifteen
years since he published *Un Homme Libre*, a volume
which struck one as grotesque in form, violent in expression and paradoxical in aim. Yet there was something
in this thorny book by an unknown youth, some quality
of the heart, some abrupt manifestation of intellectual
rectitude, which overbalanced, already and a hundred-
fold, anything repellent in so new a method of writing.

As M. Barrès began, so has he proceeded. For many

of us, the real revelation of his genius came with *Le Jardin de Bérénice*, that entrancing reverie, so childish and so profound, with its babblings of the taciturn lady of Aigues Mortes, and her symbolic donkey, and the ducks that betrayed their lowly birth in their lack of the elements of courtesy. Humour, philosophy, tenderness, irony, all were mingled to form the obscure and glittering web of that most curious book; but no one who read it, if he had any perception of the heavenly signs, could doubt that its author was a new star in the firmament.

The written work of M. Barrès is abundant and comprehensive. He has written delicious ironic pamphlets; he has published six ideological novels and he has given us seven collections of essays, partly entertaining, partly didactic, of which *Le Voyage de Sparte* is the latest. His literary activity has been great, and yet he has not confided too exclusively in literature. Perhaps no French author of his generation has come out of literature into life with so much impetuous curiosity as M. Maurice Barrès. He was brought up among the Parnassians, was taken by them into their ivory city, and heard the gates shut behind him, with the world outside. He was received, as an ardent youth, into the passionless and arrogant intimacy of Leconte de Lisle and of Heredia. But he could not breathe within those walls, and he soon broke out, occupying himself with the very thing that the poets and scholars of his youth despised, moral ideas and the relation of human thought to human conduct.

The public formed its earliest impression of M. Barrès as of a young man peacocking in an extreme and laughable vanity. His early writings were unblushingly concerned with himself and he disdained to consider whether this particular subject was at present interesting to his readers. Such titles as *L'Ennemi des Lois, Sous l'Œil des Barbares* and *Le Culte du Moi* were caps thrown with great precision at the moon. Nothing is more unaccountable than the charm or the disgust produced by egotism. Individualities are like odours, and some repel as fantastically as others attract. M. Barrès's is to his readers as that of nemophila is to cats; it simply cannot be resisted. But he is not one of those egotists who seek for nothing but a personal triumph. On the contrary, there has been no more curious example than his of an author who has captured his audience only that he may hold it under his finger and thumb. M. Maurice Barrès has danced through the villages wearing his motley and shaking his bells, but merely that he might collect a stream of followers and take them with him to church. He is still the merriest of preachers; he totters with laughter, sometimes, as he mounts the steps of his pulpit, but he makes no secret any longer of its being a pulpit, and his hearers now quite understand that they have come to him for the salvation of their souls.

For M. Barrès—as we may see now, looking back— with his exquisite refinement, his delicately-toned gradations of moral feeling, has never been, could never be, a vulgar egotist. He has gradually come to be the most charming, but the most serious teacher of his day. He has observed that the achievement of civic liberty in the nineteenth century was not accomplished without great sacrifices. He sees life in France impoverished by the removal of discipline. He has become aware that the tumultuous haste of the present has cast away all manner of precious things that were bequeathed to it by the past. He insists on the importance of tying up again the loose ends of that cord which used to bind us to history, since by forcing ourselves from it we have cruelly cut ourselves off from a stream of hereditary energy. M. Barrès, in an age which prides itself upon the independence of the living, has recalled the youth of France to the worship of the dead. In all these aspects, the work he has done, and is doing, is immense; with no exaggeration, a master of an earlier generation, M. Paul Bourget, has called him " le plus efficace serviteur, peut-être, à l'heure présente, de la France éternelle." And if the lesson of M. Maurice Barrès is pre-eminently addressed to France, there are numberless aspects in which it may be a message, in these times of crisis, to England also.

Those who are familiar with the processes of M. Barrès's mind will know what to expect in *Le Voyage de Sparte*, and they will not be disappointed. As a traveller, M. Maurice Barrès is a little less circum-stantial than Stevenson, perhaps a little more than Sterne. The chapter entitled " Je quitte Mycènes " irresistibly reminds one of a page in *Tristram Shandy*. " ' Where,' continued my father, ' is Mytilene ? What is become, brother Toby, of Cyzicum and Mytilene ? ' " What, indeed ! And the reflection of the French tourist mainly resolves itself into this Shandean formula : " It was great fun for Schliemann, no doubt, to discover the seventeen splendid corpses, but what do *I* get ? It is the truffle-dog that carries off the truffle." The Argive tombs were empty, and all that M. Barrès carried away from Tiryns was rather less emotion than the bones of an ichthyosaurus would have given him. The aim of *Le Voyage de Sparte* is to distinguish between true and false enthusiasm, to define exactly what the emotion is which the ruins of Greek civilisation inspire. Clear your minds of cant, this preacher says, and enter the great, rough Albanian village which is Athens, with an honest imagination. M. Barrès piously sees the usual sights; he visits the shrines with humility, but he is intent on a faithful analysis of his sensations. His object in travelling is not æsthetic. He has not come for the landscape; he has not come, as Leconte de Lisle would come, to reinstitute a supposititious perfection of plasticity; nor come, as Renan would come, to maintain the divinity of Pallas Athene. He has come, as a Frenchman of Lorraine, solicitous for the soul of his race, to see what *bénéfice moral* he can extract from this remote, dim world of ancient beauty. He has come, not to wash away the prose of his old life in a vague poetic flow, but to see how he can enrich it. He has come to find out what Eleusis and Corinth and Sparta have to give him, by means of which he can live a fuller life on the wooded plains of Lorraine; not be a sort of false Greek, but a wiser and more wholesome rural Frenchman. "Bénéfice moral!" How far those words, in the mouth of the most influential French writer of the day, take us from the " L'Art pour l'art " cry of five-and-twenty years ago!

1906.

M. HENRI DE REGNIER

M. HENRI DE RÉGNIER

LES JEUX RUSTIQUES ET DIVINS

THE determination of the younger French writers to enlarge and develop the resources of their national poetry is a feature of to-day, far too persistent and general to be ignored. Until a dozen years ago, the severely artificial prosody accepted in France seemed to be one of the literary phenomena of Europe the most securely protected from possible change. The earliest proposals and experiments in fresh directions were laughed at, and often not undeservedly. No one outside the fray can seriously admit that any one of the early *francs-tireurs* of symbolism made a perfectly successful fight. But the number of these volunteers, and their eagerness, and their intense determination to try all possible doors of egress from their too severe palace of traditional verse, do at last impress the observer with a sense of the importance of the instinct which drives them to these eccentric manifestations. Renan said of the early Decadents that they were a set of babies, sucking their thumbs. But these people are getting bald, and have grey beards, and still they suck their thumbs. There must be something more in the whole thing than met the eye of the philosopher. When the entire poetic youth of a country such as France is observed raking the dust-heaps, it is probable that pearls are to be discovered.

It cannot but be admitted that M. Henri de Régnier

has discovered a large one, if it seems to be a little clouded, and perhaps a little flawed. Indeed, of the multitude of experiment-makers and theorists, he comes nearest (it seems to me) to presenting a definitely evolved talent, lifted out of the merely tentative order. He stands, at this juncture, half-way between the Parnassians and those of the symbolists who are least violent in their excesses. If we approach M. de Régnier from the old-fashioned camp, his work may seem bewildering enough, but if we reach it from the other side— say, from M. René Ghil or from M. Yvanhoé Rambosson —it appears to be quite organic and intelligible. Here at least is a writer with something audible to communicate, with a coherent manner of saying it, and with a definite style. A year or two ago, the publication of his *Poèmes Anciens et Romanesques* raised M. de Régnier, to my mind, a head and shoulders above his fellows. That impression is certainly strengthened by *Les Jeux Rustiques et Divins*, a volume full of graceful and beautiful verses. Alone, among the multitude of young experimenters, M. de Régnier seems to possess the classical spirit; he is a genuine artist, of pure and strenuous vision. For years and years, my eloquent and mysterious friend, M. Stéphane Mallarmé, has been talking about verse to the youth of Paris. The main result of all those abstruse discourses has been (so it seems to me) the production of M. Henri de Régnier. He is the solitary swallow that makes the summer for which M. Mallarmé has been so passionately imploring the gods.

M. Henri de Régnier was born at Honfleur in 1864, and about 1885 became dimly perceptible to the enthusiastic by his contributions to those little *revues*, self-sacrificing tributes to the Muses, which have formed such a pathetic and yet such an encouraging feature of recent French literature. He collected these scattered verses in tiny and semi-private pamphlets of poetry, but it was not until 1894 that he began to attract general attention and that opposition which is the compliment time pays to strength. It was in that year that M. de Régnier published *Aréthuse*, in which were discovered such poems as *Péroraison* :—

> " O lac pur, j'ai jeté mes flûtes dans tes eaux,
> Que quelque autre, à son tour, les retrouve, roseaux,
> Sur le bord pastoral où leurs tiges sont nées
> Et vertes dans l'Avril d'une plus belle Année !
> Que toute la forêt referme son automne
> Mystérieux sur le lac pâle où j'abandonne
> Mes flûtes de jadis mortes au fond des eaux.
> Le vent passe avec des feuilles et des oiseaux
> Au-dessus du bois jaune et s'en va vers la Mer ;
> Et je veux que ton âcre écume, ô flot amer,
> Argente mes cheveux et fleurisse ma joue ;
> Et je veux, debout dans l'aurore, sur la proue,
> Saisir le vent qui vibre aux cordes de la lyre,
> Et voir, auprès des Sirènes qui les attirent
> À l'écueil où sans lui nous naufragerions,
> Le Dauphin serviable aux calmes Arions."

But the vogue of his melancholy and metaphysical poetry, with its alabastrine purity, its sumptuous richness, began when the poet finally addressed the world at large in two collections of lyrical verse, entitled *Poèmes Anciens et Romanesques* (1896) and *Les Jeux Rustiques et Divins* (1897), when it was admitted, even by those who are the most jealous guardians of the tradition in France, that M. Henri de Régnier represented a power which must be taken for the future into serious consideration.

It is scarcely necessary to remind ourselves, in reading *Les Jeux Rustiques et Divins*, of the Mallarméan principle that poetry should suggest and not express, that a series of harmonious hints should produce the effect of direct

clear statement. In the opposite class, no better
example can be suggested than the sonnets of M. de
Heredia, which are as transparent as sapphires or topazes,
and as hard. But if M. de Régnier treats the same class
of subject as M. de Heredia (and he often does) the result
is totally different. He produces an opal, something
clouded, soft in tone, and complex, made of conflicting
shades and fugitive lights. In the volume before us we
have a long poem on the subject of Arethusa, the nymph
who haunted that Ortygian well where, when the flutes
of the shepherds were silent, the sirens came to quench
their thirst. We have been so long habituated, in
England by the manner of Keats and Tennyson, in
France by the tradition of the Parnassians, to more or
less definite and exhaustive portraiture, that at first
we read this poetry of M. de Régnier without receiving
any impression. All the rhythms are melodious, all
the diction dignified and pure, all the images appropriate,
but, until it has been carefully re-read, the poem seems
to say nothing. It leaves at first no imprint on the
mind; it merely bewilders and taunts the attention.

It is difficult to find a complete piece short enough for
quotation which shall yet do no injustice to the methods
of M. de Régnier; but *Invocation Mémoriale* may serve
our purpose :—

> " La main en vous touchant se crispe et se contracte
> Aux veines de l'onyx et aux nœuds de l'agate,
> Vases nus que l'amour en cendre a faits des urnes !
> Ô coupes tristes que je soupèse, une à une,
> Sans sourire aux beautés des socles et des anses !
> Ô passé longuement où je goûte en silence
> Des poisons, des mémoires âcres où le philtre
> Qu'avec le souvenir encor l'espoir infiltre
> Goutte à goutte puisé à d'amères fontaines;
> Et, ne voyant que lui et elles dans moi-même,
> Je regarde, là-bas, par les fenêtres hautes,
> L'ombre d'un cyprès noir s'allonger sur les roses."

The studied eccentricity of the rhymes may be passed over; if *fontaines* and *même*, *hautes* and *roses*, satisfy a French ear, it is no business of an English critic to comment on it. But the dimness of the sense of this poem is a feature which we may discuss. At first reading, perhaps, we shall find that the words have left no mark behind them whatever. Read them again and yet again, and a certain harmonious impression of liquid poetic beauty will disengage itself, something more in keeping with the effect on the mind of the *Ode to a Grecian Urn*, or the close of the *Scholar Gypsy*, than of the purely Franco-Hellenic poetry of André Chénier or of Leconte de Lisle. Throughout this volume what is presented is a faint tapestry rather than a picture—dim choirs of brown fauns or cream-white nymphs dancing in faint, mysterious forests, autumnal foliage sighing over intangible stretches of winding, flashing river; Pan listening, the pale Sirens singing, Autumn stumbling on under the burden of the Hours, thyrsus and caduceus flung by unseen deities on the velvet of the shaven lawn —everywhere the shadow of poetry, not its substance, the suggestion of the imaginative act in a state of suspended intelligence. Nor can beauty be denied to the strange product, nor to the poet his proud boast of the sanction of Pegasus :—

> " J'ai vu le cheval rose ouvrir ses ailes d'or
> Et, flairant le laurier que je tenais encor,
> Verdoyant à jamais hier comme aujourd'hui,
> Se cabrer vers le Jour et ruer vers la Nuit."

1897.

La Cité des Eaux

It may be conceded that the publication of a new volume by M. Henri de Régnier is, for the moment, the event most looked forward to in the poetical world of France. The great poets of an elder generation, though three or four of them survive, very rarely present anything novel to their admirers, and of the active and numerous body of younger writers there is no one, certainly among those who are purely French by birth, whose work offers so little to the doubter and the detractor as that of M. de Régnier. He has been before the public for sixteen or seventeen years; his verse is learned, copious, varied, and always distinguished. Like all the younger poets of France, he has posed as a revolutionary, and has adopted a new system of æsthetics, and in particular an emancipated prosody. But he has carried his reforms to no absurd excess; he has kept in touch with the tradition, and he has never demanded more liberty than he required to give ease to the movements of his genius. By the side of the fanatics of the new schools he has often seemed conservative and sometimes almost reactionary. He has always had too much to say and too great a joy in saying it to be forever fidgeting about his apparatus.

M. Henri de Régnier is much nearer in genius to the Parnassians than any other of his immediate contemporaries. If he had been born a quarter of a century earlier, doubtless he would be a Parnassian. In his earliest verses he showed himself a disciple of M. Sully-Prudhomme. But that was a purely imitative strain, it would seem, since in the developed writing of M. de Régnier there is none of the intimate analysis of feeling and the close philosophic observation which characterise the exquisite author of *Les Vaines Tendresses*. On the other hand, in M. de Heredia we have a Parnassian whose objective genius is closely allied, on several sides, to that of the younger poet. The difference is largely one of texture; the effects of M. de Heredia are metallic, those of M. de Régnier supple and silken. A certain hardness of outline, which impairs for some readers the brilliant enamel or bronze of *Les Trophées* is exchanged in *Les Jeux Rustiques et Divins* and *Les Médailles d'Argile* for a softer line, drowned in a more delicate atmosphere. This does not prevent M. de Heredia and M. de Régnier from being the poets in whom the old and the new school take hands, and in whom the historical transition may be most advantageously studied.

La Cité des Eaux emphasises the conservative rather than the revolutionary tendencies of the writer. In two closely related directions, indeed, it shows a reaction against previous movements made by M. de Régnier somewhat to the discomfort of his readers. In the poetry he was writing five or six years ago, he seemed to be completely subdued by two enchanting but extremely dangerous sirens of style—allegory and symbol. Some of the numbers in *Les Jeux Rustiques et Divins* were highly melodious, indeed, and full of colour, but so allusive and remote, so determined always to indicate and never to express, so unintelligible, in short, and so vaporous, that the pleasure of the reader was very seriously interfered with. The fascinating and perilous precepts of Mallarmé were here seen extravagantly at work. If M. de Régnier had persisted in pushing further and further along this nebulous path, we will not venture to say that he would soon have lost himself, but he would most assuredly have begun to lose his admirers. We are heartily glad that in *La Cité des Eaux* he has seen fit to return to a country where the air is more lucid, and where men are no longer seen through the vitreous gloom as trees walking.

M. de Régnier builds his rhyme with deep and glowing

x

colour. In this he is more like Keats than any other
recent poet. Whether in the mysterious eclogues of
antiquity which it used to please him to compose, or
in the simpler and clearer pieces of to-day, he is always
a follower of dreams. If the French poets were distinguished by flowers, as their Greek predecessors were,
the brows of M. Henri de Régnier might be bound with
newly-opened blossoms of the pomegranate, like those
of Menecrates in the garland of Meleager. His classical
pictures used to be extraordinarily gorgeous, like those
in Keat's *Endymion*, purpureal and over-ripe, hanging in
glutinous succession from the sugared stalk of the rhyme.
They are now more strictly chastened, but they have
not lost their dreamy splendour.

The desolation of the most beautiful of Royal gardens
has attracted more and more frequently of late the
curiosity of men of imagination.   It inspired this year
the fantastic and elegant romance of M. Marcel Batilliat,
Versailles-aux-Fantômes. But it has found no more
exquisite rendering than the cycle of sonnets which
gives its name to the volume before us.   M. de Régnier
wanders through the pavilions and across the terraces
of Versailles, and everywhere he studies the effect of its
mossed and melancholy waters.   He becomes hypnotised
at last, and the very enclosures of turf take the form of
pools to his eyes :—

> " Le gazon toujours vert ressemble au bassin glauque.
> C'est le même carré de verdure équivoque,
> Dont le marbre ou le buis encadrent l'herbe ou l'eau :
> Et dans l'eau smaragdine et l'herbe d'émeraude,
> Regarde, tour à tour, errer en ors rivaux
> La jaune feuille morte et la cyprin qui rôde."

The vast and monumental garden stretches itself before
us in these sonnets, with its invariable alleys of cypress

and box, its porcelain dolphins, its roses floating across the wasted marble of its statues, the strange autumnal odour of its boscages and its labyrinths, and, above all, still regnant, the majestic and monotonous façade of its incomparable palace.

For English readers the matchless choruses of *Empedocles* said the final word in poetry about Marsyas, exactly fifty years ago. M. de Régnier, who has probably never read Matthew Arnold, has taken a singularly parallel view of the story in *Le Sang de Marsyas*, where the similarity is increased by the fact that the French poet adopts a form of free verse very closely analogous to that used by Arnold in *The Strayed Reveller* and elsewhere. The spirited odes, called *La Course* and *Pan*, have the same form and something of the same Arnoldian dignity. The section entitled *Inscriptions lues au Soir Tombant*—especially those lines which are dedicated to " Le Centaure Blessé "—might have been signed, in his moments of most Hellenic expansion, by Landor. It is not an accident that we are so frequently reminded, in reading M. de Régnier's poems, of the English masters, since he is a prominent example of that slender strain which runs through French verse from Ronsard to André Chénier, and on through Alfred de Vigny, where the Greek spirit takes forms of expression which are really much more English than Latin in their character. Of the purely lyrical section of this charming volume it is difficult to give an impression without extensive quotation. We must confine ourselves to a single specimen entitled *La Lune Jaune :*—

" Ce long jour a fini par une lune jaune
   Qui monte mollement entre les peupliers,
  Tandis que se répand parmi l'air qu'elle embaume
   L'odeur de l'eau qui dort entre les joncs mouillés.

Savions-nous, quand, tous deux, sous le soleil torride,
   Foulions la terre rouge et le chaume blessant,
Savions-nous, quand nos pieds sur les sables arides
   Laissaient leurs pas empreints comme des pas de sang,

Savions-nous, quand l'amour brûlait sa haute flamme
   En nos cœurs déchirés d'un tourment sans espoir,
Savions-nous, quand mourait le feu dont nous brûlâmes,
   Que sa cendre serait si douce à notre soir,

Et que cet âpre jour qui s'achève et qu'embaume
   Une odeur d'eau qui songe entre les joncs mouillés
Finirait mollement par cette lune jaune
   Qui monte et s'arrondit entre les peupliers ? "

1903.

Les Vacances d'un Jeune Homme Sage

M. Henri de Régnier is one of the most distinguished
living poets of France. But in writing *Les Vacances
d'un Jeune Homme Sage* he has attacked a new province
of literature, and has taken it by storm. M. de Régnier
has written several novels,—*La Double Maîtresse* and *Le
Bon Plaisir* in particular—which have aimed at recon-
structing past eras of society. These books have been
remarkable for their ethical insouciance, their rough and
cynical disregard of prejudice. One has formed the
impression that M. Henri de Régnier's ambition was to
be a poet like Keats grafted upon a novelist like Smollett.
And the novels, with all their vigour, were not quite
what we sympathise with in this country. Curiously
enough, without giving us the least warning, M. de
Régnier has written, in a mood of pure laughter, a refined
little picture of real life in a provincial town of to-day.
He is deliciously sympathetic at last.

A boy (I beg his pardon—a young man) of sixteen,
Georges Dolonne, has the misfortune to be plucked for
his bachelor's degree at the Sorbonne. This is due

partly to his shyness, and partly to his pre-occupations, for he is very far indeed from being stupid. It is rather a serious check, however, but his mother in her clemency carries him away to the country for the holidays, to stay with his great-uncle and aunt at the little town of Rivray-sur-Vince. The story is simply a plain account of how Georges spent this vacation, but in the course of it every delightful eccentricity of the population of Rivray is laid bare. I can imagine no pleasanter figures to spend a few hours with than M. de la Boulerie, a decayed old nobleman with a mania for heraldry; or comfortable obese Madame de la Boulerie, whose rich Avignon accent comes out in moments of excitement; or Mademoiselle Duplan, the drawing-mistress, who wears a huge hat with feathers in the depths of her own home and dashes out every few moments to drive the boys from her espaliers; or M. de la Vigneraie, coarse and subtle, with his loud voice and his pinchbeck nobility and his domestic subterfuges.

Every one will laugh with these inhabitants of Rivray-sur-Vince, but English readers must not be a little philosophical in order to appreciate young Master Georges. It is not a mere display of Podsnappery to find him curiously exotic to our ideas of decorous youth. But we ought to take a pleasure in him as a psychological specimen, although so very unlike those which flourish in our own collections. There is no cricket, of course, at Rivray-sur-Vince, and no base-ball; Georges neither rides, nor shoots, nor even fishes. He smokes quantities of little cigarettes, and he takes walks, not too far nor too fast, and always on the shady side. In fact, the notion of physical exercise does not enter into his head. Notwithstanding this, Georges Dolonne is not a milksop or a muff; he is simply a young French gentleman in an immature condition. Mentally he is much more alert, much more adroit and astute, than an English boy in his seventeenth year would be, and the extremely amusing part of the book—that part, indeed, where it rises to a remarkable originality—is where the contrast is silently drawn between what his relations and friends believe Georges to be and insist upon his being, and the very wide-awake young person that he really is. The prominent place which the appearance and company of women take in the interests of a young Frenchman at an age when the English youth has scarcely awakened to the existence of an ornamental side to sex is exemplified very acutely, but with a charming reserve, in *Les Vacances d'un Jeune Homme Sage*.

1904.

FOUR POETS

FOUR POETS

STÉPHANE MALLARMÉ

In the midst of the violent incidents which occupied
public attention during the month of September 1898
the passing of a curious figure in the literary life of
France was almost unobserved. Stéphane Mallarmé
died on the 9th at his cottage of Bichenic, near Vulaine-
sur-Seine, after a short illness. He was still in the fullness
of life, having been born 18th March, 1842, but he had
long seemed fragile. Five or six years ago, and at a
quieter time, the death of Mallarmé would have been
a newspaper " event," for in the early nineties his
disciples managed to awaken around his name and his
very contemplative person an astonishing amount of
curiosity. This culminated in and was partly assuaged
by the publication in 1893 of his *Vers et Prose*, with a
dreamy portrait, a lithograph of great beauty, by Mr.
Whistler. Then Mallarmé had to take his place among
things seen and known ; his works were no longer arcane ;
people had read *Hérodiade*, and their reason had survived the test. In France, where sensations pass so
quickly, Mallarmé has already long been taken for
granted.

It was part of his resolute oddity to call himself by
the sonorous name of Stéphane, but I have been assured
that his god-parents gave him the humbler one of
Étienne, He was descended from a series, uninterrupted

both on the father's and on the mother's side, of officials
connected with the parochial and communal registers,
and Mallarmé was the quite-unexpected flower of this
sober vegetation.   He was to have been a clerk himself,
but he escaped to England about 1862, and returned to
Paris only to become what he remained, professionally,
for the remainder of his life—a teacher of the English
language.   While he was with us he learned to cultivate
a passion for boating; and in the very quiet, unambitious
life of his later years to steal away to his *yole d'acajou*
and lose himself, in dreaming, on one of the tributaries
of the Seine was his favourite, almost his only, escapade.
In 1875 he was in London, and then my acquaintance
with him began.   I have a vision of him now, the little,
brown, gentle person, trotting about in Bloomsbury with
an elephant folio under his arm, trying to find Mr.
Swinburne by the unassisted light of instinct.

This famous folio contained Edgar Poe's *Raven*,
translated by Mallarmé and illustrated in the most
intimidating style by Manet, who was then still an
acquired taste.   We should to-day admire these illustra-
tions, no doubt, very much; I am afraid that in 1875,
in perfidious Albion, they awakened among the few
who saw them undying mirth.   Mallarmé's main design
in those days was to translate the poems of Poe, urged
to it, I think, by a dictum of Baudelaire's, that such a
translation " peut être un rêve caressant, mais ne peut
être qu'un rêve."   Mallarmé reduced it to reality, and
no one has ever denied that his version of Poe's poems
(1888) is as admirably successful as it must have been
difficult of performance.   In 1875 the *Parnasse Contemporain* had just rejected Mallarmé's first important
poem, *L'Après-Midi d'un Faune*, and his revolt against
the Parnassian theories began.   In 1876 he suddenly

braved opinion by two " couriers of the Décadence,"
one the *Faune*, in quarto, the other a reprint of Beckford's *Vathek*, with a preface, an octavo in vellum.
Fortunate the bibliophil of to-day who possesses these
treasures, which were received in Paris with nothing but
ridicule and are now sought after like rubies.

The longest and the most celebrated of the poems of
M. Mallarmé is *L'Après-Midi d'un Faune*. It appears
in the " florilège " which he published in 1893, and I
have now read it again, as I have often read it before.
To say that I understand it bit by bit, phrase by phrase,
would be excessive. But if I am asked whether this
famous miracle of unintelligibility gives me pleasure, I
answer, cordially, Yes. I even fancy that I obtain from
it as definite and as solid an impression as M. Mallarmé
desires to produce. This is what I read in it : A faun—
a simple, sensuous, passionate being—wakens in the
forest at daybreak and tries to recall his experience of
the previous afternoon. Was he the fortunate recipient
of an actual visit from nymphs, white and golden
goddesses, divinely tender and indulgent ? Or is the
memory he seems to retain nothing but the shadow of
a vision, no more substantial than the " arid rain " of
notes from his own flute ? He cannot tell. Yet surely
there was, surely there is, an animal whiteness among
the brown reeds of the lake that shines out yonder ?
Were they, are they, swans ? No ! But Naiads
plunging ? Perhaps !

Vaguer and vaguer grows the impression of this
delicious experience. He would resign his woodland
godship to retain it. A garden of lilies, golden-headed,
white-stalked, behind the trellis of red roses ? Ah !
the effort is too great for his poor brain. Perhaps if
he selects one lily from the garth of lilies, one benign

and beneficent yielder of her cup to thirsty lips, the memory, the ever-receding memory, may be forced back. So, when he has glutted upon a bunch of grapes, he is wont to toss the empty skins into the air and blow them out in a visionary greediness. But no, the delicious hour grows vaguer; experience or dream, he will now never know which it was. The sun is warm, the grasses yielding; and he curls himself up again, after worshipping the efficacious star of wine, that he may pursue the dubious ecstasy into the more hopeful boskages of sleep.

This, then, is what I read in the so excessively obscure and unintelligible *L'Après-Midi d'un Faune;* and, accompanied as it is with a perfect suavity of language and melody of rhythm, I know not what more a poem of eight pages could be expected to give. It supplies a simple and direct impression of physical beauty, of harmony, of colour; it is exceedingly mellifluous, when once the ear understands that the poet, instead of being the slave of the alexandrine, weaves his variations round it like a musical composer. Unfortunately, *L'Après-Midi* was written fifteen years ago, and his theories have grown upon M. Mallarmé as his have on Mr. George Meredith. In the new collection of *Vers et Prose* I miss some pieces which I used to admire—in particular, surely, *Placet*, and the delightful poem called *Le Guignon.* Perhaps these were too lucid for the worshippers. In return, we have certain allegories which are terribly abstruse, and some subfusc sonnets. I have read the following, called *Le Tombeau d'Edgard Poe*, over and over and over. I am very stupid, but I cannot tell what it *says.* In a certain vague and vitreous way I think I perceive what it *means;* and we are aided now by its being punctuated, which was not the case in the original form in which I

met with it.   But, " O my Brothers, ye the Workers,"
is it not still a little difficult ?

> Tel qu'en Lui-même enfin l'éternité le change,
>   Le Poëte suscite avec un glaive nu
>   Son siècle épouvanté de n'avoir pas connu
> Que la mort triomphait dans cette voix étrange !
> Eux, comme un vil sursaut d'hydre oyant jadis l'ange
>   Donner un sens plus pur aux mots de la tribu
>   Proclamèrent très haut le sortilège bu
> Dans le flot sans honneur de quelque noir mélange.
> Du sol et de la nue hostiles, ô grief !
> Si notre idée avec ne sculpte un bas-relief
>   Dont la tombe de Poe éblouissante s'orne
> Calme bloc ici-bas chu d'un désastre obscur,
>   Que ce granit du moins montre à jamais sa borne
> Aux noirs vols du Blasphème épars dans le futur.

Of the prose of M. Mallarmé, I can here speak but
briefly. He did not publish very much of it; and it
is all polished and cadenced like his verse, with strange
transposed adjectives and exotic nouns fantastically
employed.   It is even more distinctly to be seen in his
prose than in his verse that he descends directly from
Baudelaire, and in the former that streak of Lamartine
that marks his poems is lacking.

The book called *Pages* can naturally be compared with
the *Poèmes en Prose* of Baudelaire.   Several of the
sketches so named are reprinted in *Vers et Prose,* and
they strike me as the most distinguished and satis-
factory of the published writings of M. Mallarmé.   They
are difficult, but far more intelligible than the enigmas
which he calls his sonnets.   *La Pipe*, in which the sight
of an old meerschaum brings up dreams of London and
the solitary lodgings there; *Le Nénuphar Blanc*, recording the vision of a lovely lady, visible for one tantalising
moment to a rower in his boat; *Frisson d'Hiver*, the
wholly fantastic and nebulous reverie of archaic elegances
evoked by the ticking of a clock of Dresden china; each

of these, and several more of these exquisite *Pages*, give just that impression of mystery and allusion which the author deems that style should give. They are exquisite —so far as they go—pure, distinguished, ingenious; and the fantastic oddity of their vocabulary seems in perfect accord with their general character.

Here is a fragment of *La Pénultième*, on which the reader may try his skill in comprehending the New French:

" Mais ou s'installe l'irrécusable intervention du surnaturel, et le commencement de l'angoisse sous laquelle agonise mon esprit naguère seigneur, c'est quand je vis, levant les yeux, dans la rue des antiquaires instinctivement suivie, que j'étais devant la boutique d'un luthier vendeur de vieux instruments pendus au mur, et, à terre, des palmes jaunes et les ailes enfouies en l'ombre, d'oiseaux anciens. Je m'enfuis, bizarre, personne condamnée à porter probablement le deuil de l'inexplicable Pénultième."

As a translator, all the world must commend M. Mallarmé. He has put the poems of Poe into French in a way which is subtle almost without parallel. Each version is in simple prose, but so full, so reserved, so suavely mellifluous, that the metre and the rhymes continue to sing in an English ear. None could enter more tenderly than he into the strange charm of *Ulalume*, of *The Sleeper*, or of *The Raven*. It is rarely indeed that a word suggests that the melody of one, who was a symbolist and a weaver of enigmas like himself, has momentarily evaded the translator.

Extraordinary persistence in an idea, and extraordinary patience under external discouragement, these were eminent characteristics of Mallarmé. He was not understood. Well, he would wait a little longer. He

waited, in fact, some seventeen years before he admitted
an ungrateful public again to an examination of his
specimens. Meanwhile, in several highly eccentric
forms, the initiated had been allowed to buy *Pages*
from his works in prose and verse, at high prices, in
most limited issues. Then, in 1893, there was a burst
of celebrity and perhaps of disenchantment. When
the tom-toms and the conches are silent, and the Veiled
Prophet is revealed at last, there is always some frivolous
person who is disappointed at the revelation. Perhaps
Mallarmé was not quite so thrilling when his poems could
be read by everybody as when they could only be gazed
at through the glass bookcase doors of wealthy amateurs.
But still, if everybody could now read them, not everybody could understand them. In 1894 the amiable
poet came over here, and delivered at Oxford and at
Cambridge, *cités savantes*, an address of the densest
Cimmerian darkness on Music and Letters. In 1897
appeared a collection of essays in prose, called *Divagations*. The dictionaries will tell the rest of the story.

The problem may, perhaps, now be definitely stated.
Language, to Mallarmé, was given to conceal the
obvious, to draw the eye, in direct opposition to Wordsworth's axiom, away from the object. The Parnassians
had described, defined, inexorably modelled the object,
until it stood before us as in a coloured photograph.
The aim of Mallarmé was as much as possible to escape
from photographic exactitude. He aimed at illusion
only; he wrapped a mystery about his simplest utterance; the abstruse and the suggestive are his peculiar
territory. His desire was to use words in such harmonious combinations as will induce in the reader a
mood or a condition which is not mentioned in the text,
but was nevertheless paramount in the poet's mind at

the moment of composition. To a conscious aiming at this particular effect are, it appears to me, due the more curious characteristics of his style, and much of the utter bewilderment which it produced on the brain of indolent readers debauched by the facilities of realism.[1]

It seems quite impossible to conjecture what posterity will think of the poetry of Stéphane Mallarmé. It is not of the class which rebuffs contemporary sympathy by its sentiments or its subjects; the difficulty of Mallarmé consists entirely in his use of language. He was allied with, or was taken as a master by, the young men who have broken up and tried to remodel the prosody of France. In popular estimation he came to be identified with them, but in error; there are no *vers libres* in Mallarmé. He was resolutely misapprehended, and perhaps, in his quiet way, he courted misapprehension. But if we examine very carefully in what his eccentricity (or his originality) consisted, we shall find it all resolving itself into a question of language. He thought that the vaunted precision and lucidity of French style, whether in prose or verse, was degrading the national literature; that poetry must preserve, or must conquer, an embroidered garment to distinguish her from the daily newspaper. He thought the best ways of doing this were, firstly, to divert the mind of the reader from the obvious and beaten paths of thought, and secondly, to arrange in a decorative or melodic scheme words chosen or reverted to for their peculiar dignity and beauty.

It was strange that Mallarmé never saw, or never chose to recognise, that he was attempting the impossible.

---

[1] See Appendix, for a letter from M. Mallarmé himself on this subject.

He went on giving us intimations of what he meant, never the thing itself. His published verses are mere fallings from him, vanishings, blank misgivings of a creature moving about in worlds not realised. They are fragments of a very singular and complicated system which the author never carried into existence. Mallarmé has left no " works," and, although he was always hinting of the Work, it was never written. Even his Virgilian *Faune,* even his Ovidian *Hérodiade,* are merely suggestions of the solid Latin splendour with which he might have carried out a design he did no more than indicate. He was a wonderful dreamer, exquisite in his intuitions and aspirations, but with as little creative power as has ever been linked with such shining convictions.

What effect will the life and death of Mallarmé have upon poetry in France ? Must it not be hoped that his influence may prove rather temporary and transitional than lasting ? He did excellent peripatetic service. His conversation and example preserved alight, through a rather prosy time, the lamp of poetic enthusiasm; he was a glowing ember. But, on the other hand, who can deny that his theories and practice, ill-comprehended as they were, provoked a great display of affectation and insincerity ? *Prose pour les Esseintes* is a very curious and interesting composition; but it is not a good model for the young. Mallarmé himself, so lucid a spirit of so obscure a writer, was well aware of this. People, he found, were cocksure of what his poems meant when the interpretation was only dawning upon himself after a generation of study. A youthful admirer once told him, it is said, that he entirely understood the meaning of one of his most cryptic publications. " What a genius you have ! " replied Mallarmé, with his gentle

Y

smile; " at the age of twenty you have discovered in a week what has baffled me for thirty years."

Some of the eulogies on this poor, charming Mallarmé, with his intense and frustrated aspiration after the perfect manner, have been a cruel satire on his prestige. From one of these mystifications I learn that " with the accustomed Parian (flesh of death), Mallarmé associated grafts of life unforeseen, eyes of emerald or of sapphire, hair of gold or silver, smiles of ivory," and that these statues " failed to fidget on their glued-down feet, because to the brutal chisel had succeeded a proud and delicate shiver glimmering through the infinite, perceptible to the initiated alone, like the august nibbling-away of Beauty by a white mouse ! " So far as Mallarmé and his theories are responsible for writing such as this— and for the last fifteen years his name has been made the centre for a prodigious amount of the like clotted nonsense—even those who loved and respected the man most cannot sincerely wish that his influence should continue.

Mallarmé has been employed as a synonym for darkness, but he did not choose this as a distinction. He was not like Donne, who, when Edward Herbert had been extremely crabbed in an elegy on Prince Henry, wrote one himself to " match," as Ben Jonson tells us, Herbert " in obscureness." In a letter to myself, some years ago, Mallarmé protested with evident sincerity against the charge of being Lycophrontic : " excepté par maladresse ou gaucherie je ne suis pas obscur." Yet where is obscurity to be found if not in *Don du Poème ?* What is dense if the light flows freely through *Prose pour des Esseintes ?* Some of his alterations of his own text betray the fact that he treated words as musical notation, that he was far more intimately affected by their euphonic interrelation than by their meaning in logical sequence. In my own copy of *Les Fenêtres*, he has altered in MS. the line

"Que dore la main chaste de l'Infini"

to

"Que dore le matin chaste de l'Infini.'

Whether the Infinite had a Hand or a Morning was purely a question of euphony. So, what had long appeared as "mon exotique soin" became "mon unique soin." In short, Mallarmé used words, not as descriptive, but as suggestive means of communication between the writer and the reader, and the object of a poem of his was not to define what the poet was thinking about, but to force the listener to think about it by blocking up all routes of impression save that which led to the desired and indicated bourne.

He was a very delightful man, whom his friends deeply regret. He was a particularly lively talker, and in his conversation, which was marked by good sense no less than by a singular delicacy of perception, there was no trace of the wilful perversity of his written style. He had a strong sense of humour, and no one will ever know, perhaps, how far a waggish love of mystification entered into his theories and his experiments. He was very much amused when Verlaine said of him that he " considéra la clarté comme une grâce secondaire." It certainly was not the grace he sought for first. We may, perhaps, be permitted to think that he had no such profoundly novel view of nature or of man as justified procedures so violent as those which he introduced. But, when we were able to comprehend him, we perceived an exquisite fancy, great refinement of feeling and an attitude towards life which was uniformly and sensitively poetical. Is it not to be supposed that when he could no longer be understood, when we lost him in the blaze of language, he was really more delightful than ever, if only our gross senses could have followed him ?

1893–1898.

M. ÉMILE VERHAEREN

Among those poets who have employed the French tongue with most success in recent years, it is curious that the two whose claims to distinction are least open to discussion should be, not Frenchmen at all, but Flemings of pure race. The work of M. Verhaeren has not the amusing quality which has given a universal significance to the dramas and treatises of M. Maeterlinck, and he has remained obstinately faithful to the less popular medium of verse. In our English sense of the term, M. Maeterlinck is a poet only upon occasion, while M. Verhaeren never appears without his singing-robes about him. By dint of a remarkable persistency in presenting his talent characteristically to his readers, M. Verhaeren has risen slowly but steadily to a very high eminence. He has out-lived the impression, which prevailed at first, of ugliness, of squalor, of a pre-occupation with themes and aspects radically anti-poetical. He has conquered us deliberately, book by book. He has proved that genius is its own best judge of what is a good " subject," and imperceptibly we have learned to appreciate and respect him. He is true to himself, quite indefatigable, and we are beginning to realise at last that he is one of the very small group of really great poets born in Europe since 1850.

He has a local, besides his universal, claim on our respect, since he is the pioneer and captain of the brilliant neo-Belgian school which is now so active and so prominent. His first book of verses, *Les Flamandes*, of 1883, is curious to look back upon. It was thrust upon a perfectly hostile world of Brussels, a world with its eyes loyally fixed on Paris. It had just the same harsh, austere aspect which M. Verhaeren's poetry has preserved ever since. It was utterly unlike what came from Paris then, dear little amber-scented books of polished sonnets, bound in vellum, with Lemerre's familiar *piocheur* on the cover. It was the first shoot of a new tree, of Franco-Flemish imaginative literature. M. Verhaeren cared nothing for the neglect of the critics; he went on putting forth successive little volumes, no less thorny, no less smelling of the dykes and dunes— *Les Moines* in 1886, *Les Soirs* in 1887, *Les Débâcles* in 1888. It was not until 1889 that M. Maeterlinck came to his support with a first book, the *Serres Chaudes*. Meanwhile, the genius of M. Verhaeren, the product of an individuality of extraordinary strength, pressed steadily forward. He has gained in suppleness and skill since then, but all that distinguishes him from other writers, all that is himself, is to be found in these earliest pamphlets of gaunt, realistic poetry.

The following dismal impression of London is highly characteristic of the early Verhaeren of *Les Soirs* :—

" Et ce Londres de fonte et de bronze, mon âme,
Où des plaques de fer claquent sous les hangars,
Où des voiles s'en vont, sans Notre Dame
Pour étoile, s'en vont, là-bas, vers les hasards.

Gares de suies et de fumée, où du gaz pleure
Ses spleens d'argent lointain vers des chemins d'éclair,
Où des bêtes d'ennui bâillent à l'heure,
Dolente immensément, qui tinte à Westminster.

Et ces quais infinis de lanternes fatales,
Parques dont les fuseaux plongent aux profondeurs,
Et ces marins noyés, sous des pétales
De fleurs de boue où la flamme met des lueurs.

> Et ces châles et ces gestes de femmes soûles,
> Et ces alcools en lettres d'or jusques au toit,
>   Et tout à coup la mort parmi ces foules—
> O mon âme du soir, ce Londres noir que trône en toi ! "

A hundred years ago we possessed in English literature a writer very curiously parallel to M. Verhaeren, who probably never heard of him. I do not know whether any one has pointed out the similarity between Crabbe and the Belgian poet of our day. It is, however, very striking when we once come to think of it, and it embraces subject-matter, attitude to life and art, and even such closer matters as diction and versification. The situation of Crabbe, in relation to the old school of the eighteenth century on the one hand and to the romantic school on the other, is closely repeated by that of M. Verhaeren to his elders and his juniors. If Byron were now alive, he might call M. Verhaeren a Victor Hugo in worsted stockings. There is the same sardonic delineation of a bleak and sandy sea-coast country, Suffolk or Zeeland as the case may be, the same determination to find poetic material in the perfectly truthful study of a raw peasantry, of narrow provincial towns, of rough and cheerless seafaring existences. In each of these poets— and scarcely in any other European writers of verse— we find the same saline flavour, the same odour of iodine, the same tenacious attachment to the strength and violence and formidable simplicity of nature.

In *Les Forces Tumultueuses* we discover the same qualities which we have found before in M. Verhaeren's volumes. He employs mainly two forms of verse, the one a free species of Alexandrines, the other a wandering measure, loosely rhymed, of the sort which used among ourselves to be called " Pindarique." He gives us studies of modern figures, the Captain, the Tribune, the

Monk, the Banker, the Tyrant. He gives us studies of
towns, curiously hard, although less violent than those
in his earlier, and perhaps most extraordinary, book, *Les
Villes Tentaculaires.* His interest in towns and hamlets
is inexhaustible—and did not Crabbe write "The
Village" and "The Borough"? Even railway junctions
do not dismay the muse of M. Verhaeren :—

> " Oh ! ces villes, par l'or putride envenimées !
> Clameurs de pierre et vols et gestes de fumées,
> Dômes et tours d'orgueil et colonnes debout
> Dans l'espace qui vibre et le travail qui bout,
> En aimas-tu l'effroi et les affres profondes
> O toi, le voyageur
> Qui t'en allais triste et songeur,
> Par les gares de feu qui ceinturent le monde ?
>
> Cahots et bonds de trains par au-dessus des monts !
>
> L'intime et sourd tocsin qui enfiévrait ton âme
> Battait aussi dans ces villes, le soir; leur flamme
> Rouge et myriadaire illuminait ton front,
> Leur aboi noir, le cri, le han de ton cœur même;
> Ton être entier était tordu en leur blasphème,
> Ta volonté jetée en proie à leur torrent
> Et vous vous maudissiez tout en vous adorant."

The superficially prosaic has no terrors for M. Verhaeren. He gives us, too, of course, studies of the sea-
coast, of that dreary district (it can never have dreamed
that it would nourish a poet) which stretches from
Antwerp westward along the Scheldt to the North Sea,
that infinite roll of dunes, hung between the convulsive
surf and the heavy sky, over which a bitter wind goes
whistling through the wild thin grass towards a vague
inland flatness, vast, monotonous, and dull beyond all
power of language to describe. This is a land which
arrives at relevancy only when darkness falls on it, and
its great revolving lights give relation to its measureless
masses.

The habitual gloom and mournfulness of M. Verhaeren's pictures are only relieved once in this powerful
volume. The poem called *Sur la Mer* strikes a different
note, and resembles one of those rare sunshiny days when
the creeks of Northern Flanders are in gala. We watch
the brilliantly-coloured ship stirring her cordage and
fluttering her pennons, like some gay little Dutch garden
putting merrily out to sea. All is a bustle of scarlet and
orange and blue; but it would not be a picture of M.
Verhaeren's if it did not offer a reverse side :—

> " Le vaisseau clair revint, un soir de bruit
> Et de fête, vers le rivage,
> D'où son élan était parti ;
> Certes, les mâts dardaient toujours leur âme,
> Certes, le foc portait encore des oriflammes,
> Mais les marins étaient découronnés
> De confiance, et les haubans et les cordages
> Ne vibraient plus comme des lyres sauvages.
> Le navire rentra comme un jardin fané,
> Drapeaux éteints, espoirs minés,
> Avec l'effroi de n'oser dire à ceux du port
> Qu'il avait entendu, là-bas, de plage en plage,
> Les flots crier sur les rivages
> Que Pan et que Jésus, tous deux, étaient des morts."

For those who seek from poetry its superficial consola-
tions, the canticles of M. Verhaeren offer little attraction.
But for readers who can endure a sterner music, and a
resolute avoidance of the mere affectations of the
intellect, he is now one of the most interesting figures
in contemporary literature. And to deny that he is a
poet would be like denying that the great crimson
willow-herb is a flower because it grows in desolate
places.

1902.

ALBERT SAMAIN

The influence of Baudelaire, which so gravely alarmed the critical sanhedrim of forty years ago, has proved more durable than was expected, but at the same time singularly inoffensive. There seemed to be something in the imagination of Baudelaire which fermented unpleasantly, and an outbreak of pestilence in his neighbourhood was seriously apprehended. He was treated as a sort of plague-centre. It would be difficult to make the young generation in London realise what palpitations, what tremors, what alarms the terrible *Fleurs du Mal* caused in poetic bosoms about 1860. But the Satanic dandyism, as it was called, of the poet's most daring verses was not, in reality, a very perdurable element. Most of it was absurd, and some of it was vulgar; all of it, with the decease of poor Maurice Rollinat, seems now to have evaporated. What was really powerful in Baudelaire, and what his horrors at first concealed, was the extreme intensity of his sense of beauty, or, to be more precise, his noble gift of subduing to the service of poetry the voluptuous visions awakened by perfume and music and light.

It is this side of his genius which has attracted so closely the leaders of the poetic revival in France. A lofty, if somewhat vaporous dignity; a rich, if somewhat indefinable severity of taste; these are among the prominent qualities of the new French poetry, which is as far removed in spirit from the detestable " *manie d'étonner* " of *Les Fleurs du Mal* as it is possible to be. Yet in recounting the precursors to whom the homage of the new school is due, every careful critic must enumerate, not only Lamartine and Alfred de Vigny, but unquestionably Baudelaire.

In the unfortunate Albert Samain, for instance, whose death has deprived France prematurely of a nature evidently predestined, as few can be said to be, to the splendours of poetic fame, this innocuous and wholesome influence of Baudelaire may be very clearly traced. It does not interfere with Samain's claim to be treated as an original writer of high gifts, but it is impossible to overlook its significance. The crawling corruption of Baudelaire has, in fact, in the course of time, not merely become deodorised, but takes its place, as a pinch of " scentless and delicate dust," in the inevitable composition of any new French poet.

In the course of the winter of 1893, a good many persons, of whom the present writer was one, received a small quarto volume, bound in sage-green paper, from an unknown source in Paris. The book, which was privately printed in a very small issue, was called *Au Jardin de l'Infante*, and it transpired that this was the first production of a clerk in the Préfecture de la Seine, named Albert Samain. Born at Lille in 1859, Samain was no longer very young, but he had no relations with the world of letters, and a shy dissatisfaction with what he had written gave him a dislike to publication. The sage-green volume, already so rare, was, as it now appears, printed and sent out by a friend, in spite of the poet's deprecations. A copy of it came into the hands of M. François Coppée, who, to his great honour, instantly perceived its merits, and in the second series of *Mon Franc-Parler* attracted attention to it. In 1897 an edition of *Au Jardin de l'Infante* placed the poems of Samain within the range of the ordinary reader, and in 1898 he published another volume, *Aux Flancs du Vase*. His health, however, had failed, and he had by this time retired to the country village of Magny-les-

Hameaux, where he died on the 18th of August, 1900. Since his death there have appeared a third volume of poems, *Le Chariot d'Or* (1901), and a lyrical drama, *Polyphème* (1902).

The existence of Albert Samain left scarcely a ripple on the stream of French literary life. He stood apart from all the coteries, and his shyness and indigence prevented him from presenting himself where he might readily have been lionised. Of the very few persons who ever saw Samain I have interrogated one or two as to his appearance and manners. They tell me that he was pale and slight, with hollow cheeks and preponderating forehead, and of a great economy of speech. Excessively near-sighted, he seemed to have no cognisance of the world about him, and the regularity of his life as a clerk emphasised his dreamy habits. He is described to me as grave, and, when he spoke, somewhat grandiloquent; his half-shut eyes gave an impression of languor, which was partly physical fatigue. I think it possible that future times may feel a curiosity about the person of Albert Samain, and that there will be practically nothing to divulge, since his dreams died with him. This small city clerk, with his poor economies and stricken health, habitually escaped from the oppression of a life that was as dull and void as it could be, into the buoyant liberty of gorgeous and persistent vision.

He expresses this himself in every page of *Au Jardin de l'Infante*. He says :—

> " Les roses du couchant s'effeuillent sur la fleuve;
>   Et dans l'émotion pâle du soir tombant,
>   S'évoque un parc d'automne où rêve sur un banc
>   Ma jeunesse déjà grave comme une veuve; "

and in a braver tone :—

" Mon âme est une Infante en robe de parade,
    Dont l'exil se reflète, éternel et royal,
    Aux grands miroirs déserts d'un vieil Escurial,
Ainsi qu'une galère oubliée en la rade."

Everywhere the evidences of a sumptuous and enchanted past, everywhere the purity of silence and the
radiance of royal waters at sunset, everywhere the
incense of roses that were planted for the pleasure of
queens long dead and gone, and Albert Samain pursuing
his solitary way along those deserted paths and up the
marble of those crumbling staircases. Such is the
illusion which animates the Garden of the Infanta.
Sometimes the poet is not alone there; other forms
approach him, and other faces smile; but they are the
faces and the forms of phantoms :—

" L'âme d'une flûte soupire
    Au fond du parc mélodieux;
Limpide est l'ombre où l'on respire
    Ton poème silencieux,

Nuit de langueur, nuit de mensonge,
    Qui poses d'un geste ondoyant
Dans ta chevelure de songe
    La lune, bijou d'Orient.

Sylva, Sylvie et Sylvanire,
    Belles au regard bleu changeant,
L'étoile aux fontaines se mire,
    Allez par les sentiers d'argent.

Allez vite—l'heure est si brève !
    Cueillir au jardin des aveux
Les cœurs qui se meurent du rêve
    De mourir parmi vos cheveux."

His aim was to express a melancholy and chaste
sensuousness in terms of the most tender and impassioned symbolism. No one has succeeded more
frequently than Samain in giving artistic form to those

vague and faint emotions which pass over the soul like a breeze. He desired to write verses when, as he said, " l'âme sent, exquise, une caresse à peine," or even—

> " De vers silencieux, et sans rythme et sans trame,
>   Où la rime sans bruit glisse comme une rame,—
> De vers d'une ancienne étoffe exténuée,
> Impalpable comme le son et la nuée."

In this mood his poetry occasionally approaches that of Mr. Robert Bridges on the one side and of Mr. Yeats on the other. It has at other times a certain marmoreal severity which reminds us of neither. I desire the reader's close attention to the following sonnet, called *Cléopatre*, in which the genius of Albert Samain seems to be all revealed. Here, it may at first be thought, he comes near to the old Parnassians; but his methods will be found to be diametrically opposed to theirs, although not even M. de Heredia would have clothed the subject with a nobler beauty :—

> " Accoudée en silence aux créneaux de la tour,
>   La Reine aux cheveux bleus, serrés de bandelettes,
>   Sous l'incantation trouble des cassolettes,
> Sent monter dans son cœur ta mer, immense Amour.
>
> Immobile, sous ses paupières violettes,
>   Elle rêve, pâmée aux fuites des coussins;
>   Et les lourds colliers d'or soulevés par ses seins
> Racontent sa langueur et ses fièvres muettes.
>
> Un adieu rose flotte au front des monuments.
> Le soir, velouté d'ombre, est plein d'enchantements;
>   Et cependant qu'au loin pleurent les crocodiles,
>
> La Reine aux doigts crispés, sanglotante d'aveux,
> Frissonne de sentir, lascives et subtiles,
>   Des mains qui dans le vent épuisent ses cheveux."

There is much in the history and in the art of Albert Samain which reminds me of an English poet whom I knew well when we both were young, and who still awaits the fullness of recognition—Arthur O'Shaughnessy. Each of them was fascinated by the stronger genius of two poets of an older generation—Baudelaire and Edgar Allan Poe. But each had a quality that was entirely his own, a quality which the passage of time will certainly emphasise and isolate.

1904.

M. PAUL FORT

The instinct which impels every energetic talent to emancipate itself as far as possible from the bondage of tradition is a natural one, and it is even not so dangerous as we suppose. For, if there is a centrifugal force ever driving the ambition of youth away from the conventional idea of beauty, this is easily reversed by the inherent attraction of purity and nobility in form. The artist makes a bold flight and wheels away into the distance, but he returns; he is true, like Wordsworth's skylark, to the kindred points of heaven and home. In a writer, therefore, who starts in open rebellion to the tradition of style, we have but to wait and see whether the talent itself is durable. It is only presumptuous Icarus, whose waxen wings melt in the sun, and who topples into the sea. It is only the writer who makes eccentricity the mantle to hide his poverty of imagination and absence of thought who disappears. To the young man of violent idiosyncrasies and genuine talent two things always happen—he impresses his charm upon our unwilling senses, and he is himself drawn back, unconsciously and imperceptibly, into the main current of the stream of style.

While M. Paul Fort was merely an eccentric experimentalist, it did not seem worth while to present him to an English audience. The earliest of his published volumes, the *Ballades Françaises* of 1897, was a pure mystification to most readers. It was printed, and apparently written, as prose. It asserted the superiority of rhythm over the artifice of prosody, which is precisely what Walt Whitman did. The French conceive poetry, however, very rigidly in its essential distinction from prose. There are rules for writing French verse which are categorical, and these must be taken *en bloc*. It is far more difficult in French to imagine a thing which could represent, at the same moment, poetry and prose, than it would be in English. But M. Paul Fort determined to create this entirely new thing, and when one read his effusions first it is only fair to admit that one was bewildered. Here, for instance, is, in its entirety, one of the *Ballades Françaises* :—

" Être né page et brave vielleur d'amour, en la gentille cour d'un prince de jadis, chanter une princesse follement aimée, au nom si doux que bruit de roses essaimées, à qui offrir, un jour, en lui offrant la main pour la marche à descendre avant le lac d'hymen, l'odorant coffret d'or sous ses chaînes de lys, plein de bleus hyalins ès anneaux de soleil et d'oiselets de Chypre ardents pour embaumer, à qui donner aux sons des fifres et des vielles, pour notre traversée en la barque d'hymen, le frêle rosier d'or à tenir en sa main ! "

The only way to make anything of this is to read it aloud, and it may be said in parenthesis that M. Fort is a writer who appeals entirely to the ear, not to the eye. Spoken, or murmured in accordance with Mr. Yeats's new method, the piece of overladen prose disengages itself, floats out into filaments of silken verse, like a bunch of dry seaweed restored to its element. In this so-called ballad the alexandrine dominates, but with

elisions, assonances, irregularities of every description.
It is therefore best to allow the author himself to define
his method.   He says in the preface to a later poem, *Le
Roman de Louis XI*. :—

   " J'ai cherché un style pouvant passer, au gré de
l'émotion, de la prose au vers et du vers à la prose : la
prose rythmée fournit la transition.   Le vers suit les
élisions naturelles du langage.   Il se présente comme
prose, toute gêne d'élision disparaissant sous cette
forme."

   In short, we have heard much about " free verse "
in France, but here at last we have an author who has
had the daring to consider prose and verse as parts of
one graduated instrument, and to take the current
pronunciation of the French language as the only law
of a general and normal rhythm.   It is a curious experiment, and we shall have to see what he will ultimately
make of it.

   But one is bound to admit that he has made a good
deal of it already.   He has become an author whom we
cannot affect or afford to ignore.   Born so lately as 1872,
M. Paul Fort is in some respects the most notable, as he
is certainly the most abundant, imaginative author of
his age in France.   The book which lies before us, a
romance of Parisian life of to-day in verse, is the sixth
of the volumes which M. Fort has brought out in less
than six years, all curiously consistent in manner, all
independent of external literary influences, and all full
of exuberant, fresh and vivid impressions of nature.
The eccentricities of his form lay him open, of course,
to theoretical objections which I should never think
unreasonable, and which I am conservative enough to
share.   But these do not affect his ardour in the contemplation of nature, his high gust of being.   I scarcely

know where to point in any recent literature to an author so full of the joy of life. He does not philosophise or analyse, he affects no airs of priest or prophet; his attitude is extraordinarily simple, but is charged with the ecstasy of appreciation. In two of his collections of lyrics in rhythm, in particular, we find this ardour, this enchantment, predominating; these are *Montagne*, 1898, and *L'Amour Marin*, 1900, in which he sings, or chants, the forest and the sea.

In *Paris Sentimental* M. Paul Fort has written a novel in his peculiar and favourite form. We have had many examples of the dangers and difficulties which attend the specious adventure of writing modern fiction in metrical shape. Neither *Aurora Leigh* nor *Lucile* nor *The Inn Album* is entirely encouraging as more than the experiment of a capricious though splendidly accomplished artist. Yet *Paris Sentimental* is more nearly related to these than to any French poem that I happen to recollect. There is, indeed, as it seems to me, something English in M. Fort's habit of mind. His novel, however, is much less elaborate than either of the English poems I have mentioned, and certainly much less strenuous than the first and third. It is a chain of lyrical rhapsodies in which a very plain tale of love and disappointment in the Paris of to-day is made the excuse for a poetical assimilation of all the charming things which Paris contains, and which have hitherto evaded the skill of the poets, such as the turf in the Square Monge, and the colour of an autumn shower on the Boulevard Sébastopol, and the Tziganes singing by moonlight at the Exposition. Here is an example of how it is done :—

" Le couchant violet tremble au fond du jour rouge. Le Luxembourg exhale une odeur d'oranger, et Manon
z

s'arrête à mon bras; plus rien ne bouge, les arbres, les passants, ce nuage éloigné. . . .

"Et le jet d'eau s'est tu : c'est la rosée qui chante, là-bas, dans les gazons, où rêvent les statues, et pour rendre, ô sens-tu ? la nuit plus défaillante, les orangers en fleurs ont enivré la nue."

It would be an easy exercise to search for the metre here, as we used to hunt for blank verse in the *Leaves of Grass*. But M. Paul Fort is less revolutionary than Whitman, and more of an artist. Although he clings to his theories, in each of his volumes he seems to be less negligent of form, less provocative, than he was in the last. The force of his talent is wheeling him back into the inevitable tradition; he is being forced by the music in his veins to content himself with cadences that were good enough for Racine and Hugo and Baudelaire. And, therefore, in the last quotation which I offer from *Paris Sentimental*, I take the liberty of disregarding the typographical whims of the author, and print his lines as verse :—

"Par les nuits d'été bleues où chantent les cigales,
Dieu verse sur la France une coupe d'étoiles.
Le vent porte à ma lèvre un goût du ciel d'été !
Je veux boire à l'espace fraichement argenté.

L'air du soir est pour moi le bord de la coupe froide
Où, les yeux mi-fermés et la bouche goulue,
Je bois, comme le jus pressé d'une grenade,
La fraîcheur étoilée qui se répand des nues.

Couché sur un gazon dont l'herbe est encore chaude
De s'être prélassée sous l'haleine du jour,
Oh ! que je viderais, ce soir, avec amour,
La coupe immense bleue où le firmament rôde ! "

1902.

THE INFLUENCE OF FRANCE
UPON ENGLISH POETRY

THE INFLUENCE OF FRANCE UPON ENGLISH POETRY

Address delivered, February 9, 1904, before the Société des Conférences, in Paris.

BEFORE I begin to discuss with you the particular subject of my discourse this afternoon, I cannot refrain from expressing my emotion at finding myself, in consequence of your gracious invitation, occupying this platform. It has been said that, for a man of letters, consideration in a country not his own is a foretaste of the verdict of posterity. If there be any truth in this, then surely, in the particular case where that country happens to be France, it should be more—it should be something very like a dangerous mirage of immortality. When the invitation of your committee first reached me, it seemed for a moment impossible that I could accept it. In no perfunctory or complimentary sense, I shrank, with an apprehension of my own twilight, from presenting myself in the midst of your blaze of intelligence. How could I be sure that any of my reflections, of my observations, could prove worthy of acceptance by an audience accustomed to the teachings of the most brilliant and the most learned critics of the world? If there be an obvious lack of sufficiency in my words this afternoon, then, on yourselves must be the blame, and on your own generosity, since in venturing to stand before you, it is your commands which I obey in all simplicity. I obey them as some barbarous Northern minstrel might, who, finding himself at the court of Philippe de Valois, should be desired, in the presence of the prince and of his ladies, to exhibit a specimen of his rough native art.

The subject of our inquiry to-day is not the nature of the change which occurs when a new literature rises out of the imitation of an older one, as occurred with such splendid results when Latin poetry was deliberately based on Greek poetry, in the second century before Christ, or when, in the early Middle Ages, the vernacular literatures of modern Europe sprang out of the decay of Latin. In such cases as these the matter is simple; out of the old stock there springs a new bud, affiliated to it, imitative and only gradually independent. It is not difficult to see Ennius, in the dawn of Rome, sitting with the Greek hexameter before him, and deliberately fashioning a similar thing out of the stubbornness of his own rough tongue. It is not difficult to see some student-minstrel of the eleventh century debating within himself whether he shall put down his thoughts in faded Latin or in the delicate *lingua Tusca, communis et intelligibilis*. Influences of this kind are a part of the direct and natural evolution of literature, and their phenomena are almost of a physical kind. When a new language breaks away from an old language into the forms of a creative literature, its earliest manifestations must be imitative. It is original in the very fact that it copies into a new medium instead of continuing in an old one.

But the problem is much more subtle and the phenomena more delicate and elusive when we have to deal with the influences mutually exercised on one another by contemporary literatures of independent character and long-settled traditions. In the case before us, we have one great people building up for the expression of their joys and passions a language out of Anglo-Saxon materials, and another great people forging out of low Latin a vehicle for their complicated thoughts. The literatures so created have enjoyed a vivid and variegated vitality for century after century, never tending the one towards the other, neither at any time seriously taking a place subordinate to the other, nor even closely related. The image that may help to suggest to us what it is that we must look for in observing the mutual influences of French and English literature upon one another is that of two metallic objects, of different colour, pursuing a long parallel flight through space. We are not to count upon their touching one another, or their affecting the direction or speed of either, but we may expect, on occasion, to observe along the burnished side of the one a dash of colour reflected from the illuminated surface of the other.

It would take us too far from our proper theme this afternoon—a theme which at best we can but very hurriedly investigate—were I to dwell on the essential differences which distinguish the poetry of England from that of France. But it may be pointed out that these differences make themselves most clearly felt exactly wherever the national idiosyncrasy is most searchingly defined. The extraordinary perfection of the verse of Coleridge in its concentrated sweetness and harmony of vision, has never appealed to any French student of our literature. Perhaps no French ear could be trained to understand what the sovereign music of Coleridge means to us. In like manner it is probable that, with all our efforts, English criticism has never understood, and never will understand, what the effect of the astonishing genius of Racine is upon the nerves and intelligence of a Frenchman. On the other hand, it is easy to see that Mr. Swinburne approaches thought and style from a point of view eminently appreciable by the French, while France contains one great poet, Charles Baudelaire, whose oddity of mental attitude and whose peculiar treatment of verse-music and of imagery are perhaps more easily comprehended by an English reader than by an academic Frenchman.

A matter which might be pursued, in connection with this, but which time forbids me to do more than indicate, is that, while in France poetry has been accustomed to reflect the general tongue of the people, the great poets of England have almost always had to struggle against a complete dissonance between their own aims and interests and those of the nation. The result has been that England, the most inartistic of modern races, has produced the largest number of exquisite literary artists.

The expression of personal sensation has always been dear to the English poets, and we meet with it in some of the earliest babblings of our tongue. From Anglo-Saxon times onward, the British bard never felt called upon to express the æsthetic emotions of a society around him, as the Provençal troubadour or Carlovingian jongleur did. He was driven to find inspiration in nature and in himself. The mediæval conquest of England by the French language did not modify this state of things in any degree. When the French wave ebbed away from us in the fourteenth century, it left our poets of pure English as individual, as salient, as unrepresentative as ever. What every poet of delicate genius, whether he be Chaucer or Milton, Gray or Keats, has felt in the existing world of England, has been the pressure of a lack of the æsthetic sense. Our people are not naturally sensitive to harmony, to proportion, to the due relation of parts in a work of imaginative artifice. But what is very curious is that our poets have been peculiarly sensitive to these very qualities, and that no finer or subtler artists in language have risen in any country than precisely the poetic representatives of the densely unpoetic England.

The result of this fantastic and almost incessant discord between our poets and our people—a discord dissolved into harmony only at one moment around the genius of Shakespeare—the result of this has been to make our poets, at critical epochs, sensitive to catch the colour of literatures alien from their own. In the healthier moments of our poetry we have gained brightness by reflections from other literatures, from those of Greece and Rome, from those of Italy and Spain and France. In moments when our poetry was unhealthy it has borrowed to its immediate and certain disadvantage from these neighbours. But it will, I think, be seen that in the latter case the borrowing has invariably been of a coarser and more material kind, and has consisted in a more or less vulgar imitaticn. The evil effect of this will, I believe, be found to be as definite as the effect of the higher and more illusive borrowing is beneficial. For purposes of convenience I propose in the following remarks to distinguish these forms of influence as consisting in colour and in substance.

A few words may serve to define what I understand here by " substance " and by " colour." By the first of these I wish to indicate those cases in which influence has taken a gross and slavish form, in which there has been a more or less complete resignation of the individuality of the literature influenced. An instance of this is the absolute bondage of Spanish drama to French in the eighteenth century, when a play had no chance on the stage of Madrid unless it were directly modelled on Racine or Voltaire. We shall presently have to point to something similar in the drama of our own Restoration. These are cases where an exhausted literature, in extreme decay, is kept alive by borrowing its very body and essence from a foreign source, the result being that such life as it presents is not really its own, but provided for it, ready-made, by the genius of another country. This species of influence I hold to be invariably the sign of a diseased and weakly condition.

On the other hand, it is precisely when the poets of a country desire to clothe in new forms the personal sensations which are driving them to creative expression, that they are very likely to turn to a neighbouring literature, which happens to be at a stage of æsthetic development different from their own, for superficial suggestions. The ornaments of form which they bring back with them, when they are in this healthy and lively condition, are what I describe as " colour." In the early history of European poetry, none of the great poetic powers disdained to import from Italy the radiance and tincture of her executive skill. The introduction of the sonnet to England and to France, that of blank verse to England, that of prose comedy to France, these were instances of the absorption by living and vigorous literatures of elements in the literary art of Italy which were instinctively felt by them to be strengthening and refining, but not subjugating. In these cases influence does nothing to lessen the import-ance of that delicate distinction of individual style which

is the very charm of poetry, but rather gives that
distinction a more powerful apparatus for making its
presence felt.

We have a very instructive example of this wholesome reflex action of one literature upon another, in
the history of the fourteenth century. No one will
pretend that France possessed at that epoch, or indeed
had ever yet possessed, a poet of very high rank, with
the exception of the anonymous artist who bequeathed
to us the *Chanson de Roland*. But, in the thirteenth
century, she had produced that amazing work, *Le Roman
de la Rose*, half of it amatory, the other half of it satirical,
and the whole of it extraordinarily vivid and civilising.
It would be too much to call the *Roman de la Rose* a
great poem, or even two great poems fused into one.
But it certainly was one of the most influential works
which ever proceeded from the pen of man. Its influence, if we look at it broadly, was in the direction
of warmth and colour. It glowed like a fire, it flashed
like a sunrise. Guillaume de Lorris deserves our eternal
thanks for being the first in modern Europe to write
" pour esgaier les cœurs." He introduced into poetry
amenity, the pulse of life, the power of Earthly Love.

It is useful for us to compare the *Roman de la Rose*
with what the best English poets were writing at the
same time. What do we find ? We find a few dismal
fragments of Scriptural morality and one or two sermons
in verse. We may speculate in what spirit a dulled
English minstrel of the end of the thirteenth century
would read the bold and brilliant couplets of Jean de
Meung. He would certainly be dazzled, and perhaps
be scandalised. He would creep back to his own
clammy *Ayenbite of Inwyt* and his stony *Cursor Mundi*
to escape from so much dangerous warmth and colour.

It seems as though for nearly a hundred years England steadily refused to enter that fair orchard where Beauty and Love were dancing hand in hand around the thorny hedge that guarded the Rosebud of the World. But the revelation came at last, and it is not too much to say that English poetry, as it has since become, in the hands of Shakespeare and Keats and Tennyson, sprang into life when the English poets first became acquainted with the gallant, courteous, and amatory allegory of the Worship of the Rose.

It is very interesting to see that, apparently, it was no less a person than Chaucer who led English readers first to the grassy edge of the fountain of love. The evidence is curiously obscure, and has greatly exercised Chaucerian scholars. But the truth seems to be that Chaucer translated *Le Roman de la Rose*, as he tells us himself in *The Legend of Good Women*, but that of this translation only a fragment now survives. The other two fragments, always printed together with Chaucer's, are now considered to be not his, and indeed to come from two different hands. Into this vexed question we must not go, but it is worth noticing that although the three fragments which make up the fourteenth-century *Romaunt of the Rose* only cover, together, one-third of the French text, Chaucer constantly quotes from and refers to passages from other parts of the poem, showing that he was familiar with it all.

English poetry, we may observe, had more to learn from Guillaume de Lorris than from Jean de Meung, greater and more vigorous writer though the latter might be. What modern English poetry, in fact, in its restless adolescence, was leaning to France for was not so much vigour as grace. It had satiric vigour of its own in its apocalyptical Langland. But what beamed and glowed upon Chaucer from the *Roman de la Rose* was its human sweetness, its perfume as of a bush of eglantine in April sunshine. It was the first delicate and civilised poem of modern Europe, and its refinement and elegance, its decorated beauty and its close observation of the human heart were the qualities which attracted to it Chaucer, as he came starved from the chill allegories and moralities of his formless native literature.

It was in the autumn of 1359 that Chaucer, as a page in the retinue of Prince Lionel, paid what is supposed to have been his earliest visit to France. He took his part in the luckless invasion of Champagne, and he was captured by the French, perhaps at Réthel. Until March 1360, when King Edward III. ransomed him for the sum of £16, he was a prisoner in France. During these five or six months we have to think of Chaucer as a joyous youth of nineteen, little cast down by the fortunes of war, but full of sentiment, poetry, and passion. Up to that time, doubtless, he had read few or none but French books. We cannot question that he was familiar with the *Roman de la Rose*, and it is just possible that it was at this time that he came in contact with the lyrical writers whose personal poetry affected him so much later on. I am inclined, however, to think this unlikely, because Eustache Deschamps was a youth of about Chaucer's own age, and although Guillaume de Machault was considerably older, there had been little public distribution of his verses so early as 1360.

We must put the date of Chaucer's coming under the influence of the French writers of *chants royaux* and *lais* and *ballades* a little later. In the summer of 1369 he was once more in France, and this time, it would appear, on some pacific embassy. Perhaps he

escaped from the plague which decimated England in
that year, and carried off even Queen Philippa herself.
Perhaps he was engaged on a diplomatic mission. We
have to walk carefully in the darkness of these mediæval
dates, which offer difficulties even to the erudition of
M. Marcel Schwob. At all events, Chaucer was certainly
then "in partibus Franciæ," and it can hardly but
have been now that he fell under the influence of
Machault, whom he admired so much, and of Eustache
Deschamps, in whom he awakened so enthusiastic a
friendship.[1] There was an *entente cordiale* indeed when
Deschamps and Froissart complimented Chaucer, and
Chaucer imitated Machault and Oton de Granson. We
find the English poet passing through France again in
1373, and again in 1377. We have a vague and accidental
record of at least seven of these diplomatic journeys,
although after 1378 the French interest seems entirely
swallowed up in the far more vivid fascination which
Italy exercised over him.

To a poet who was privileged to come beneath the
intellectual sway of Petrarch and Boccaccio at the
glorious close of their careers, it might well be that
such suns would seem entirely to eclipse the tapers of
those who composed *ballades* and *virelais* in the rich
provinces north of the Loire. Himself a man of far
greater genius than any French writer of the fourteenth
century, we might be prepared to find Chaucer disdaining
the gentle balladists of France. He had, to a far
greater degree than any of them, vigour, originality,
fulness of invention. Eustache Deschamps is some-

---

[1] Mr. Fitzmaurice-Kelly reminds me that, in his celebrated
letter to the Constable of Portugal, the Spanish poet Santillana
goes into raptures about four of the writers whom Chaucer
admired—Guillaume de Lorris, Jean de Meung, Machault, and
Granson.

times a very forcible poet, but he sinks into insignificance
when we set him side by side with the giant who wrote
the *Canterbury Tales*. Yet if Chaucer brought vigour
to English poetry, he found in France, and among these
rhetorical lyrists, precisely the qualities which were
lacking at home. What it was essential for England
to receive at that most critical moment of her intellectual history was an external, almost a superficial,
matter. She did not require the body and bones of
genius, but the garments with which talent covers
them. These robes are what we name grace, elegance,
melody and workmanship, and these delicate textiles
were issuing in profusion from the looms of France.

This is the secret of the strong influence exercised
on a very great poet like Chaucer, and through him
upon the poetry of England, by a writer so essentially
mediocre as Guillaume de Machault. It was the
accomplished tradition, the picturesque and artistic
skill of the lesser poet, which so strongly attracted the
greater. From Machault English poetry took that
heroic couplet which had hitherto been unknown to it,
and which was to become one of its most abundant
and characteristic forms. In a variety of ways the
prosody of Great Britain was affected by that of France
between 1350 and 1370. The loose and languid forms
in which British poets had hitherto composed were
abandoned in delight at the close metre of the French,
and about 1350 John Gower produced his *Cinquante
Balades* not merely in the form but in the very language
of Eustache Deschamps. His *Mirour de l'Omme*, a
long and important poem first printed by Mr. Macaulay
in 1899, is an instance of pure Gallicisation. Chaucer
did not imitate the French thus grossly. Indeed, he
went to France for nothing interior or essential, but,

sensitively conscious that his own country lacked most
of all the æsthetic graces, he borrowed from writers
like Machault and Granson the external colour and the
technical forms.   But the substantial forces which
awakened the splendid *bourgeois* genius of Chaucer were
the aristocratic influences of Dante, Petrarch, and
Boccaccio.

Two hundred years later, at the next great crisis of
English literature, a very similar condition is apparent,
though exposed with less intensity.   The mediæval
forms of poetry, allegorical, didactic, diffuse, had now
worn themselves out.   There was a total abandonment
of " gardens " of rhetoric, of *plaisances* of morality.
These efforts of exhausted fancy continued to please
English readers longer than they did French ones,
and it is to be noted that their decay was sudden with
us, not gradual as with you.   Not only, for instance,
did the traditional rhetoricians of the beginning of the
sixteenth century exercise no influence on English
thought, but there is no evidence that a single person
in England read a line of Jean Le Maire des Belges.
But a little later all is different.   A recent critic has
said that the writings of Wyatt and Surrey, though
not epoch-making, were " epoch-marking."   They were
not men of genius, but they were of eminently modern
taste.   They perceived that everybody was tired of
long-winded allegory and rhetoric, and they set themselves to write verse " in short parcels," that is to say,
in brief lyrics.   So they looked to France, where Wya t
passed, probably, in 1532.   What did he find ?   Doubtless he found Clément Marot in the act of putting forth
L'Adolescence Clémentine.   It is probable that Marot,
with his " elegant badinage," was too gay for these
stiff English nobles, so solemn and rigid.   His want

of intellectual ambition would strike them, and they passed on to Italy. But something of the perfume of France was left upon their fingers, and they seem to have borrowed, perhaps from Melin de Saint-Gelais, but more probably from Marot, the sonnet-form, hitherto unknown in England. It cannot be pretended that in the great awakening of English lyrical poetry in the middle of the sixteenth century France had any great share, but what there was tended in the æsthetic direction. The ugly hardness of the last mediæval poets was exchanged for a daintiness of expression, a graceful lucidity, in the merit of which Clément Marot's rondeaux and epigrams had a distinct share.

We have now considered two instances—the one important, the other slight—in which English poetry received, at critical moments, a distinct colour from the neighbouring art of France. In each case the influence was exercised at a time when the poetic ambition of our country greatly exceeded the technical skill of its proficients, and when the verse-writers were glad to go to school to masters more habituated to art and grace than themselves. But we have now another and a very curious phenomenon to note. Fifty years later than the revival of Wyatt and Surrey, when Elizabethan literature was beginning to rise into prominence, several very strenuous efforts were made to take advantage of contemporary French accomplishment, and with one accord these attempts conspicuously failed. We find in 1580 that the French were " highly regarded " by the school of versifiers at Cambridge, and before this Edmund Spenser had translated the *Visions* of Joachim Du Bellay. It might be supposed that this would be the beginning of a consistent imitation of the *Pléiade* by the English poets—just, for instance, as modern

A A

Swedish poetry was at this moment started by Rosen-
hane's imitations of Ronsard. But on the vast wave
of Elizabethan literature, now sweeping up with irresistible force and volume, we find scarcely a trace of
the *Pléiade*. The one important writer who borrowed
from the French was Samuel Daniel, whose famous
Delia of 1592 obviously owes both its title and its form
to Maurice Scève's *Délie* of 1544. Daniel also imitates
Baïf and Pontus de Thyard, and had a vast admiration for
his more immediate contemporary, Philippe Desportes.[1]

The experiments of Jodelle and Garnier in Senecan
drama were examined by the English dramatists of
the end of the sixteenth century—by Kyd and Daniel
in particular—and were deliberately rejected. The
pathway taken by classical French tragedy was even
touched for a moment, in *Titus Andronicus*, by Shakespeare himself, but it was instantly quitted for the
utterly divergent road which led to *Othello* and *King
Lear*. The sententious and rhetorical character of
French drama was rejected by all the great Elizabethans,
and the only contemporary influence accepted from
France by our poetry at this time was that of Du Bartas,
whose violent and grotesque style gratified a growing
taste for exaggeration among the courtiers. Du Bartas
pointed the way to that decadence which fell only too
swiftly for English poetry, like a plague of insects upon
some glorious summer garden. But it is interesting
to observe that from 1580 to 1620, that is to say during
the years in which the æsthetic sense was most widely
and most brilliantly developed in English poetry,
French influences of the best kind knocked at its door

---

[1] Since this was written, however, Mr. Sidney Lee, in a valuable
essay on " The Elizabethan Sonnet-Literature " (printed in June
1904), has drawn attention to Lodge's indebtedness to Ronsard.

in vain.   In its superfluous richness, it needed no further
gifts.   It had colour enough and substance enough to
spare for all the world.

Very different was the condition of things fifty years
later.   English poetry in the Jacobean age was like a
plant in a hothouse, that runs violently to redundant
blossom, and bears the germs of swift decay in the
very splendour of its buds.   Already, before the death
of James I., the freshness was all gone, and the tendency
to decline was obvious.   Under Charles I. the development of literature was considerably warped, and at
length completely arrested, by the pressure of political
events.   Then the Civil War broke out, and the English
Court, with its artistic hangers-on, was dispersed in
foreign countries.

As early as 1624, on the occasion of the Marriage
Treaty, the attention of the English poets may probably
have been directed to Paris, but there had followed
grave estrangements between the Courts of France and
England, and in 1627 a disastrous rupture.   The
earliest verses of Edmund Waller celebrate incidents
in Buckingham's expedition, and seem to prove that
Waller had even then been made aware of the reforms
in French prosody instituted by Malherbe.   The Civil
War broke out in 1642, and the raising of the king's
standard at Nottingham was the signal to the Muses
to snatch up their lyres and quit this inhospitable
island.   The vast majority of our living poets were
Royalists, and when Charles I. was defeated they either
withdrew into obscurity or left the country.   Suckling
was already in Paris; he was followed there by Cowley,
Waller, Davenant, Denham, and Roscommon, that is
to say, by the men who were to form poetic taste in
England in the succeeding generation.   From 1645 to

1660 the English Court was in Continental exile, and it carried about it a troop of poets, who were sent, like so many carrier-pigeons, upon wild diplomatic errands.

It was a great misfortune for English poetry that it was flung into the arms of France at this precise moment. What the poets found in Paris was not the best that could be given to them, and what there was of the best they did not appreciate. Their own taste in its rapid decadence had become fantastical and disordered. We have but to look at the early Odes of Abraham Cowley to see into what peril English style had sunken. It had grown diffuse and yet rugged; it had surrendered itself to a wild abuse of metaphor, and, conscious of its failing charm, it was trying to produce an impression by violent extravagance of imagery. Its syntax had all gone wrong; it had become the prey of tortured grammatical inversions.

It is strange that in coming to France the English poets of 1645 did not see the misfortune of all this. They should have found, if they had but had eyes to perceive it, that French poetry was on the high road to escape the very faults we have just mentioned. The fault of poetry such as that of Waller and Davenant is that it is complicated and yet not dignified. Well, the English Royalists who waited upon Queen Henrietta in Paris might have observed in the verses of Malherbe and Racan poetry which was majestic and yet simple, an expression of true and beautiful sentiments in language of pure sobriety. But these were the new classics of France, and the English exiles had been educated in a taste which was utterly anti-classic. They could not comprehend Malherbe, who was too stately for them, but unfortunately there were other influences which exactly suited their habits of mind. There can be no doubt that they were pleased with the posthumous writings of Théophile de Viau, whose nature-painting has left its mark on Cowley, and unquestionably, like the rest of the world, they were enchanted with the fantastic, almost burlesque talent of Saint-Amant, who ruled the salons of Paris during the whole of the English Exile, and who seemed to his admirers of 1650 a very great poet whom it was a distinction to imitate.

The English ear for rhythm is not constituted like the French ear. We have a prosodical instinct which is entirely unlike yours. This was ill comprehended, or rather not comprehended at all, by the English Exiles. They were confronted by the severity of Malherbe and the uniformity of Maynard, and they were unable to appreciate either the one or the other. The English sublimity, as exemplified at that very hour by the majesty of Milton, is obtained by quite other means. The sympathy of the English poets was with what is irregular, and they never were genuine classics, like the French, but merely, in ceasing to be romantic, became pseudo-classical. The very type of a pseudo-classic in revolt against romance is Denham, in his extravagantly-praised *Cooper's Hill*. To compare this with the exquisite *Retraite* of Racan, with which it is almost exactly contemporaneous, is to realise what the difference is between a falsely and a genuinely classical poem. Racan's lines seem to be breathed out without effort from a pure Latin mind; the couplets of Denham are like the shout of a barbarian, who has possessed himself of a toga, indeed, but has no idea of how it ought to be worn.

It is noticeable that foreigners are seldom influenced in their style by their immediate contemporaries in another country. The prestige of public acceptance is

required before an alien dares to imitate. Hence we
search almost in vain for traces of direct relation between
the Parisian *Précieux* and their British brethren.   There
is little evidence that Voiture or Benserade had admirers
among the Exiles, although they returned to England
with ideas about pastoral, which I think they must have
owed to the *Églogues* of Segrais.   But it is certain that
they were infatuated by the burlesque writers of France,
and that Scarron, in particular, was instantly imitated.
The *Virgile Travesti* was extravagantly admired and
promptly paraphrased in England, and in Cotton we
had a poet who deliberately and with great popular
success set out to be the English Scarron.   Trivial
in French, these burlesque exercises became in English
intolerably heavy and vulgarly obscene.   The taste for
rhymed burlesque was a poor gift for the Exiles to
bring back with them from the country which already
possessed the *Adonis* of La Fontaine.

   In offering to their countrymen the forms of French
poetry, without giving them any of its enchanting
dignity and harmony, the English poets of the Restoration were doing the exact opposite of what Chaucer
had done in the fourteenth century.   They imported
the substance without the colour; they neglected precisely the gift which our neighbour has always had to
bestow, namely, the charm of æsthetic proportion.
They were partly unfortunate, no doubt, in the moment
of their return to London.   It was in the very year
1660 that the great revival of poetic taste began in
Paris, and, by coming back to their exciting duties
and pleasures at that moment, the English exiles
excluded themselves from participation in Boileau,
Molière, and Racine.   But would they have learned
to appreciate these great masters if the restoration

of the House of Stuart had been delayed for twenty
years? It is permissible to believe that they would
not.

The invasion of the British stage by French drama
between 1665 and 1690 is the most striking example
of the influence of French taste which the history of
English poetry has to offer. The theatres had been
closed by an ordinance of the Puritan government,
and all performance of plays forbidden throughout
England in 1642. So fierce was the enactment that
the theatres were dismantled, in order to make acting
impossible, while all actors in plays, even in private,
were liable to be publicly whipped, and the audiences
individually fined. The result of this savage law was
that the very tradition of histrionics died out in England,
which had been the most theatrical country in Europe.
It was not one of the least satisfactions to the banished
Royalists in Paris that they could enjoy their beloved
entertainment there, as it was no longer possible to
do in London. They could not sit through performances
of Fletcher and Massinger and Ford, but they could
delight their eyes and their ears with the tragedies of
Scudéry and Tristan l'Hermite and La Calprenède.
You will remind me that they could do better than
this by attending the dramas of Rotrou and ten times
better by studying those of Corneille. But the curious
thing is that while there are definite traces of La Calprenède and Scudéry on our English drama, there is
not, so far as I know, a vestige of Rotrou, and the
English attitude to Corneille is very extraordinary. A
poetaster, named Joseph Rutter, translated *Le Cid*
as early as 1637, that is to say, in the midst of Corneille's
original triumph; it is interesting to note that Rutter's
version was made at the command of the English king

and queen. This bad translation, which enjoyed no success, sufficed for English curiosity. On the other hand, *Les Horaces* was a great favourite in England, and was carefully translated into verse by three or four poets. Some couplets by Sir John Denham, accompanying the version made about 1660 by the "Matchless Orinda," have a particular interest for us. Denham (who was, we must remember, the Racan of the classical movement in England) says of *Les Horaces* :

> " This martial story, which through France did come,
> And there was wrought on great Corneille's loom,
> Orinda's matchless muse to Britain brought,
> And foreign verse our English accents taught."

The total ignoring of the *Cid*, while *Les Horaces* received boundless admiration, is a curious fact, which can only, I think, become intelligible when we observe that to an English audience in 1665 the chivalry and *panache* of the former play were unintelligible, while the showy patriotism and high-strung amorosity of the other were exactly to the English taste. Wherever Corneille's psychological study of the human heart became subtle, he rose above the range of the Royalist exiles. In the English tragedies of the Restoration we see the predominant part which violent passion took in the interest of the age. This, together with the laborious and unflagging emphasis which becomes to us so tedious in these dramatic writers, the English poets borrowed, not from Corneille, whom they may have venerated but hardly comprehended, but from the lesser heroic dramatists of the same age.

A little later in the seventeenth century, when the great men had made their appearance in France, the English dramatists could no longer overlook Molière and Racine; but the luminous wit of the one and the

harmonious and passionate tenderness of the other were
beyond their reach. There is evidence of the favour
which Quinault, especially for his Roman tragedies,
enjoyed in London, and there was something in his
colourless, melodious, and graceful style which attracted
and did not terrify the contemporary English translator.
The want of interest shown by the London adapters
in the successive masterpieces of Racine is quite extraordinary. A solitary attempt was made in 1675 by
John Crowne, or under his auspices, to bring *Andromaque*
on the English stage, but shorn of all its tender beauty.
This, amazing as it sounds, is practically the only
evidence remaining to show that our Gallicised playwrights were conscious of the existence of Racine.
The fact is, no doubt, that he soared above their reach
in his celestial emotion, his delicate passion and his
penetration into the human heart. English versification in 1675 was capable of rough and vigorous effects,
music of the drum and the fife; but it had no instrument
at its command at that time which could reproduce
the notes of Racine upon the violin. Here was an
instance of colour which was evanescent and could not
be transferred. The substance of Molière, on the other
hand, offered no technical difficulties. It is extraordinary how many of Molière's plays were imitated
or adapted on the English stage during his life-time
or very shortly after the close of it. Our great Dryden
mingled *L'Étourdi* with the *Amant Indiscret* of Quinault,
and as the result produced *Sir Martin Mar-all* in 1667.
He used the *Dépit Amoureux* and *Les Précieuses Ridicules*
in adapting Thomas Corneille's arrangement of *El
Astrólogo fingido* of Calderon, in 1668. The English
playwrights, however, had no real appreciation of
Molière, though they stole from him so freely. The

poetess, Mrs. Aphra Behn, being accused in 1678 of borrowing scenes from the " *Malad Imagenere* " (as she called it), admitted frankly that she had done so, but " infinitely to Moleer's advantage."

The poetry of France in the third quarter of the seventeenth century is pre-eminently characteristic of a grave and polished system of society. The age of Racine was, and could not but be, an age of extreme refinement. It was useless for the crude contemporary dramatists of London to take the substance of the Parisian masterpieces, since their spirit absolutely evaded them. English society under Charles II. had elements of force and intellectual curiosity, but it lacked exactly what Paris possessed—the ornament of polished, simple, and pure taste. In the jargon of the time Racine and Molière were " correct," while even English poets of genius, such as Dryden and Otway, hardly knew that " correctness " existed. Hence Boileau, in whom " correctness " took the form of a doctrinal system, made no impression at all upon the English poetry of his own time. He could not act upon English social thought until England ceased to be barbarous, and it is, therefore, not until the age of Queen Anne that the powerful influence of Boileau, like a penetrating odour, is perceived in English poetry, and above all in the verse of Pope. In the *First Epistle of the Second Book*, published in 1737, that great poet reviews the literature of the last seventy years in lines of extraordinary strength and conciseness :—

> " We conquered France, but felt our captive's charms;
> Her arts victorious triumph'd o'er our arms :
> Britain to soft refinements less a foe,
> Wit grew polite, and numbers learned to flow.
> Waller was smooth; but Dryden taught to join
> The varying verse, the full-resounding line,

> The long majestic march and energy divine.
> Though still some traces of our rustic vein
> And splay-foot verse remained, and will remain.
> Late, very late, correctness grew our care,
> When the tired nation breath'd from civil war.
> Exact Racine and Corneille's noble fire
> Showed us that France had something to admire.
> Not but the tragic spirit was our own,
> And full in Shakespeare, fair in Otway shone.
> But Otway failed to polish or refine,
> And fluent Shakespeare scarce effaced a line."

When Pope wrote these vigorous verses, he had reached the meridian of his art. He was the greatest living poet not only of England, but of the world. He had to look back over a literary career of nearly forty years, which had been a perpetual triumph, yet in the course of which he had been steadily conducted by the genius of Boileau, who had died in body exactly at the moment when Pope was giving new lustre to his spirit. No critic of authority will question that Pope was a greater writer than Boileau, excellent as the latter is. In the innumerable instances where direct comparison between them is invited, the richness of Pope's language, the picturesque fulness of his line, transcends the art of Boileau. But there is always due a peculiar honour to the artist who is a forerunner, and this belongs to the author of *Le Lutrin*.

The qualities which entered the English poetry of the eighteenth century came through Pope, but they had their source in Boileau. From him, enemy as he was to affectation, pedantry, and spurious emphasis, we learned that a verse, whether good or bad, should at least say something. Boileau's attitude of " honest zeal " commended itself, theoretically if not always practically, to the mind of Pope, who is never tired of praising the Frenchman, " that most candid satirist." Both imitated Horace, but even Pope's vanity could not conceal the fact that he studied the great Roman master mainly in the *Épîtres* of Boileau.   We have here an excellent example of the kind of influence of which we found an example so many centuries back in Chaucer. Here it is not a dull transference of material, ill-comprehended, ill-digested, from one literature to another. It is the capture of the transient charm, the colour and odour of a living art.   Few exercises in criticism would be more instructive than an analysis of French influences on the splendid poetry of Pope.   They mainly resolve themselves into the results of a patient and intelligent study of Boileau.   If we compare the *Essay on Criticism* with the *Art Poétique* we see the young Pope at the feet of the ancient tyrant of letters; if we place *Le Lutrin* by the side of *The Rape of the Lock* we see the knack of mock-heroic caught, and developed, and raised to a pinnacle of technical beauty.   The *Epistle to Dr. Arbuthnot* is vastly superior to the poem *A son Esprit*, but Pope would never have traversed the road if Boileau had not pointed out the way.   Pope captured the very touch of Boileau, but he heightened it, and he made it English.   How English he made it can be seen from the fact that the manner spread, as Pope's and as English, to the literatures of Italy, Sweden, and even Russia.

It spread, moreover, to the whole of the fashion of poetry to be written in Pope's own England through the remainder of the eighteenth century.   Even where that fashion turned to forms more unclassical or even languidly romantic, a faint varnish of Pope's precision continued to characterise it.   But during the eighteenth century (that epoch so curious in the history of poetry, where everything seemed to combine to hold the imagination in a static if not in a semi-paralysed condition) there

was no more display of influence from France on England.
What influence there was was exercised all in the reverse
direction. The moral disquisition in exquisitely-serried
couplets gave way in some degree to descriptive poetry
as Thomson devised it, to lyrical poetry as it was conceived by Gray. But these writers, eminent enough in
their place and their degree, not only owed nothing to
France, but they exerted an immediate influence on the
poets of that country. The Abbé Delille, with his
olives and his vines, his corn-fields and his gardens
and his bees, was inspired in the second degree, no
doubt, by Virgil, but in the first degree, unquestionably,
by the natural descriptions of the English poets of the
preceding generation.

When we come to the dawn of a new age, when we
examine for exotic impressions the writings of the
pioneers of the romantic revival, we find that the
prestige is still all on the side of Great Britain. On
Cowper and Burns and Blake we discover no trace of
any consciousness of foreign influence, other than is
indicated by an occasional and usually hostile acknowledgment of the existence of Voltaire and Rousseau on
the prosaic confines of the art. Quite different is the
case in France, when we approach a writer in some
respects more modern than either Cowper or Burns,
namely, André Chénier, the more conventional parts
of whose works display, to an English reader, a far
greater pre-occupation with English poetry than, I
believe, any French critic has noted. In the later
part of the eighteenth century the deplorable didacticism
of verse, with the tedium of its topographical and
descriptive pieces, of its odes to *Inoculation* and to
The Genius of the Thames, of its epics on the cultivation
of the sugar-cane, and the breeding of sheep and the

navigation of sailing-vessels, although it took its start from a misconception of the teaching of Boileau, had long ceased to be definitely French, and had become technically British in character. But the group of Parisian poets, so solemn and so deadly dull, who formed the court of Delille after the French Revolution, were the disciples of the verse of Thomson, in fact, as much as in theory they were the pupils of the prose of Buffon.

The reaction against dryness and flatness in imaginative literature was complete and systematic in England long before it had been accepted by the intelligent classes in France. The authority of Chateaubriand, although most of his important work was published already, was not in any wide degree accepted until after 1810, even if this be not too early a date to suggest for it, while the formular tendency of the whole work of the author of *Atala* and *René* was rather to the revival of a vivid, picturesque, and imaginative prose than to the study of verse. But in England, before 1810, the revolution was complete in the essential art of poetry itself. Wordsworth and Coleridge had completed their reform, and it was of a nature absolutely radical. In 1798 they had determined that " the passions of men should be incorporated with the beautiful and permanent forms of nature," and they had, working on those lines, added to the poetry of the world some of its most perfect and its most durable ornaments. Crabbe, Campbell, even Sir Walter Scott, had completely revealed the nature of their genius before France was awakened to the full lesson of Chateaubriand. When the second romantic epoch was revealed in France, the great era in England was over. The year 1822, which saw Alfred de Vigny, Victor Hugo, and Lamartine ascend the

Parisian horizon as a new constellation of unequalled effulgence, saw the burial of Shelley in that Roman garden of death where Keats had shortly before been laid, and saw the retirement of Byron to Genoa, his latest Italian home.

It was physically impossible, therefore, that the belated Romantiques in France, at the beginning of the nineteenth century, could exercise any influence o˙ er their British brethren, who had been roused from slumber one watch earlier than they had. Far north, in the valleys of Somerset, by the Isis at Oxford, long before there was any motion of life by the Seine or by the Rhône, the spirit of living poetry had arisen, singing, from the ground, and the boyish Lamartine and Vigny, had they been aware of the fact, might have whispered of their English predecessors in 1810 :—

> " By rose-hung river and light-foot rill
>   There are who rest not, who think long
> Till they discern as from a hill
>   At the sun's hour of morning song,
>   Known of souls only, and those souls free,
> The sacred spaces of the sea."

The English Romantics of the beginning of the nine teenth century earnestly and pointedly repudiated the influence which French poetry had exercised in England a hundred years earlier. This deliberate revolt finds a very interesting expression in the *Sleep and Poetry* of Keats, a poem of much importance in the history of criticism. *Sleep and Poetry* was written in 1816, six years before the first Cénacle was formed in Paris, and four years before the publication of Lamartine's *Méditations Poétiques*. In the course of it, Keats describes the practice of the Anglo-Gallic writers of verse in picturesque and stringent language, culminating

in an attack on the impeccable Boileau himself. He
says :—

> " A schism
> Nurtured by foppery and barbarism
> Made great Apollo blush for this his land.
> Men were thought wise who could not understand
> His glories : with a puling infant's force
> They swayed about upon a rocking-horse
> And thought it Pegasus. . . . Ill-fated race !
> That blasphemed the bright Lyrist to his face
> And did not know it,—no, they went about,
> Holding a poor, decrepit standard out,
> Mark'd with most flimsy mottoes, and in large
> The name of one BOILEAU ! "

During the ninety years which separate us from the
early enthusiasms of Keats and Shelley, it cannot be
said that this influence of France has to any marked
degree asserted itself on the poetry of England. It
would be in the highest degree fantastic to pretend
that it can be traced on the texture of Tennyson or
of the Brownings. It is a remarkable fact that the
genius of Victor Hugo, although of such overwhelming
force among the Latin nations, failed to awaken the
least echo in the poets of the North. The allusions
to Hugo in the writings of his greatest immediate
contemporaries in England are ludicrously perfunctory
and unappreciative. Tennyson addressed to him a
well-intentioned sonnet which is a monument of tact-
lessness, in which Victor Hugo is addressed as " Weird
Titan " and in which the summit of the French poet's
performance appears to have been reached in his having
been polite to one of Tennyson's sons. " Victor in
drama, victor in romance," the English poet sings in
artless wit, and shows no appreciation whatever of the
unmatched victories in the splendour and perfection
of lyrical melody. It was Mr. Swinburne who, about

1866, earliest insisted on the supremacy of Victor
Hugo :—

> " Thou art chief of us, and lord ;
>   Thy song is as a sword
> Keen-edged and scented in the blade from flowers ;
>   Thou art lord and king ; but we
>   Lift younger eyes, and see
> Less of high hope, less light on wandering hours."

In spite, however, of Mr. Swinburne's reiterated
praise of that " imperial soul," and of the respectful
study which has been given to the poet in England
for the last forty years, Victor Hugo has asserted little
or no influence on English poetry. Much lesser talents
than his, however, have offered in the later years of
the century a colour to a certain school of our poets,
and it is in Théophile Gautier and Théodore de Banville
that our English Parnassians found something of the
same æsthetic stimulus that their predecessors of the
fourteenth century found in Guillaume de Machault
and Eustache Deschamps.

But our hour is over, and this brief and imperfect
discourse must come to an end. We have very lightly
touched on the events of six hundred years. Are we
to speculate, imperfect prophets that we are, on the
future relations of the two great countries of the west,
which, far beyond all others, have always been in the
vanguard of liberty and light ? That is a feat of daring
beyond my limited imagination. But I cannot help
nourishing a confident belief that in the future, as well
as in the past, the magnificent literatures of France
and of England will interact upon one another, that each
will, at the right psychological moments, flash colour
and radiance which will find reflection on the polished
surface of the other. To facilitate this, in ever so small

B B

and so humble a degree, must be the desire of every
lover of England and of France.   And in order to adopt
from each what shall be serviceable to the other, what
is most needful must be a condition of mutual intelligence.   That *entente cordiale* which we value so deeply,
and which some of us have so long laboured to pro-
mote,—it must not be confined to the merchants and
to the politicians. The poets also must insist upon
their share of it.

APPENDIX

APPENDIX

M. MALLARMÉ AND SYMBOLISM

IT was with not a little hesitation that I undertook to unravel a corner of the mystic web, woven of sunbeams and electrical threads, in which the poet of *L'Après-Midi d'un Faune* conceals himself from curious apprehension. There were a dozen chances of my interpretation being wrong, and scarcely one of its being right. My delight therefore may be conceived when I received a most gracious letter from the mage himself; Apollonius was not more surprised when, by a fortunate chance, one of his prophecies came true. I quote from this charming paper of credentials, which proceeds to add some precious details :—

"Paris, Mardi 10 *Janvier* 1893.

" . . . Votre étude est un miracle de divination . . . Les poëtes seuls ont le droit de parler; parce qu'avant coup, ils savent. Il y a, entre toutes, une phrase, où vous écartez tous voiles et désignez la chose avec une clairvoyance de diamant, le voici : ' His aim . . . is to use words in such harmonious combination as will suggest to the reader a mood or a condition *which is not mentioned in the text*, but is nevertheless paramount in the poet's mind at the moment of composition.'

" Tout est là. Je fais de la Musique, et appelle ainsi non celle qu'on peut tirer du rapprochment euphonique

373

des mots, cette première condition va de soi ; mais
l'au delà magiquement produit par certaines dispositions
de la parole, où celle-ci ne reste qu'à l'état de moyen
de communication matérielle avec le lecteur comme
les touches du piano. Vraiment entre les lignes et
au-dessus du regard cela se passe, en toute pureté, sans
l'entremise de cordes à boyaux et de pistons comme à
l'orchestre, qui est déjà industriel ; mais c'est la même
chose que l'orchestre, sauf que littérairement ou silen-
cieusement. Les poëtes de tous les temps n'ont jamais
fait autrement et il est aujourd'hui, voilà tout, amusant
d'en avoir conscience. Employez Musique dans le sens
grec, au fond signifiant Idée du rythme entre les rapports ;
là, plus divine que dans son expression publique ou
Symphonique. Très mal dit, en causant, mais vous
saisissez ou plutôt aviez saisi tout au long de cette
belle étude qu'il faut garder telle et intacte. Je ne
vous chicane que sur l'obscurité ; non, cher poëte,
excepté par maladresse ou gaucherie je ne suis pas
obscur, du moment qu'on me lit pour y chercher ce
que j'énonce plus haut, ou la manifestation d'un art
qui se sert—mettons incidemment, j'en sais la cause
profonde—du langage : et le deviens, bien sûr ! si l'on
se trompe et croit ouvrir le journal. Riez, et je vous
serre la main, sur ma clarté.—Votre.

STÉPHANE MALLARMÉ.''

INDEX

Abbé Mouret, L', Zola, 130

Abbé Roitelet, L', Fabre, F., 157, 166

Abbé Tigrane, L', Fabre, 151, 157–162, 165

Ablancourt, *Mémoires* of, 74

Adélaïde du Guesclin, Voltaire's, 44, 55

Adolescence, Clémentine, L', Marot, 352

Aïssé, Mademoiselle, 35–62

Alcaforada, Mariana, 68. *See* Mariana.

Aléxis, Paul, 129, 130, 138

Amaïdée, d'Aurevilly's, 91, 92

Amant Indiscret, Quinault's, 361

Amitiés Francaises, Les, Maurice Barrès', 288–290

Amour Impossible, L', d'Aurevilly, 91, 92

Amour Marin, L', M. Paul Fort, 337

Amoureuses, Les, Daudet, 110, 120

Ancien Régime, L', Taine, 256

Andromaque, Racine's, 361

Anneau d'Améthyste, L', 264

Annunzio, G. D', 193, 241

Aphrodite, Pierre Louÿs, 265

Après-Midi d'un Faune, L', Mallarmé, 314–316, 373

Aréthuse, M. de Régnier, 301

Argental, Comte d', 38, 49, 50, 56, 57

Arnold, Matthew, 4, 28, 194, 264, 287, 307

Art Poétique, Boileau, 364

Asse, M. Eugène, 47, 82

Atala, Chateaubriand's, 366

Athées, A un Diner d', Aurevilly's, 93, 100, 101

Au Maroc, P. Loti, 220

Aumont, Duc d', 54

Aurevilly, Jules Barbey d', 89–102

Avec Trois Mille Cent Francs, Daudet's, 109

Aventures du Grand Sidoine, Zola's, 132

d'Aydie, Chevalier Blaise Marie, 43–46, 53–54, 57, 58, 60–62

Aziyadé, Pierre Loti, 202, 216

Baïf, 354

Bal, Vigny's, *Le*, 7

Ballades Françaises, Paul Fort, 335

Balthasar, A. France, 188

Balzac, Honoré de, 122, 241

Balzac (Jean Louis Guez), 66, 67

Banville, Théodore de, 369

Barante, M. de, 47

Barbin, Paris Publisher, 67

Barnabé, Fabre's, 157

Barrès, M. Maurice, 254, 265, 287–295

Batilliat, M. Marcel, 306

Baudelaire, C., 113, 317, 329, 334, 338

Bazin, M. René, 261–283

Beauvois, M., 71, 72, 82–84

Bédarieux (Birthplace of Fabre), 152, 153, 156, 168, 174

Beerbohm, Mr. Max, 96

Behn, Mrs. Aphra, 362

375

Beja, Canoness of, 67, 68, 73, 83, 85
Bennett, James Gordon, 248
Benserade, 358
Bercail, Fabre, F., *Le*, 157
Bernard, Claude, 147
Bernhardt, Madame Sarah, 251
Berry, Mme. la Duchesse de, 44
Boccaccio, 350, 352
Boileau, 80, 358, 362, 363, 364, 366, 368
Boissier, Gaston, 56
Boissonade, 68
Bolingbroke, Lady, 41, 45
——, Lord, 40, 43, 46, 55
Bonheur dans le Crime, Le, d'Aurevilly's, 94, 101,
Bon Plaisir, Le, H. de Régnier's, 308
Boufflers, Stanislaus, Chevalier de, 128
Bouillon, Duchesse de, 56
Boule de Suif, Guy de Maupassant's, 138
Bourges, M. Élémir, 267
Bourget, M. Paul, 91, 109, 235–258, 294
Bournonville, Mme. la Princesse de, 49
Boursault, Père, 62
Bouton, Noël, Count of St. Léger-sur-Dheune, 69. See Chamilly.
Brummell, Du Dandyisme et de Georges, d'Aurevilly, 91, 96
Brunetière, 263
Buffon, 97, 366
Bunbury, Miss Lydia, *later* Comtesse de Vigny, 13
Byron, Lord, 7, 11, 13, 14, 29, 94, 96, 326, 367

CALANDRINI, Madame, 46–49, 53, 55, 58, 62
Calderon de la Barca, Pedro, 361
Calprenède. Gautier la, 359

Canterbury Tales, Chaucer, 351
Cantilènes, Les, Moreas, 182
Capitaine Burle, Le, Zola's, 142
Carnet de Danse, Le, Zola's, 128
Céard, M. Henri, 138
Celle qui m'aime, Zola's, 131, 132
Chamilly, Marquis of, 68–71, 80–83
Chanson de Roland, 8, 347
Charcot, the physician, 106
Charist d'Or, Le, A. Samain, 331
Chateaubriand, F. de, 6, 90–92, 366
Chats, Les Paradis des, Zola's, 135
Chatterton, Thomas, 19–23
Chatterton, Vigny's, 20, 21
Chaucer, Geoffrey, 344, 348–352, 358
Chénier, André, 4, 6, 19, 307, 365
Chesterfield, Lord, 210
Chevrier, Le, Fabre, 157, 171–174
Christianisme, Génie du, Chateaubriand, 6
Cid, Corneille's, 360
Cinq-Mars, Vigny's, 13
Cinquante Balades, John Gower's, 351
Cité des Eaux, La, M. H. de Régnier's, 303, 305
Claretie, Jules, 113, 151
Clélie, Mdlle. de Scudéry's, 66
Coignard, Jérôme, Anatole France, 190
Coleridge, S. T., 8, 343, 366
Collingwood, Lord, 25
Complications Sentimentales, Bourget's, 244–246
Confession d'un Enfant du Siècle, de Musset's, 283
Contes à Ninon, Zola's, 128, 132

Contes Choisis, Daudet's, 110, 122

Contes du Lundi, Daudet's, 110

Cooper's Hill, Sir John Denham's, 357

Coppée, François, 330

Cor, Vigny's *Le*, 8

Corneille, Pierre, 359, 363

——, Thomas, 361

Cotton, Charles, 358

Courbezon, Les, Fabre's, 156

Cowley, Abraham, 355–357

Crabbe, George, 326, 366

Crébillon, Claude, 128

Crime d'Amour, Bourget's, *Un*, 235

Criticism, Pope's *Essay on*, 364

Croquis de France, Bazin's, 282

Croquis d'Orient, Bazin's, 282

Crowne, John, 361

Culte du Moi, M. Barrès, 293

Dame Romaine, Vigny's *La*, 7

Dandy d'avant les Dandys, d'Aurevilly's *Un*, 96

Dandyisme et de Georges Brummell, d'Aurevilly's *Du*, 91, 96

Daniel, Samuel, 354

Dante, 4, 129, 352

Daudet, Alphonse, 105–123

——, Ernest, *Mon Frère et Moi*, 108

Davenant, Sir William, 355, 356

Débâcles, Les, Verhaeren's, 325

Deffand, Madame du, 43, 44, 56, 61

Delavigne, Casimir, 16, 90

Delia, Daniel's, 354; Maurice Scève's, 354

Delille, Abbé, 365, 366

Deluge, Vigny's *Le*, 9–11

Denham, Sir John, 355, 357, 360

De Quincey, Thomas, 288, 291

Déracinés, M. Barrès' *Les*, 254, 255, 265

Dernier Jours de Pékin, Les, Loti's, 228–232

Deschamps, Émile, 8

——, Eustace, 350, 351, 369

Désert, Le, Pierre Loti's, 202–207, 213

Desportes, Philippe, 354

Dessous des Cartes, d'Aurevilly's *Le*, 100, 101

Destinées, Vigny's *Les*, 27–28

Destouches, N., 36, 55

De Tocqueville, A., 247, 249

De Toute son Âme, René Bazin's, 274–276

Dévouée, La, Hennique, 138

Diaboliques, Les, d'Aurevilly, 101

Dickens, Charles, 98, 116, 241

Disraeli, B., 94

Divagations, Stéphane Mallarmé's, 319

Don Juan, Le Plus Bel Amour de, d'Aurevilly's, 95, 101

Donne, John, 322

Dorval, Marie, 16–18, 20, 26, 27

Double Conversion, La, Daudet, 110

Double Maitresse, La, M. H. de Régnier, 208

Dryden, John, 180, 361, 362

Du Bartas, 354

Du Bellay, Joachim, 353

Dubreuil, l'Abbé, 154

Duchesse Bleue, La, Bourget's 239–243, 264

Éloa, Vigny's, 9, 11–12, 18

Embarrassments, Mr. Henry James's, 239

Empedocles, Matthew Arnold's, 307

Endymion, Keats', 306

English Poetry, the influence of France upon, 341–370

Ennemi des Lois, L', M. Barrès', 293

Ensorcelée, L', d'Aurevilly's, 93
Epistle to Dr. Arbuthnot, Pope's, 364
Espinasse, Mademoiselle de l', 36, 37, 46
Essay on Criticism, Pope's, 364
Étape, L', Bourget, 253–258
Étourdi, L', Molière's, 361
Évangeliste, L', Daudet's, 106, 114

FABRE, L'Abbé Fulcran, 153
——, Ferdinand, 151–175
Faërie Queen, Spenser's, 4
Fantôme d'Orient, P. Loti's, 202, 223
Fée Amoureuse, La, Zola's, 128
Femmes d'Artistes, Les, Daudet's, 122
Ferriol, Baron d'Argental, Charles, 37, 38, 40
——, Madame de', 37, 38, 42–46, 49, 58, 59, 61
Feuillet, Octave, 145, 263
Figures et Choses qui passaient, Pierre Loti, 217, 222
FitzJames, Duchess of, 54
Fitzmaurice-Kelly, Professor James, 350
Flamandes, Les, Émile Verhaeren's, 325
Flancs du Vase, Aux, M. Albert Samain's, 330
Flaubert, G., 113, 122, 138, 264
Fletcher, John, 359
Fleurs d'Exil, Loti's, 229
Fleurs du Mal, Baudelaire's, 329
Fleury, Cardinal de, 52
Forces Tumultuenses, Les, Émile Verhaeren's, 326
Ford, John, 359
Forgeron, Zola's *Le*, 135
Fort, M. Paul, 334–338
France, M. Anatole, 169, 187–197, 263
Friendship's Garland, Matthew Arnold's, 194, 264

Froissart, 350
Fromont Jeune et Risler Ainé, Daudet's, 108, 114, 115, 116

Galilée, P. Loti's *La*, 213–216, 223, 229
Garnier, Robert, 354
Gautier, Théophile, 128, 369
Gay, Delphine, 8, 13
Génie du Christianisme, Chateaubriand's, 6
Gesvres, Duc de, 38, 39
Ghil, M. René, 300
Gilbert, poet, 19
Goethe, 91, 99
Goncourt, Edmond de, 46, 113, 133, 264
——, Jules de, 133
Gower, John, 351
Grandeur et Servitude Militaires, Vigny's, 7, 23–25
Granson, Oton de, 350, 352
Gray, Thomas, 56, 344, 365
Grignan, Madame de, 48, 66
Guerin, Maurice de, 90, 91
Guerres, Zola's *Trois*, 139
Guilleragues, Pierre Girardin de, 80
Gulliver's Travels, Swift's, 55

HACHETTE, M., 129, 130
Haggard, Sir Henry Rider, 207
Halévy, Ludovic, 151, 268
Hardy, Mr. Thomas, 152, 171, 174, 263
Harland, Henry, 179, 181
Hennique, Léon, 138
Heredia, M. de, 292, 302, 304, 305, 333
Hermite, Tristan l', 359
Hérodiade, Mallarmé's, 313
Hervieu, M. Paul, 264
Histoire Comique, M. Anatole France's, 193–197
Histoire d'une Grecque Moderne, Prévost's, 55
Histoire sans Nom, Une, d'Aurevilly's, 92, 94, 100

Homme d'Affaires, Un, M. Bourget's, 264
Homme Libre, Un, M. Barrès', 288, 291
Hommes, Les Œuvres et les, d'Aurevilly's, 99
Horaces, Les, 360
Howell, James, 65–66
Hugo, Victor, 3, 7–9, 11, 16, 90, 181, 326, 338, 366, 368, 369
Humble Amour, M. René Bazin's, 277
Huysmans, Joris Karel, 138, 265

Idylle Tragique, Une, Bourget's, 245
Immortel, L', Daudet's, 115
Isez, the surgeon, 51, 52
Italie, Bourget's *Sensations d'*, 247

Jack, Daudet's, 109, 114
James, Mr. Henry, 44, 201, 239, 242
Jardin de Bérénice, M. Barrès' *Le*, 289, 292
Jardin d'Épicure, Le, M. Anatole France's, 188, 195
Jardin de l'Infante, Au, Albert Samain's, 330, 331
Jean Gourdon, Zola's *Les Quatre Journées de*, 135, 144
Jephté, La Fille de, Vigny's, 7
Jérôme Coignard, M., M. Anatole France's, 188
Jerusalem, Pierre Loti's, 208–213, 220, 228, 229
Jeux Rustiques et Divins, Les, M. H. de Régnier's, 299–301, 305
Jonson, Ben, 322
Jusserand, M., 71

Kahn, M. Gustave, 181
Karr, Alphonse, 290
Keats, John, 8, 106, 302, 306, 308, 344, 348, 367, 368

Kilmorey, Earl of, 27
Kipling, Rudyard, 116, 175
Kyd, Thomas, 354

Lacordaire, 159
La Fontaine, Jean de, *Adonis*, 358
Lamartine, Alphonse de, 3, 329, 366, 367
Lammenais, F., 13, 159
Langland, William, 348
Le Terre, Zola's, 127
Leblond, Célénie, 45, 58, 59
Lecouvreur, Adrienne, 56
Lee, Sir Sidney, 354
Legend of Good Women, Chaucer's, 348,
Lemaître, M. Jules, 151, 283
Leopardi, Giacomo, 4
L'Estrange, Sir Roger, *Five Love Letters from a Nun to a Cavalier*, 84
Letters from a Nun to a Cavalier, 65–85
Letters, Mademoiselle Aïssé's, 40
Lettres de mon Moulin, Daudet's, 110, 111, 120
Lettres Portugaises, 65–85
Lisle, Leconte de, 292, 295
Lodge, Thomas, 354
Lorres, Guillaume de, 347, 348, 350
Loti, Pierre, 134, 151, 201–232
Lucifer, Fabre's, 157, 162, 165
Lutrin, Le, Boileau's, 363
Lys Rouge, Le, M. A. France's, 189, 195

Machault, Guillaume de, 350, 351, 352, 369
Madame Corentine, M. Bazin's, 276
Ma Douleur, Daudet's, 105
Maeterlinck, 324, 325
Maintenon, Madame de, 80
Malherbe, F., 356, 357
Mallarmé, Stéphane, 179, 300, 313–323
——, and Symbolism, 373, 374

Mannequin d'Osier, Le, M. A. France's, 169, 188, 189, 191
Manon Lescaut, 55, 115
Mariage de Loti, Le, P. Loti's, 201
Mariana Alcaforada, the Portuguese Nun, 65–85
Marivaux, Pierre, 235
Marot, Clement, 352, 353
Ma Tante Giron, M. Bazin's, 268, 269
Matelot, P. Loti's, 202, 223
Maupassant, Guy de, 109, 122, 138, 145, 239, 264
Ma Vocation, Fabre's, 153
Médailles d'Argile, M. H. de Régnier's, 305
Méditations Poétiques, Lamartine's, 367
Mémoires d'un Homme de Qualité retiré du Monde, Prévost d'Exiles', 55
Meung, Jean de, 347, 348, 350
Milton, John, 4, 11, 13, 128, 344, 357
Mirour de l'Omme, Eustache Deschamps, 351
Moines, Les, M. Emile Verhaeren's, 325
Moïse, Vigny's, 9
Molière, 55, 62, 358, 360–362
Mon Frère Yves, P. Loti's, 223
Monsieur de Camors, O. Feuillet's, 145, 263
Monsieur Jean, Fabre's, 170
Montagne, M. Paul Fort's, 337
Montaigne, 172, 190
Montesquieu, 36
Moore, Thomas, 11, 12, 14
Moréas, Jean, 180, 181, 184
Moreau, Hégésippe, 22
Motteville, Madame de, *Mémoires*, 77
Moulin, Zola's *L'Attaque du*, 139
Muse Française, La, 11
Musset, Alfred de, *Confession d'un Enfant du Siècle*, 283

Nabab, Le, Daudet's, 114, 121
Nana, Zola's, 127
Nanthia, Vicomtesse de, 46
Nichina, La, Hugues Rebell's, 265
Ninon, Nouveaux Contes à, Zola's, 133–135
Nodier, C., 7, 13
Noellet, Les, M. Bazin's, 277
Norris, Mr. W. E., 271
Notre Cœur, Guy de Maupassant's, 239
Nouveaux Lundis, Sainte-Beuve's, 5
Numa Roumestan, Daudet's, 114, 115, 121, 122
Nun's Love Letters, see *Portuguese Letters : see* Mariana Alcaforada

Oncle Célestin, Mon, Fabre's, 153, 157, 168
Orinda, The Matchless, 360
Orleans, Duke of, 41
Orme du Mail, L', M. Anatole France's, 189–191, 264
O'Shaughnessy, Arthur, 334
Othello, Shakespeare, 261, 354
Otway, Thomas, 362, 363
Outre-Mer, M. Paul Bourget's, 247–253

PACK, Major Richardson, 84
Paléologue, M., 13, 26,
Parabère, Madame de, 42, 46, 49, 54, 60, 61
Paris : Elevation, Vigny's, 23
Paris, Gaston, 263
Paris Sentimental, M. Paul Fort's, 337
Parnasse Contemporain, 314
Parnassians, 292, 302, 304, 333, 369
Pascal, 17
Pater, Walter, 173, 174
Pattison, Mark, 72
Pécheur d'Islande, P. Loti's, 223, 277
Pékin, Pierre Loti's, 228–232

Pellissier, operatic star, 30
Penruddock, Mrs., 67
Perraud, Cardinal, 151
Petit Chose, Le, Daudet's, 108, 116, 117
Petrarch, 350, 352
Philosophe Marié, Le, Destouche's, 55
Pichot, M. Amédée, 156
Piedagnal, M., 47
Plato's *Timæus,* 255
Pléiade, the, 353, 354
Poe, Edgar Allan, 314, 334
Poèmes Anciens et Romanesques, M. de Régnier's, 300, 301
Poèmes Antiques, Judaïques, et Modernes, Vigny's, 7
Polyphème, A. Samain's, 331
Pont-de-Veyle, Marquis de, 38, 50, 56, 57
Pontmartin, M. de, 89
Pope, Alexander, 4, 362–364
Portuguese Letters, the, 65–85
Précieuses Ridicules, Les, Molière's, 361
Prêtre Marié, Le, d'Aurevilly's, 92, 93
Prévost, M. Marcel, 264
Prévost d'Exiles, L'Abbé, 55
Propos d'Exil, P. Loti's, 222
Prose pour les Esseintes, S. Mallarmé's, 321
Puits de Sainte Claire, Le, M. A. France's, 188

Quélen, Archbishop de, 159
Quinault, 361

Racan, 357
Racine, Jean, 338, 344, 346, 358, 360, 361, 362, 363
Rambosson, M. Yvanhoé, 300
Ramuntcho, Pierre Loti's, 222, 223
Rape of the Lock, Pope's, 364
Régnier, M. Henri de, 299–310
Renan, Ernest, 151, 295
René, Chateaubriand's, 366

Retraite, La, Racan's, 357
Richardson, Samuel, 46, 235
Rideau Cramoisi, Le, d'Aurevilly's, 95, 100
Rieu, Mademoiselle, 44, 45
Rod, Édouard, 266
Rois en Exil, Les, Daudet, 114
Rollinat, Maurice, 329
Roman de la Rose, Lorris's, 347, 348, 349
Roman de Louis XI, M. Paul Fort's, 336
Roman d'un Enfant, Le, P. Loti's, 220
Roman d'un Spahi, Loti's, 203, 223
Roman Expérimental, Le, Zola's, 262
Ronsard, 307, 354
Rose et Ninette, Daudet's, 115
Rosny (Les Frères), 266
Rôtisserie de la Reine Pédauque, La, M. Anatole France's, 188, 196
Rotrou, 359
Rougon-Macquart series of Zola, 127, 132, 133–135, 189, 262
Rousseau, J. J., 82, 365
Route d'Émeraude, La, Eugène Demolder's, 265
Ruffec, Duc de, 49
Ruskin, John, 35, 207
Rutter, Joseph, 359

Saint-Amant, 357
Sainte-Beuve, C. A., 5, 6, 37, 99, 156, 157
Sainte Claire, Le Puits de, M. Anatole France's, 188
Sainte-Gelais, Malin de, 353
Saint-Simon, Duc de, 68, 80, 81
Saint-Victor, Paul de, 101
Samain, Albert, 329–334
Sand, George, 18, 130, 152, 157, 262
Sandeau, Jules, 157
Santillana, 350

Sapho, Daudet's, 106, 115, 117
Sarcelle Bleue, La, Bazin's, 267, 271–273
Scarron, Paul, 107, 358
Schomberg, Count of, 70
Schwob, Marcel, 350
Scott, Sir Walter, 13, 14, 366
Scudéry, Mademoiselle de, 66, 359
Séché, M. Leon, 6, 13
Segrais's *Églogues*, 358
Sensations d'Italie, M. Bourget's, 247
Serao, Matilde, *Il paese di Cuccagna*, 241, 242
Serres Chandes, Les, Maeterlinck's, 325
Sévigné, Madame de, 36, 48, 66, 77
Shakespeare, 15, 345, 348, 354, 363
Shelley, P. B., 4, 367, 368
Sir Martin Mar-all, Dryden's, 361
Sleep and Poetry, Keats', 367
Soirs, Les, M. E. Verhaeren's, 325
Soumet, A., 13
Sous l'Œil des Barbares, M. Barrès', 293
Spectator, The, 84
Spenser, Edmund, 353
Stanley, Dean, 204, 205
Stello, Vigny's, 18–20
Sterne, Laurence, 294
Stevenson, Robert Louis, 116, 140, 174, 294
Suckling, Sir John, 355
Surrey, Henry Howard, Earl of, 352, 353
Swift, Dean, 191, 194
Swinburne, Algernon, 344, 369
Symons, Mr. Arthur, 179

Tache d'Encre, Une, René Bazin's, 268, 269, 271, 287
Taine, H., 151, 152, 159, 174, 255, 256, 287

Tartarin of Tarascon, Daudet's, 118, 119
Tencin, Madame de, 46, 54, 61
Tennyson, 194, 302, 348, 368
Terminations, Mr. Henry James's, 242
Terre d'Espagne, M. Bazin's, 281
Terre qui Meurt, La, M. Bazin's, 277–280, 282
Thais, M. A. France's, 188
Thérèse Raquin, Zola's, 133
Thyard, Pontus de, 354
Tissot, M. Ernest, 99
Tocqueville, A. de, 247, 249
Tolstoi, 25, 136, 140, 141, 187, 193, 241
Touissaint Galabru, Fabre's, 171
Trente Ans de Paris, Daudet's, 107
Trebutien, M., 91
Trois Ames d'Artistes. See *Duchesse Bleue*, 242
Trollope, Anthony, 116, 165

ULBACH, Louis, 133

Vacances de Pâques, Pierre Loti's, 220
Vacances d'un Jeune Homme Sage, M. H. de Régnier's, 308–310
Vaines Tendresses, Les, Sully Prudhomme's, 304
Vathek, Beckford, with preface by Mallarmé, 315
Verhaeren, M. Emile, 324–328
Verlaine, Paul, A first sight of, 179–184, 323
Versailles-aux-Fantômes, M. Batilliat's, 306
Vers et Prose, S. Mallarmé's, 313, 316
Viau, Théophile de, 357
Vie Littéraire, La, M. Anatole France's, 188
Vielle Maitresse, Une, d'Aurevilly's, 94
Vieux, Les, Daudet's, 111, 112

Vigny, Alfred de, 3–31, 90, 307, 329, 366, 367
Villes Tentaculaires, Les, M. Verhaeren's, 327
Villette, Mademoiselle de, 45
——, Marquise de, 41
Vogüé, Melchior de, 238
Voiture, Vincent, 66, 67, 358
Voleurs et l'Âne, Les, Zola's, 130
Voltaire, 36, 44, 47, 50, 56, 60, 346, 365
Voyage de Sparte, Le, M. Barrès', 292, 294

Voyageuses, M. Paul Bourget's, 235–239, 244–253

WALLER, Edmund, 355, 356
Whitman, Walt, 335, 338
Wood's Town, Daudet's, 117
Wordsworth, William, 4, 19, 28, 334, 366
Wyatt, Sir Thomas, 352, 353

YEATS, Mr. W. B., 237, 333, 335

ZOLA, Emile, 113, 127–147, 187, 241